ACE of ACES
The Dick Bong Story

ACE of ACES

The Dick Bong Story

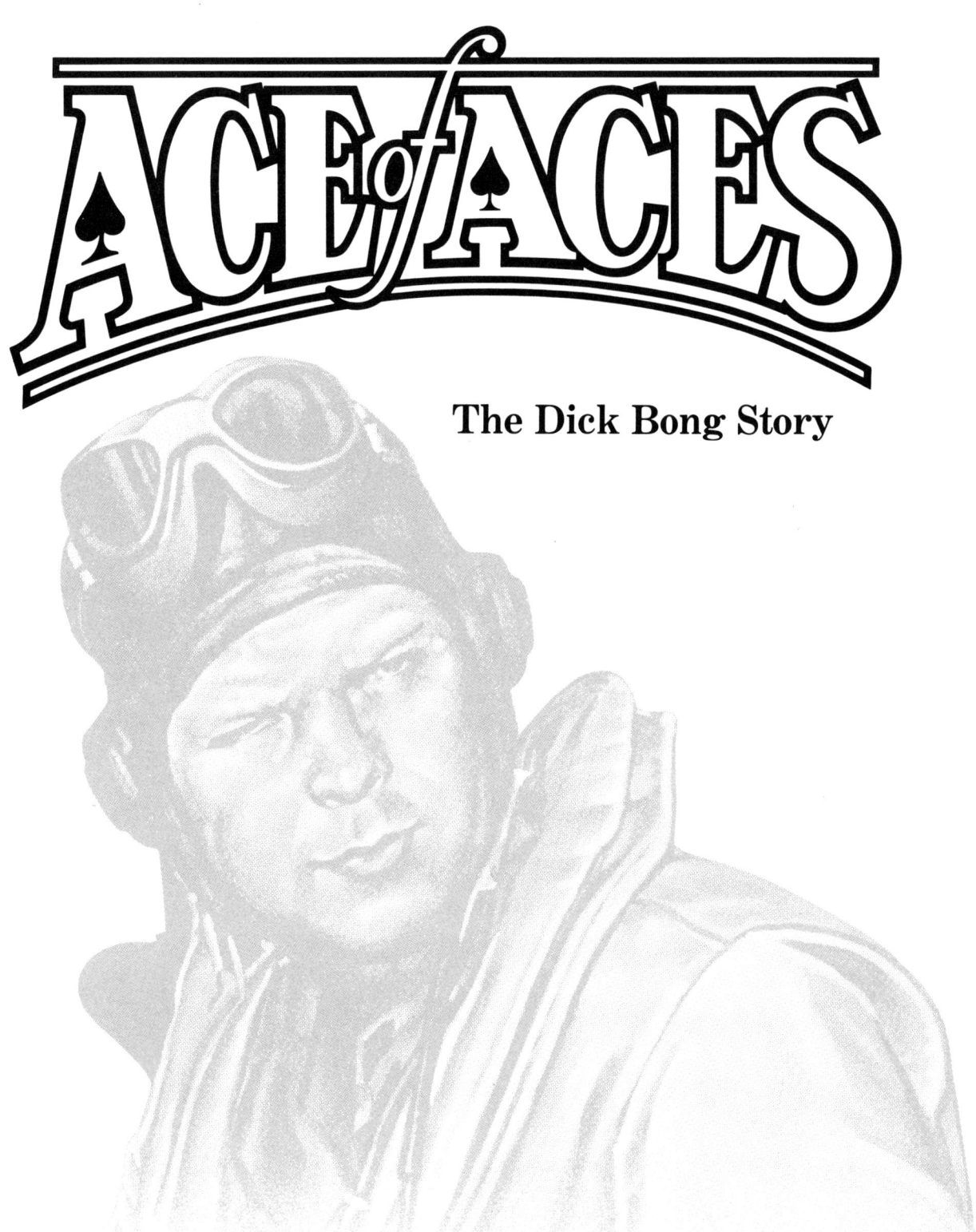

by

Carl Bong and Mike O'Connor

Champlin Fighter Museum

Copyright © 1985 by Carl Bong and Mike O'Connor

All rights reserved. This book, or parts thereof, must not be reproduced in any form without permission of the publisher.

Library of Congress Catalog Number
International Standard Book Number
Printed and bound in the United States of America.

Library of Congress Cataloging-in-Publication Data

Bong, Carl, ca. 1925-
    Ace of aces.

    Includes index.
    1. Bong, Richard I. 2. Fighter pilots — United States — Biography. 3. United States. Army Air Forces — Biography. 4. World War, 1939 - 1945 — Aerial operations, American. 5. World War, 1939 - 1945 — Pacific Area. I. O'Connor, M. J. (Michael J.), 1945 - II. Title. III. Title: Dick Bong story.
UG6262.B66B66 1985   358.4'14'0924 [B] 85-14677
ISBN O-912173-06-8

Dedications:

To Jim Bong, whose interest sparked the extensive research that resulted in this book. CB.

To Gracie, Maureen, Marilyn and Pat. MOC.

Contents

Acknowledgements

Introduction

Chapter 1	Atsugi, Japan (August 30, 1945)	1
Chapter 2	Poplar (September 1920 - May 1941)	2
Chapter 3	Learning the Trade (May 1941 - May 1942)	6
Chapter 4	Countdown to Combat (May - September 1942)	13
Chapter 5	Into Combat (September 1942 - February 1943)	18
Chapter 6	With the Flying Knights (February - March 1943)	45
Chapter 7	Dobodura Days (April - June 1943)	52
Chapter 8	The Score Mounts (July - November 1943)	57
Chapter 9	Stateside Leave (November 1943 - February 1944)	67
Chapter 10	Return to Combat (February - April 1944)	70
Chapter 11	Breaking the Record (April - October 1944)	89
Chapter 12	Balikpapan to Tacloban (October - November 1944)	96
Chapter 13	Medal of Honor (December 1944)	104
Chapter 14	Test Plot (January - August 1945)	109
Chapter 15	"It was a Terrible Sight" (August 6, 1945 and after)	128
Epilogue	"There is a Time for Patriots" (Jay Reed)	134
Notes		136
Appendix A	Decorations and Promotions of Major Richard I. Bong	139
Appendix B	Combat Record of Major Richard I. Bong	140
Appendix C	Aircraft Flown by Major Richard I. Bong	143
Appendix D	Richard Bong Memorial	145
Index		149

Acknowledgments

The authors would like to thank the following individuals, organizations and government agencies for their assistance in the production of this book.

Aerospace Audiovisual Service, Norton AFB
Air Force Inspection and Safety Center, Norton AFB
Air Force Office of Information
Carroll Anderson
Stanley Andrews
Clyde Barnette
Erland Bjork
William Bleeker
Jim Bong
Gregory Boyington
Nial Castle
William Caldwell
Frederick Champion
J. A. Chandler
Chicago Tribune
Ken Clark
Louise Colby
William Coleman
Russell Collins
Barbara Curtis
Warren Curton
Cecil Davis
Defense Audiovisual Agency
Robert DeHaven
John DuPilka
Charles Earnhart
Gene Edgette
Charles Ehrmann
Donald Fisher
Nelson Flack
Thomas Fowler
Raymond Fredette, Office of Air Force History
Royal Frey, Air Force Museum
Del Furgason
General Services Administration, Audiovisual Archives Division
Barry Goldwater
Hal Gray

Acknowledgments Continued

William Greenhalgh
Cheatham Gupton
Alvin Hagen
Charles Hale
Mel Hanisch
James Harvey
Philip Head, Lockheed - California
William Hess
Ray Holman
S. D. Huff
Donald Hutchinson
James Ince
Infantry Journal Publishing
Fred Johnson
Robert S. Johnson
C. L. Jones
Wallace Jordan
George C. Kenney
Charles King
King Features Syndicate
M. F. Kirby
Norb Krane
Carl Lambert
John Lane
C. J. Langmack
Tony LeVier
Peter Madison
Marge
Walter Markey
Charles McElroy
Robert McFarland, Combat Pilots Association
Robert McMahon
Milwaukee Journal
Milwaukee Sentinel
William Morris Agency
Robert Morrissey
Robert Murphy
Duncan Myers
New York Times Company
Frank Nickerson
Walt Olson
Frank Olynyk
Clinton Palmer
Samuel F. Pearce, Lockheed Corporation
Edward Peck

Acknowledgments Continued

Jesse Peaslee
George Pegg
Sammy Pierce
Carl Planck
Wayne Pryor, Lockheed Corporation
Jack Purdy
Jay Reed, Milwaukee Journal
Art Rogers
James Rorrison
Yale Saffro
Henry Sakaida
Sam Scher
William Schmidt, Lockheed Corporation
J. C. Selman
Albert F. Simpson, Historical Research Center, Maxwell AFB
Edward H. Sims
C. M. Smith
R. E. Smith
C. Clifford Stahl II
John Stanaway
Floyd Stith
Osamu Tagaya
United Press International, Inc.
Ralph Wandrey
James Watkins
Norman Wilford
Sidney Woods
Zenger Publishing

Introduction

Forty years later, my memory of Dick Bong is a fresh-faced kid from Wisconsin whose skill in a P-38 was matched only by his bad luck at poker. Those of us flying with the 475th Fighter Group in the Philippines during 1944-45 saw a lot of talent up close. Among the three Lightning groups were "Colonel Mac" MacDonald, Tommy McGuire, Jerry Johnson, Jay Robbins, Cy Homer and Jim Watkins to name just a few. All were experienced, aggressive leaders who provided crucial know-how to younger pilots breaking into combat.

Much has been written of the rivalry between Bong and McGuire and their eagerness to run up their scores. But in truth, most of us felt that way. Competition was keen, as we preferred to fly the "gravy missions" when strong aerial opposition was expected. It's still amazing to me how well morale held up under those conditions, but leadership made the difference.

Dick Bong wasn't a notable combat leader but there were compensations. He showed by example how to fight and survive in the P-38, and let it be remembered he was still flying combat long after he could have honorably accepted a cushy job in the States.

For all the glory which passed his way, Dick Bong remained unchanged and unruffled. He kept that farmboy demeanor about him which fooled many people. There was tempered Scandanavian steel below that cherubic Wisconsin exterior, and General Kenney recognized it. Early on, he identified Bong as the fighter pilot with enough stamina to become an ace of aces.

If Dick were alive today, he would be right in the middle of the American Fighter Aces Association. Certainly he would endorse the Champlin Museum in Mesa, Arizona as "home of the aces," for it provides the focal point of our organization and activities. We believe it is the finest fighter museum in the world, but more than that, we have a message.

Throughout her history, America has been kept free by men with the willingness and ability to defend her from external enemies. But the price of freedom comes high, and those of us who have seen war know only too well how dear the price can be. It is the belief of the American Fighter Aces Association that as long as we produce men like Dick Bong, and maintain the peace through strength, we'll never have to fight another world war.

John E. Purdy
President
American Fighter Aces Association

Chapter 1

Atsugi, Japan
(August 30, 1945)

At 4:15 p.m. on August 30, 1945, the first of eight Lockheed P-38 Lightnings from the American 49th Fighter Group touched down at Atsugi airstrip southeast of Tokyo. The eight Lightnings, all drawn from the group's 9th Fighter Squadron, had been designated as an honor guard for transports bearing Army and Air Force staff officers to Atsugi, the first American airfield in Japan. Although hostilities against Japan had ceased, the final surrender documents had yet to be signed in Tokyo, hence the need for fighter protection.

The eight pilots chosen for this mission were all combat veterans with service dating from the fierce fighting on Leyte and beyond. Major Pete Petrovich, the commander of the 9th FS, led the formation, his radio call-sign: Red One. Leading White Flight, the second section of four P-38s, was Captain Ed Howes, squadron operations officer. Flying wing on Howes was Captain Ken Clark. Clark was not flying his regularly assigned aircraft on August 30th, his usual mount being in the shop for inspection. Instead, Clark had been assigned a "show aircraft," a Lightning painted with special ace markings for the benefit of the press on Okinawa where the 49th FG was based.

As the P-38s turned off the runway at Atsugi Colonel Jerry Johnson, former 49th Group commander, directed the aircraft to parking sites. Aside from Johnson and a few press photographers on hand to record the P-38s' arrival, the only other witnesses to this historic event were several Japanese policemen who were to guard the aircraft. Johnson and the photographers left soon after, leaving the eight fighter pilots feeling very isolated in the midst of an enemy numbering in the millions.

As the pilots turned to and began unloading their aircraft the Japanese policemen dropped their normal reserve and came closer, peering intently at the first Americans they had ever seen and their menacing-looking fighters. As they beheld the markings on Clark's aircraft they began gesturing and talking animatedly, for here was clearly the machine of a great ace!

Stretching in even rows from the nose to the wing fairing and halfway down from the glare shield to the ammunition ejector chutes were 40 Japanese flags, each designating a confirmed kill. Chattering excitedly amongst themselves the Japanese glanced back and forth from the P-38 to the American pilots, respect in their eyes. Then, their curiosity satisfied, they moved off, still talking about the fearsome American pilots and their mighty aircraft.

The Japanese had no way of knowing that the 40 victories displayed on that P-38L were not Clark's. Nor could they have known that the man whose score was reflected by those 40 kill flags was not even among the eight pilots busily unloading their aircraft. That man would never set foot in Japan nor enjoy the fruits of a victory he had worked so hard to achieve, having perished in an air crash only three weeks previously.

Yet his record of service to his country, as symbolized by those 40 flags, would stand as a legacy. It would bring to mind desperate air battles fought over Pacific locales with tongue-twisting names like Dobodura, Bena Bena, Lae, Balikpapan and Tacloban. It would stir memories of ordinary men named Johnson, McGuire and Lynch performing extraordinary feats of bravery in a rugged, twin-engined "fork-tailed devil" of a fighter made by Lockheed Aircraft. Most of all, it would rekindle thoughts of a quiet Wisconsin farm boy named Bong.

Chapter 2

Poplar
(September 1920 - May 1941)

In the late 1800s settlers began moving into the raw, untamed areas of northern Wisconsin. One such settler was Gust Bong, a native of Sweden, who sailed to America in 1896 and purchased land near the tiny logging and farming community of Poplar in the upper northwestern corner of the state. One year later the rest of the Bong family, including Gust's son Carl, journeyed to Poplar. In 1919, after service in France during World War I, Carl returned to Poplar and married Dora Bryce, a slim, energetic woman with a tomboy air. Carl and Dora moved into a two-story frame house located on an 80-acre spread two-and-a-half miles south of Poplar. On September 24, 1920 their first child was born, a son they named Richard Ira.

Dick was the first of nine children, a population explosion that strained the Bong household to bursting. A year after Dick's arrival a sister - Nelda - was born. In short order Nelda was followed by Betty, Geraldine, Carl, Joyce, Barbara, Sue and Jim.[1] The Bong family was a big, bustling household bound together by love, laughter, music and lots of hard work.

Carl Bong's main livelihood was building roads, a trade he learned during World War I while in the Army Engineers. In the winter he logged, contracting to skid pulp wood. Initially farming was a sideline, providing enough to meet the needs of the family. In time the farming grew to the point where the Bongs owned or leased five farms with a total acreage of 200 acres. As the eldest child, Dick soon learned that he was expected to play a leading role in the farm's operation.

Gene Edgette, a childhood friend, supplied the following description of life on the Bong farm: "Being a village boy with no farm responsibilities, I marveled at the organization of a farm family with daily chores to perform seven days a week, come rain or come shine. Dick was responsible for feeding the hogs, milking the cows, feeding and watering them, cleaning the barn and bedding them down. Very often his dad was doing construction work and Dick had full responsibility for these chores. Then it was up in the morning, before six, to repeat the process before catching the school bus.

"Everyone in the family had an assignment either to prepare the meal, make beds, do dishes, do the chores or make the lunches. Everything moved like an assembly line. With nine kids it had to be that way. Dick's mother was on top of them like a WAC sergeant but you could always see the love and pride in her eyes."

The daily routine of chores coupled with more taxing duties such as combining, haying and helping his dad haul firewood out of the woods toughened Dick's compact frame over the years. Standing 5'6" tall, Dick normally weighted in at 155 pounds, depending on whether he had had too much of his mom's fricasseed chicken to eat! As soon as he was tall enough to reach the pedals, Dick's father put him behind the wheel of the Farm-all tractor owned by the Bongs. By the time he was 14 Dick was quite adept at manhandling the Farm-all F-12 tractor around the back forty. The time Dick spent as a tractor jockey helped develop his arm muscles and also helped develop good hand-foot coordination.

Farm life was not only beneficial from a physical standpoint. The farm family environment nurtured individual development while emphasizing the need for and importance of teamwork and common goals. Farm life, through daily example, brought out the value of hard work, fair play, duty, honor and self-worth.

And finally it wrapped the whole learning experience in a protective covering of laughter and love, joy and sorrow, tenderness and caring (along with a smack on the behind when needed!)

Farm chores aside, there always seemed to be time for other activities. Dick and the others, for instance, were very active in 4-H affairs, Dick joining 4-H when he was ten years old. His first project was in forestry and involved planting 300 evergreens to serve as a windbreak between the farm and the north fields. In 1936 Dick was elected president of the local 4-H chapter.

Hunting and fishing were a way of life in northern Wisconsin, the menfolk being expected to supplement the family diet with fresh game and fish. The northwoods abounded in rabbit, squirrel, ruffed grouse and deer. Hunting regulations were observed more in spirit than in fact, no-one questioning Dick's dad, for example, when fresh venison appeared on the family table in September! Dick developed into a pretty fair shot himself, taking the field with his Model 90 Winchester .22 caliber, a present on his 12th birthday. Trout lurked in the Poplar River, part of which ran through the Bong property. On one memorable opening day in 1933 Dick hauled in a 13½-inch brookie, a record that stood for six years in the Bong clan.

Then, too, exploring the wilds of nearby woods with childhood pals brought many hours of pleasure as related by Erland Bjork: "Many a time Dick and I ran away from his sisters and brothers so we could be alone fishing at Erickson's Hole. A lot of times we went hunting together with that old Winchester pump .22 of his. One time we even came across a still in the pasture where a friend of Dick's dad was making moonshine. A couple of days later we stopped back and almost every crock was gone! I guess somebody didn't dare take a chance on having two kids knowing about that."

When the winter snows melted the skates and hockey sticks were put away and out came baseball gloves, bats and balls. The end of the school year brought with it American Legion and town team baseball. Like his dad, Dick liked to pitch and, in time, developed a pretty good curve ball. Dick was active in sports, playing on the high school baseball and basketball teams and, later, the Poplar hockey and baseball teams.

Gene Edgette remembered Dick's love of sports, commenting that Dick "loved hockey because it combined speed, agility, individual skill, team play and physical contact. He skated well and was extremely competitive.

"Dick could hit a baseball or softball with real authority. Not only in Legion ball but later in the Vacationland League he could match any hitter in averages or distance (except me, of course.) At the plate he was very tenacious. He would foul off a dozen balls until he got the one he wanted. I pitched against him in the Vacationland League and he was extremely difficult to strike out or get out in any fashion. He had keen eyesight, which certainly helped him as a pilot.

"I wouldn't call him a great basketball player because he lacked height but he could shoot, pass and lead a team exceptionally well. Having a keen mind and leadership ability, he analyzed the game carefully and directed the team well."

Music played a large part in Dick's life. The Bong household boasted a piano which the girls took turns playing. Family singalongs at the end of the day were quite common. Dick also sang in the choir of Poplar's Bethany Lutheran Church. Reverend Arvid Hoorn recalled that "Dick had a fine tenor voice and he wasn't afraid to sing out. But there were some folks who said the only time they ever heard Dick use his speaking voice was when he gave the answers the day he was confirmed."

In high school, band and the occasional play production were just about Dick's only extracurricular activities. His efforts at taming a musical instrument - he played clarinet in the high school band - drew mixed reactions. His mother gave him credit but later admitted he was "not much of a player." Dick later rued the day he signed up for one particular play. In it he played a character named Pinky. His classmates picked up on the nickname and, agreeing that the moniker fitted Dick with his rosy complexion, hereafter christened him "Pinky" Bong. Such activities aside, farm chores limited Dick's free time, especially in his senior year when he commuted to Superior Central High School, a 44-mile round trip. Despite a hectic work schedule Dick finished 18th in his class of 428.

In the fall of 1938 Dick began classes at the Superior State Teachers College. The school offered courses for training teachers from kindergarten through senior high level. Graduates of the four-year program received a Bachelor of Education degree. When Dick entered Superior State his mother, among others, assumed he would pursue engineering studies. His father wanted Dick to become a civil engineer. Dick, however, had already set his mind on a different goal, a career far removed from the mundane world of engineering.

It is difficult to pinpoint the exact moment when Dick first became enamored of flying. His sister Nelda remembered that as a boy Dick would stop work whenever an airplane passed nearby, following it with rapt attention until it passed from sight. In Nelda's words: "Dick wasn't interested in hopped-up autos. All he could think about was planes." During the long winter months Dick would toil over models of World War I Nieuports and Spads along with Ryan STs and Mono-Coupes.

Certainly the period immediately after World War I witnessed advances in aviation that thrilled and inspired millions of people around the world. In May 1919 an American flying boat flew the Atlantic, the first aircraft to accomplish this feat. One month later Alcock and Brown, in a Vickers Vimy, made the crossing non-stop. A month after that, a British airship made the first round-trip crossing of the Atlantic. The new decade would witness even more daring flights. In 1922 Jimmy Doolittle sped across the United States in under 24 hours. The first around-the-world flight came two years later. In 1926 Richard Byrd became the first person to see the North Pole from the air. And in May 1927 Charles Lindbergh made what is arguably the most influential flight in history when he soloed the Atlantic.

Aviation dominated national and world headlines during the 1920s and 30s. Colorful characters like Roscoe Turner, Wiley Post and Amelia Earhart were front-page news. Travel-Airs, Laird Super Solutions and Gee Bee racers tore through the skies, competing for fame and glory. Not to be outdone, the Army Air Corps staged various goodwill and record-breaking flights along with airpower demonstrations. Newsstands featured the adventures of *G-8 and His Battle Aces, Bill Barnes, Air Adventurer* and countless others. Movie audiences thrilled to *Wings, Hell's Angels* and *The Dawn Patrol*. Aviation permeated everywhere and it was heady stuff, intoxicating to many.

For Dick the turning point came in 1928. President Calvin Coolidge was vacationing in the area, his "summer White House" being located in the Superior Central High School. Every day Coolidge's mail was flown up to Superior, the aircraft's track coincidentally taking it right over Poplar. Some years later Dick recalled that the mail plane "flew right over our house and I knew then I wanted to be a pilot."

So, as Dick began his studies at Superior Teachers College in 1939, he had already decided on a career in aviation. Considering his lack of finances, Dick had given himself a difficult feat to accomplish. Fortunately he was able to utilize the government-sponsored Civilian Pilot Training Program in his last semester at Superior to obtain the flying experience he desired.

The CPT Program had been established by President Franklin Roosevelt in 1938 as a response to the growing menace of the Axis powers. Roosevelt, feeling war was inevitable, wanted to beef up America's military might before the event. The CPT Program, which entailed training 20,000 private pilots a year at America's colleges and universities, was one way to build up a cadre of pilots should war come. The program was run under the auspices of the Civil Aeronautics Authority.

At this time the Army Air Corps was accepting cadet applications for flight training, the only prerequisite being two-and-a-half years of college. Dr. Paul Miller, one of Dick's college instructors who also taught the pre-flight segment of the CPT course, felt that Dick "only wanted enough college work to qualify him for the Air Force. Soon as he had his civilian pilot certificate, he was on his way." In fact, Dick was so committed to obtaining his certificate that he excluded all else, Dr. Miller observing: "I don't think he knew there were any girls in the college!"

Regrettably few details have surfaced about Dick's training in the CPT Program. Like thousands of others, Dick's training came at the controls of a Piper J-3 Cub, his first flight being on September 24, 1940. Entries in his logbook by various instructors provide brief glimpses into the developing pilot. It was noted that overall Dick "was cooperative, relaxed, alert and consistent." He possessed "good control touch, good coordination and good speed sense." However, his instructors also noted he "skids on turns" and "climbs too steep." In all Dick logged some 36 hours of CPT flight time. As his confidence grew he occasionally flew to Poplar, where he would put on an impromptu air show for friends and family.

The fall 1940 semester was Dick's last at Superior State. In early 1941 he applied for the Army Air Corps' Aviation Cadet Program. There is little evidence that Dick took this step because of an interest in getting into combat. Rather, all indications point to Dick following his plan of action - service in the Air Corps followed by a career in commercial aviation. On May 29, 1941 Dick reported for induction at Wausau, Wisconsin and soon after was on his way west, bound for Tulare, California and Primary School.

Chapter 3

Learning the Trade
(May 1941 - May 1942)

Prior to his assignment to the Rankin Aeronautical Academy at Tulare, Dick had rarely been out of the state. Consequently, the train trip west was an education and an eye opener for him. Dick, who became an avid letter writer while in service, described the journey in a letter to his family:

"At Chicago we stopped at Northwestern Station and were taken by taxi to LaSalle Station. I was in Chicago about five-and-a-half hours and wanted to go to the Field Museum but didn't figure I had time. We got in just in time to see the last part of the Memorial Day parade on Michigan Boulevard. The town is so noisy you can hardly hear yourself think. There are street cars on the street level and subways and elevated streetcars all making a lot of noise. At night the town is actually brighter than it is in the daytime. I didn't like Chicago in the daytime but it looked pretty good at night.

"We pulled out on the *Californian* about 8:00 p.m. Memorial Day. Sleeping on a train is the berries and I don't mean maybe. The porter called the berths a honey-moon bed when we asked him how two are going to sleep in them. They are a honey-moon bed all right because you have to sleep close together or the outside one will fall into the aisle. We crossed the Mississippi during the night so I didn't see it.

"Kansas is just one mess of wheat fields where we went through. There are some gullies and stuff that slightly remind you of the Badlands of the Dakotas. I slept right through Oklahoma so I don't know what it looks like.

"The next stop was El Paso which was as close as we got to Mexico. It's a pretty nice town. There was an awful lot of horses at Fort Bliss just outside of El Paso. What little bit of Texas I saw was range country. I saw quite a few horses and cattle grazing along the tracks.

"New Mexico was about the most barren country I ever saw next to Arizona. We began to run into the mountains in New Mexico and cactus began to appear. In Arizona we saw a lot of cactus of all kinds. That prickly pear really looks like dangerous stuff. I slept through the rest of Arizona and woke up next morning in California. Along the tracks were endless orchards of oranges, grapes and tangerines.

"We were in sight of the mountains until we got near Los Angeles. At Los Angeles we stopped for about one hour and 20 minutes but it was so early in the morning there wasn't much traffic yet. I did go through the post office and some other large buildings. I noticed one thing though, and that was that you could see a double feature for five cents.

"On the way out of Los Angeles we saw the Lockheed Aircraft Corporation and one other. At one field that we passed there were about 200 camouflaged planes of the light bomber class for Britain. We left Los Angeles through a mountain pass and went through about 30 tunnels before we got into the San Joaquin Valley which is were we are now."

Dick would be based at the Rankin Aeronautical Academy at Tulare, California for the next three months. Rankin was one of the civilian flying schools scattered across the country being used for Primary flight training of Army Air Corps students. Under the program set up by General "Hap" Arnold, the Air Corps was responsible for the training program and supplied the students, aircraft and curriculum. All ground school

Learning the Trade

and flight instruction was given by civilian instructors. The civilian operators would provide housing and food for the cadets along with other facilities and services stipulated by the Army Air Corps.

The Rankin school had only begun operations as an Air Corps flight training center in May 1941, so when Dick reported for duty construction was still going on. Located eight miles southeast of Tulare, the school sprawled over some 900 acres of sun-baked, coyote-infested prairie land. The school was operated by Robert Norswing and a larger-than-life stunt pilot named John Gilbert Rankin, known to one and all as "Tex."

To Dick and the other cadets "Tex" Rankin was the personification of a hot pilot. Physically Rankin looked more like a businessman, being rather heavy-set with black hair thinning at the top. He even wore gold-rimmed eyeglasses. But Rankin was a character, having run away from home at age 16 to join the Northwest Mounted Police. The Mounties, not unexpectedly, sent him back home to Breham, Texas. Rankin had served in World War I in the Aviation Section of the Army Signal Corps. He had first come to prominence in 1930 when he set a record of 19 consecutive outside loops. During the 30s he toured with various air shows, thrilling crowds with his stunt flying. Previously he had owned and operated the Rankin School of Flying based at Van Nuys, California.

Dick arrived at Tulare on June 2, 1941 and quickly became immersed in Primary Training. Primary would be followed by Basic and then Advanced, with more complex aircraft awaiting the cadet as he progressed through the system.

Dick's letters home recorded his progress at Rankin. On June 2nd he wrote: "I have finally arrived and have just finished making my bunk and cleaning up the barracks. We have very wonderful quarters. My roommate and I have a room about 16 by 12 by 8 feet with a shower and toilet next door. We have a list of instructions a mile long to learn besides having to march on the double quick wherever we go and saying sir to all the upper classmen. There will be about 60 boys in our class. We have 32 Stearman biplane trainers and an instructor for every four boys. We start flying next week on Monday."

The start of Dick's Primary training was delayed as he recorded in a letter dated June 7th: "I have been confined to quarters or with a special detail of myself and three other boys ever since Wednesday night. It seems that after we left Fort Sheridan an epidemic of scarlet fever broke out so we are quarantined for 12 days. The rest of the 'dodoes,' as the new men are called, will start flying Monday but we don't start until Thursday."

Again, on June 15th: "I didn't fly last Thursday after I got out of quarantine because the instructor was sick. However, the chief pilot took me up on Friday the 13th and I had to do spins and stalls and a take-off besides a bunch of turns. I got in 50 minutes of flying and I got a little bit air-sick but not very much."

The training schedule at Rankin was tough going. Normally Dick and the other cadets rolled out of bed at 5:30 a.m. with a half-hour of calisthenics at 6:00 and breakfast at 6:40. At 7:25 the cadets fell in and marched off to the flight line where the Stearmans were waiting. Flying was done in the morning from 7:30 to 12:30. Ground school ran from 1:30 to 4:30 followed by drill and calisthenics till 6:00. Retreat was sounded at 6:45 with call to quarters at 8:00. The remainder of the evening was spent on ground school lessons ranging from theory of flight to trigonometry, meteorology, navigation and engine structure.

Along with technical terminology Dick learned a number of new expressions peculiar to flying. As previously mentioned, the new cadets at Rankin were termed "dodoes" and were subject to hazing by the upperclassmen. A senior would yell at Dick to "get in a brace" and he would stand rigidly at attention until the upperclassman let him go. Another favorite game was "red light." A cadet, perhaps on his way to the flight line or classes, would freeze at attention when a senior called out "red light." He couldn't move until the upperclassman gave him the green light. A cadet also learned about "hedge hopping" (flying at very low altitude), "sinkers" (down-drafts that pushed an aircraft's nose down), "stuffed clouds" (a mountain with a cloud wrapped around it) and the dreaded "washout" (being dropped from the program.)

John T. Africa, coordinator of training operations at Rankin, recalled that Dick "took a lot of punishment without flinching." Africa remembered that Dick was called "Mister" Bong because of his boyish looks. He summed up Dick in the following words:

"He talked low but was quick on the trigger. Bong had a hell of a good mind. He had a great deal of curiosity. He wanted to learn. He wanted to know all there was to know about flying an airplane. He'd spend his leisure time in the control tower to learn how traffic was controlled. Yet, with all of that, he wasn't an outstanding student. He was one of the herd. Nobody would select him as a hot pilot or a hot shot. There were 60 cadets in his class and he didn't stand out. He had a nice personality, not forward. He wasn't the kind to shoot the breeze."[1]

Dick soloed on June 25th with six hours of Primary time under his belt. Some cadets weren't doing as well, as Dick reported in a letter home, mentioning that "two of the boys ground-looped their planes today and wrecked the wing on both planes a little. My instructor demonstrated a couple of chandelles today and they were fun. Not that I'm boasting or anything but my instructor tells me I'm one of the best students he ever had that has had previous flying time." By the first of July eight men had washed out of Dick's class.

On July 12th Dick became an upperclassman when the old class rotated out. He and several other classmates celebrated their new status by taking a side trip to Sequoia National Park, a welcome change from Tulare where temperatures often ranged in the high 90s. Dick had a little trouble adjusting to his new status, reporting that "we've got a bunch of about 52 dodoes here now. It's just as hard for me to get used to them calling me Sir as it was for me to get used to our calling our upperclassmen Sir."

By the end of July Dick had passed his 40-hour check ride, commenting: "I'm having great fun now because I'm getting lots of flying upside down. It certainly gives you a new perspective and a peculiar sensation to be hanging by your safety belt with your head straight down. I'm getting so used to steep turns and upside down flying that I don't get a thrill out of it anymore."

As the new month dawned Dick's time at Tulare drew to a close. On August 3rd he told his family that "two weeks from now we leave Tulare. I don't know where we are going yet so I can't tell you that. I haven't anything new to tell you about me out here. I've got about 47 hours in now, about 25 hours solo and 22 hours dual. I'm doing acrobatics now all the time. I've blacked myself out a couple of times diving out of a half roll. It only lasts a few seconds and then I'm normal again.

"I'm getting kind of fat out here now. I weigh 162 pounds now which is about two pounds more than I ever weighed at home. I had a T-bone in town tonight for supper which is not going to help me from getting fat.

"I'm afraid there is not much chance of me getting home for hunting season but I have hopes of getting home for Christmas. It may be that I can't get home until after I'm commissioned. If that is so, why I won't get home until February sometime."

A week later Dick's orders came through. He was ordered to report to Gardner Field near Taft, California at noon on August 19th to begin Basic training. After Dick passed his 60-hour check ride on the 11th he began preparing for the move to Taft, feeling pleased that he had made the grade at Rankin. Almost a third of the cadets in Dick's class had been washed out by this time. On graduation day Dick and his classmates were treated to an air show put on by "Tex" Rankin, who topped off the show by writing the class numerals in the sky. And then it was on to Gardner Field.

When he first arrived at Gardner Field Dick wasn't too enthused about what he found, describing it as "much worse looking than Tulare. The barracks aren't as good and there is only one drinking fountain in each barracks building." The lack of watering holes for the cadets was important since "Taft is hotter than it was at Tulare, if such a thing is possible." Dick may have been overly critical about Taft because he was impatient to try out the BT-13 trainers which he would fly in Basic. On August 25th he could finally report: "I've been here six days now and I finally got up in an airplane today. They are swell. We cruise along at 120 mph in these planes."

Dick's stay at Taft turned out to be fairly pleasant, in part because friends and relatives lived in nearby Los Angeles. On those weekends when Dick could get away he would explore Los Angeles, Anaheim, Santa Barbara and Long Beach in the company of friends. He really enjoyed L.A., admitting that he wouldn't mind living there. Dick had looked forward to seeing the Pacific Ocean but perhaps built his hopes too high, since he wrote home that "it wasn't very inspiring. It looks just like Lake Superior."

The schedule at Taft was a demanding one, Dick and the other cadets being introduced to cross-country flights, formation flying and instrument flying. Of the three Dick felt "that instrument flying is the hardest. I have to fly the airplane when I can't see the ground and have to fly it by looking at the instruments only. Formation flying is kind of hard too because you have to keep the planes so close together. We fly with the parts of the different airplanes about four feet apart and you have to watch the plane beside you all the time." Dick rated night flying as "quite a thrill" but instrument flight was "just plain hard work."

Ironically, Dick's first airplane accident took place on the ground. On September 22nd he had just landed and "was rolling quite fast. There was an airplane parked way down near the end of the field. I was looking down in the cockpit when I heard a yell. I looked up and saw a bunch of mechanics running. My wing was about three feet from the other airplane's wing. I slammed on the brakes because I was still going between 15 and 20 miles an hour. The plane nosed over and the propeller started digging a hole in the ground. Then the tail settled down again and I stopped my engine and got out of the airplane. My left wing went right under his left wing. If I would have been two feet to the left I would have ruined a whole wing on the parked airplane and ruined the engine on mine. As it was there wasn't much damage done and I only got five stars for the incident. The instructor bawled me out some..."

As the training intensified Dick began putting in some long hours, as he recounted in a letter dated October 9th: "Oh, what a day. I got in the airplane at 1:15 p.m. and didn't get out of it until 5:30, that is 4:15 in one sitting. I left on the cross country at 1:30 and got back at 4:30. When I got back I took off right away for 45 (min.) of aerobatics. That was a relief because I wasn't sitting all the time in that. I was upside down half the time. Over in the Mojave Desert there is a bunch of bombing targets. They look so small I don't see how they can hit them at all. I flew formation with one of the other boys part of the way. I'm all done with cross country now and I have 59.00 hours. I've got 45 (min.) of aerobatics, 1:15 instruments, 3:00 formation and 6:00 hours of just plain flying left."

As Dick neared the end of the course at Taft rumors began circulating as to where he would be sent next, the likely candidates being Phoenix, Stockton or Mather Field. Dick speculated that he had "about a 50-50 chance of being an instructor. I'm pretty sure that I wouldn't get sent out of the U.S. because they are getting almost enough volunteers now for that." This last statement may have been made to allay fears that Dick would be involved in a combatant role should war break out. Yet even as Dick was writing, Japan had put its plans for an attack on the American naval base at Pearl Harbor into effect. In this same letter Dick, perhaps with his eye still on a career in aviation, mentioned: "I'm trying to get into twin-engine flying in advanced because twin-engine time will be the most valuable when I get out of here." That twin-engine time Dick spoke of would prove valuable, but in a totally different context than what he intended.

Although Dick had thought he would go straight to Advanced after he finished at Taft, events turned out otherwise, enabling him to spend some time with his family in late October. The time in Poplar was a welcome break but getting back to Taft proved quite an adventure. Dick later related that he "got to Minneapolis all right and got to the airport. I met my CAA instructor at the field down there. About 8:00 a.m. Champion (another Taft cadet) showed up and we got all set to go. We took off and flew above the clouds all the way to Sioux City, Iowa and landed there ok. We were then informed that we would have to wait until about 3:00 p.m. before we could get to Omaha. The weather was worse than before so we took a train to Omaha.

"At Omaha we waited five hours for another train and got out of there at 3:50 a.m. Saturday. I didn't sleep any Thursday night on the train and I didn't get to sleep Friday night either. I slept most of the way across Nebraska on Saturday morning. We got to Cheyenne and tried and tried to get a plane and couldn't so we hurried up and bought a ticket on the train for Salt Lake City. While we were on the train we got a telegram from United Air Lines saying that we could get a plane out of there Sunday morning. We got off the train at Salt Lake City at 3:30 in the morning. They made us a couple of beds to sleep on so we slept until eight o'clock. We finally got out of Salt Lake City at 1:15 p.m.

"We got to Los Angeles at 4:30 p.m. and took a bus to Taft. We arrived at Taft at 9:30 p.m. Sunday night. We got a hotel room and stayed there all night then went to the post first thing in the morning. We reported in two days late..."

Fortunately for the two junior birdmen the Army had been well aware of the bad weather covering mid-America and took no action against them. Time was of the essence however, Dick leaving Taft that very day for his next duty station - Phoenix, Arizona.

On November 4, 1941 Dick, having finished the Basic course at Taft, reported in at Luke Field near Phoenix for Advanced training. Luke was the final step in the training process, graduates being posted to operational Army Air Force units.[2] The prime trainer at Luke was the North American AT-6 Texan,

America's best-known training aircraft. On November 7th Dick had his turn at the Texan and reported: "I had my first ride in the AT-6A yesterday and it is a lot more airplane than the BT-13A. They have about 100 planes here of all types. Some BTs, quite a few ATs, two P-64s and even a few PT-13s that we flew in primary. There is one bomber here also.

"We get training in the Link trainer here too. We will get formation, night flying, cross-country, night cross-country, instrument work, aerial gunnery at both ground targets and moving targets. They have one machine gun on each of the AT-6As.

"There were two guys killed here a week before we got here. They were flying instruments and the guy in the front seat wasn't paying enough attention."

By the 14th Dick had soloed and was making good progress. Others were not so fortunate, Dick mentioning: "We've been having a lot of accidents here this week. There have been about eight planes cracked up on the ground but nobody has been hurt. One of the upperclassmen took a P-64 up yesterday and ran out of gas up north of here about 60 miles. He made a forced landing and got down safely."

Ground school started at the end of November but Dick sometimes had trouble concentrating on the information being presented. In Wisconsin it was hunting season - deer hunting season - and Dick grew homesick at the thought of missing the action, writing home: "Boy do I wish I was there to run around and hunt."

Several days later Dick found time to dash off a hasty letter detailing his progress: "We finish up ground school this week and then start shooting skeet and flying the Link trainers. I guess we start gunnery next week. Tomorrow or next day I'm going on a high altitude hop. We go up to 24,000 feet, oxygen and everything and cold weather, of course. Takes half an hour to get up that high and 17 seconds to get back down again. That's moving right along. I'm kind of looking forward to it as a new experience because I've never been up higher than about 13,000 feet before."

Normally in his letters home Dick rarely discussed the worsening world situation, preferring to keep his letters full of questions about home and family along with progress reports on his training. In this same letter, however, he made an indirect allusion to the war in Europe and the part he might play should America become involved, reporting that "15 of (the upperclassmen) are going to ferry P-40s over to Southeast Africa for six months. Our class is going to do that but we don't know who or how many. I guess most of us are going to put in for combat groups, most likely foreign."

Four days after Dick penned those lines, 353 warplanes from the Japanese aircraft carriers *Akagi*, *Kaga*, *Soryu*, *Hiryu*, *Shokaku* and *Zuikaku* devastated Pearl Harbor and plunged America into world war. Initial reports of the disaster at Pearl Harbor were confusing, sometimes contradictory but always horrifying. In the weeks immediately following the "Day of Infamy" Dick's letters reflected the comparative isolation he and the other cadets lived in. They also reflected an almost all-encompassing determination on Dick's part to ignore outside events, however world-shaking, and concentrate on the most important goal in his life - graduating from Luke.

On December 8th he wrote: "Well it seems from the radio this afternoon that we are having a little trouble with Japan. A paper just came in and the headlines say that Japan declared war on the U.S. Well that just about cinches the Christmas situation. Our graduation day may be set up a ways."

Six days later he opened with: "So we have a war. I never see a paper so you know more about it than I do. We have rumors here that we are going to be moved. Don't know where to yet... Has the war made any changes back there? It hasn't here except that everything is fitted up for blackout and the guard is a lot more strict."

On December 19th he asked: "How is the war coming? I never see a paper and don't hear the radio very much so I don't know as much about it as you do... There is some talk of sending our class to Alaska and there is also some talk that we will be Basic instructors. I'm getting so that I don't care anymore. One thing is as good as another and you haven't any choice any way."

In mid-December the rumor mill died as the official word went out. Graduation would be advanced two weeks to January 2nd. By that time Dick was "in ground school now so you can see I didn't get my instrument check. All the rest of my flying time will be night flying, ground gunnery and aerial gunnery. I've got $57\frac{1}{2}$ hours already and will probably get about 25 or 30 more. It's going to be rather a busy schedule because we've only got two weeks to do it in."

As events turned out graduation was actually a week later, on January 9th. On December 31, 1941 Dick completed his training at Luke, reporting: "I finished flying yesterday and passed my instrument check. I've got 205 hours and 30 minutes of army flying now and 36 hours of CAA. I've been up in the air quite a while now. I finish ground school tomorrow and I passed my code test quite a while ago. I'm still awful bad at skeet shooting. Every time I shoot at those clay pigions I get worse." This last comment is interesting in that much later, when Dick was a top-scoring ace, reporters thought he was pulling their legs when he kept maintaining he really wasn't a very good aerial shot.

One of Dick's instructors at Luke Field was Barry Goldwater. Senator Goldwater recalled: "I had him in ground school, where I was teaching the fundamentals of air-to-air gunnery or, as we call it, fighter gunnery. He was a very bright student, I can remember, but the most important thing came from a check pilot who flew the first P-38 into Luke Field and went up to check out different cadets in evasive tactics." He said that Bong was probably the finest natural pilot that he had ever met. There was no way in the world he could keep Bong from getting on his tail, even though Bong would be flying an AT-6, a very slow airplane, and he was flying the P-38 which Bong later became a Medal of Honor winner in.

"Being such a natural pilot, it was just a certainty that he would wind up one of our top aces, which he did. I happen to have had a date to play golf with him on the day that he crashed and was killed in taking off from Burbank. He was a wonderful young man, probably one of the finest we had in World War II."

On January 9, 1942 graduation exercises for the Class of 42-A were held, one of the graduates being Aviation Cadet Richard I. Bong, serial number 16022192. Dick's diploma was signed by the Commandant of the Advanced Flying School, Lieutenant Colonel Ennis C. Whitehead. Whitehead had already decided to keep Dick at Luke as an instructor because "Bong could simply fly an AT-6 better than his contemporaries and for that reason made a much better score on tow targets. He was good enough so that we kept him as an instructor for several months. He was a good one."

Initially Dick, now a second lieutenant, was disappointed in being retained at Luke as an instructor. Many months later, after he had become America's ranking ace, he reflected back on the Luke assignment. Dick admitted that it was an "assignment I hated at the time but now (I) realize it was the best thing that ever happened to me. When I graduated from flight school, they made me an instructor - that hurt my pride and I didn't like the assignment at all. But about the second week I began learning how very little I really knew about flying. The fastest way to recognize your own shortcomings is to try to teach someone else the right way of doing something."[3]

Whatever Dick's feelings about the Luke assignment, the Air Force didn't give him much time to ruminate about the posting. Within the month Dick was leading flights of cadets over the Arizona countryside as he recounted to his family: "Well I have finally finished instructors school (on the 23rd). I flew 37 hours in seven days. That includes about 12 hours of night flying, a cross-country trip to El Paso and back and a lot of instrument flying.

"Last night I started instructing. I took charge of five cadets and took them on a cross country to Yuma and back and then gave them some night formation. It's a great life if you don't weaken."

Despite the tongue-in-cheek comment about the "great life" Dick found instructing a curious combination of fun, hard work and tragedy. On February 17th he spoke of one night when "we lost five airplanes and four cadets. We lost another airplane and cadet yesterday. He was flying and shooting aerial gunnery and ran into the cable of the tow target. The cable cut his wing off and he spun in.

"I've been out searching for three more airplanes that are lost around here somewhere. They are not from Luke Field though. It's a lot of fun flying on search missions because in order to see anything you have to fly close to the ground. I flew for about four hours at altitudes between 10 and 100 feet off the ground. It's great fun but kind of dangerous in the mountains."

In early March Dick and another instructor decided to pay the Grand Canyon a visit in their AT-6s, Dick marveling: "It certainly is a big hole in the ground. I was flying over the ground at 180 miles per hour and just barely over the tree tops when we came to the edge of the canyon. The ground just simply dropped away from me. It sure gave me a funny feeling. The ground just drops almost straight down for a mile at the place that we hit the canyon. The canyon isn't much to see after the first look through. I was flying down in it and did a loop in it and never got to the top of the wall on the whole loop."

March also brought a surprising development, Dick and the other Luke instructors being offered a chance to be in a Hollywood movie! Fox Studios was shooting a flick entitled *Thunder Birds* at nearby Thunderbird Field, one of the largest primary flight schools in the Training Command. Directed by William Wellman, the movie starred Preston Foster as a hardbitten flying instructor and John Sutton as a Royal Air Force flying cadet. Between aerial hops the two competed for the hand of Gene Tierney. *Thunder Birds* was pretty standard fare, but it did benefit from some marvelous stunt work by Paul Mantz and the presence of Air Force trainers.

Dick recounted his days in front of the cameras in several of his letters home. On March 21st he opened with: "What do you think I was doing today? I was over at Thunderbird Field flying PT-17s in formation for a movie. 20th Century Fox is making a movie over there called *Thunderbirds* with Gene Tierney, Preston Foster and Jack Holt. Fifteen instructors from Luke went over to do the flying scenes for them. We didn't get more than 500 feet off the ground at any time. They gave us a big steak dinner and it sure was good. I hope I get a chance to see that picture."

And on April 1st: "The name of that show will be *Thunderbirds*. My ship was 231 and I flew a couple others, too. However I'll probably see it before you do so I'll be able to tell you what scenes to look for."

Lastly, on April 5th: "I was over to Thunderbird Field today flying for the movies again. Same picture but we flew AT-6As today and I was flying 305. I think it will show up in the camera quite well because I was pretty close to it a few times. I understand we are going to get paid $25 a day for that flying so that makes $50 I've got coming." (Dick collected his money at the end of the month.)

As previously mentioned, instructing duty could be fun (as in stunting for the movies) or it could turn dangerous. On March 21st Dick had a fairly close call in bad weather, recounting that: "I'm darned lucky to be back at all because on our way back the weather was so bad we had to fly close to the ground along the railroad tracks. We ran into some fog. I couldn't see the telephone poles along the railroad tracks when I was only ten feet above them flying at 160 miles an hour. I came out of the fog right over a little town and there was a grain elevator right in front of me so I had to pull up to get over the top of it. If I hadn't got out of the fog I would have ran right into the grain elevator."

On April 24th Dick's first class of cadets graduated. He had pretty well adjusted to life as an instructor and was even talking about buying a car "so I can come and go as I please without having to wait around and bum a ride." There were a number of officers with cars "but most of them are guys who want to go to town and drink and stay out late and that isn't quite to my liking." If his dad could help him with a loan, Dick was thinking about a "club coupe or sedan (1940-41) with good tires." Unfortunately, the Air Force had other plans and were already cutting orders for him, orders that would have far-reaching effects on Dick's Air Force career.

Chapter 4

Countdown to Combat
(May - September 1942)

On May 6, 1942 Dick reported to the 49th Pursuit Squadron, 14th Pursuit Group stationed at Hamilton Field, San Francisco. The 14th PG had been activated at Hamilton on January 15, 1941 and spent the remainder of the year training at March Field and other bases. Dick's assigned unit, the 49th PS, had flown a mixture of Curtiss P-40s and Vultee P-66s until early December 1941 when several Lockheed P-38 Lightnings, borrowed from other West Coast units, arrived. The squadron was not brought up to full strength until February 1942 when it fielded 25 P-38s, mostly E models. In May 1942 the squadron, commanded by Major Kenneth Wade, moved to Hamilton Field.

The 14th PG was assigned to the Fourth Air Force which was responsible for the defense of the West Coast. The stay at Hamilton, as most suspected, was to be a short one. In his first speech to the 49th Squadron Major Wade informed the men that the 14th PG was destined for overseas duty. The rumor mill indicated, in Dick's words, "a crack at the Japs" but that was incorrect. The unit was actually destined for the North African front. In a letter home Dick speculated that at best "we will be in Frisco for about two or three months and then sent to foreign duty."

In any case, Major Wade's announcement brought about a surge of activity in the squadron. The squadron history recorded. "There was an air of intensity around the hangars as new men were converted into armorers, crew chiefs, assistant line-men and engineering specialists. There were new pilots to be trained and new enlisted men to be instructed in the intricacies of servicing an airplane. And there was formation flying, gunnery and combat tactics to be learned. Everyone knew that the time was limited, that the day of departure was not far off." The tense atmosphere was heightened on June 2nd when the entire West Coast was put on alert. Japanese forces had attacked Dutch Harbor in the Aleutians! The 14th PG went on 24-hour alert. All passes were cancelled. All aircraft were loaded with live ammunition. As information on the Aleutians situation filtered down, the air of tension passed and the group turned once again to its impending deployment.

Dick's logbook reflected this air of frantic activity. After brief check-out flights in twin-engined AT-14s and C-40s he logged his first flight time in a P-38 on May 12th, a brief 40-minute orientation hop. Dick rapidly built up his time in the Lockheed fighter, regularly flying twice daily. The P-38 was quite a step up from the AT-6s Dick was used to flying. After his first flight in the Lightning, on the 12th, Dick exuberantly wrote home: "Wooey! What an airplane! That's all I can say but that is enough." In a subsequent letter he added: "It's the fastest I have ever flown and is also the easiest plane to fly that I have ever flown. However, it is nothing to get careless with. One boy was killed in one here yesterday."

The Lockheed P-38 Lightning owed its existence to a 1937 Army Air Corps specification calling for a long-range high-altitude interceptor with a speed of 360 mph at 20,000 feet. Lockheed responded with a winning design that radically differed from contemporary American fighters - a twin-engined fighter that housed the pilot in a centrally-located nacelle. The Lightning bristled with innovations such as tricycle landing gear, centrally-mounted armament of cannon and machine guns, bubble canopy, Fowler flaps and leading edge induction coolers. Compared to contemporary fighters the P-38 was massive, 150% the size of a P-39 or

P-40. In its XP-38 form the aircraft spanned 52 feet, stood nine feet six inches high and weighed in (empty) at 11,507 pounds! Luftwaffe pilots would christen the P-38 the "forked-tail devil." In the South Pacific Theater Japanese pilots would come to fear the P-38 as well.

By the time Dick reported to the 49th PS the P-38 had progessed through several models, the latest being the E model. The P-38E was the first true combat version of the Lightning and the first to see action. Its twin Allison V-1710 engines gave it a top speed of 395 mph, a service ceiling of 39,000 feet and a range of 500 miles. Armament was a lethal quartet of .50 caliber machine guns and a 20mm cannon. By way of comparison, the Curtiss P-40E, then the standard Air Force fighter, was 41 mph slower, had a service ceiling of 29,000 feet and much shorter range.

The Lightning therefore was a formidable warplane and initially enjoyed a reputation as being a "hot" aircraft to handle. The P-38's engines rotated in different directions to counteract torque. However, if one engine failed on takeoff the aircraft normally rolled inverted in split seconds and crashed. With the good engine churning out 3,000 rpm few pilots could react fast enough to contain the emergency. Two 14th PG pilots died in crashes, a third was seriously injured. Lieutenant Colonel Ben Kelsey, from Wright Field's Material Division, visited Hamilton Field on May 18th and 19th, giving lectures on the P-38 and staging an acrobatic display to bolster the confidence of the pilots in the Lightning.

As revealed in Dick's letters, home life at Hamilton Field had its pleasant moments. On May 12th he wrote: "We have a pretty nice setup here. One big hangar is devoted to athletic stuff with a basketball floor, several ping-pong tables, a couple of badminton courts, three handball courts, six bowling alleys and a boxing room. Then there are outdoor tennis courts and swimming pools." In another letter he marvelled that "about all I do around here is bowl and play ping-pong and sleep when I don't have to be on the flight line."

As the intensive training continued Dick and his fellow pilots grew more proficient in the Lightning. The late Charles Earnhart supplied the following account of Dick's growing mastery of the P-38.

Earnhart recalled: "Jim Butler, Dick and I used to fly and practice dogfights near San Francisco when we were stationed at Hamilton Field after the war started. Dick was on the quiet side, as I remember, and I never got to know him well.

"Dick, Jim and I loved to go out of the area and practice dogfights like regular combat between fighters but not using our guns. We had gun cameras but at the time the film wasn't available. We didn't need it, anyhow.

"We would climb to 15 to 20,000 feet and start from there on oxygen. With only two of us we would go in opposite directions then come back head-on at high speed in level flight. As we passed we would then go into any maneuver we could dream up to try to get on the tail of the other P-38.

"Once you were latched on to, you had to do violent maneuvers to keep the guy tailing you from getting a lead to shoot you down. You could tell this by glancing back. If the P-38 behind you was getting a good lead you just figured you were dead if it was the real thing. Of course if you were good at dogfights there wasn't any such thing as getting shot down in straight and level flight. Now when three of us flew the practice dogfights we did the same thing except it would be two P-38s against one. It was fun.

"How was Dick? He was like a cat chasing a mouse, harder than hell to shake him and get on his tail, almost impossible. He was good and, of course, the war proved it. You had to have an inborne ability to fly that fighter like you were a part of it, a born aerial acrobat. Dick had that ability 100%.

"On the ground he never had much to say that I can remember. In fact, I only remember him in the air trying to shake him off my tail. If I got on his tail I had to work like hell to stay there and many times he shook me. We came down wet with sweat. I don't even remember how many days he was with us but I don't think it was too long. I only wish the three of us could have been together all during the war."

Sadly, Charles Earnhart did not get his wish. In July the 14th Pursuit Group, now assigned to the Eighth Air Force in England, left Hamilton for colder climes. Dick did not accompany the group, having been transferred out of the 49th Squadron a month earlier. After serving briefly with Eighth Air Force, the 14th Group was committed to Operation Torch. The heavy North African fighting inevitably brought losses. Charles Earnhart was shot down after four victories and ended the war in a POW camp. Jim Butler, with two, was killed in action, hence the special poignancy of Earnhart's wish that "the three of us could have been together all during the war."

As far as can be ascertained, Dick was transferred from the 49th Squadron for breaking a standing order forbidding military aircraft from flying near the Golden Gate Bridge. Of all the flights and fights Dick was involved in as an Air Force pilot, none are more colorful or controversial than his alleged flight under the Golden Gate. Its importance to Dick's subsequent military career cannot be overemphasized since it brought him together with the man who would play a dominant role in shaping that career, General George C. Kenney. Considering its notoriety, however, the flight itself has never been explored in any depth - until now.

For many years the only description available on the alleged Golden Gate flight was found in Kenney's biography by Dick entitled *Dick Bong, Ace of Aces*. In his book Kenney recalled that he had to reprimand Dick for "looping the loop around the center span of the Golden Gate Bridge in a P-38 and waving to the stenographic help in the office buildings as he flew along Market Street. There was plenty of evidence indicating that a large part of waving had been to people on some of the lower floors of the buildings. Streetcars had stopped, taxis had run up on the sidewalks and pedestrians had fled to the nearest doorways to get indoors and under cover. (Lastly) a woman on the outskirts of Oakland was quoted as saying that she didn't need any help from Kenney's fighter pilots in removing her washing from the clothesline unless they would like to do it on the ground."[1] Such is the stuff legends are made of.

In actual fact it appears that Dick - and several other pilots - were guilty of unauthorized low-level flying in the San Francisco area. From the entries in Dick's logbook it appears the "Golden Gate flight" took place on June 11, 1942. Dick and at least three other pilots, including Lieutenant John "Jump" O'Neill, took off on a routine training mission. One eyewitness, Corporal Russell Collins, a 49th PS mechanic, claimed that Dick led the flight since he was senior officer. Collins also recalled that Dick flew the aircraft regularly assigned to Lieutenant O. G. Bluher. Collins was on the flight line when Dick landed, as was "a staff car with a major and a bird colonel (who) met Lieutenant Bong after he landed. I heard the order given to him that he was grounded as of the moment."

Aside from O'Neill, it has proven impossible to identify the other 49th PS pilots who flew that day. The only other eyewitness account available on the incident was a newspaper article penned by Dick and reporter Lee Van Atta in 1944 in which Dick denied flying under the Golden Gate. He wrote that while he "was waiting for orders to go overseas I met General Kenney. We were finishing our training in Lightnings at Hamilton Field - we being Lieutenant John O'Neill of Gasport, N.Y. and myself - and we were out cutting up in the air one day.

"O'Neill got hauled up before the Hamilton commandant for flying under San Francisco's Golden Gate Bridge. They nabbed me because I buzzed over a friend's house in San Anselmo, near the field. My friend didn't object but the neighbors next door were preparing supper and it seems that my buzz job completely upset the lady of the house, who spilled the dinner all over the kitchen.

"She wrote a letter, and with O'Neill already tagged we both went before the commandant. There was considerable talk of courtmartial. Finally General Kenney called for us and we went to San Francisco to see him - he was commanding general of the Fourth Air Force then.

"He gave us quite a lecture but admitted he went under the Brooklyn Bridge the day he won his own wings so he didn't regard buzzing a bridge a crime meriting capital punishment. He sent us back to Hamilton Field with orders to write a 5,000-word thesis on safe flying. Then we had to stand up and read the thesis to the entire squadron."

However, harsher punishment was meted out to Dick and O'Neill. Both were dropped from the 49th Squadron, Dick being assigned to the Interception Center at Fourth Air Force headquarters in San Francisco. The grounding order was in force a full six weeks, not being lifted until July 23rd.

The actual sequence of events that took place during the "Golden Gate flight" may never be known. The flight did gain Dick some notoriety among the pilots based at Hamilton but he was very reticent about talking of the flight. Walter Markey recalled that he "never remembered Dick admitting to that incident. He would simply get a sheepish grin on his face and pass on to another subject." However, in late 1943, when Dick had returned home from his first combat tour, he talked of the incident to family members and stated that he had not flown under the Golden Gate. For the time being that must remain the final word on the subject.

Soon after his encounter with Dick, General Kenney was on his way to the Pacific to take over and revitalize the rag-tag American air force in Australia and New Guinea. Kenney regarded the assignment as a "number one trouble-shooting job" since the Japanese outnumbered the Allies in the air and fielded superior aircraft and more experienced crews. Before he left for his new command, Kenney and General "Hap" Arnold worked out an agreement whereby Kenney, a firm supporter of the P-38, would get 50 Lockheeds and his pick of West Coast Lightning pilots. One of his first picks was his "stunt flying bad boy, Second Lieutenant Richard I. Bong."

Dick, of course, was unaware of the events taking place in Washington between Kenney and Arnold. Grounded indefinitely and assigned to the Intercept Center, Dick tried to make the best of the situation. Writing home on the 4th of July he commented that he "didn't know how long I'm going to be here working on the intercept board but not too long I hope. I'm off now until Monday afternoon until 4 p.m. then I work from 4 till 12 every night next week. Great fun I must say . . . I guess I'm nearly out of the doghouse now and from rumors floating around I might go to the east coast."

Unfortunately, the east coast rumors were groundless and were soon replaced by talk that had Dick being assigned to the *west* coast "up around Yakima someplace I guess." As the rumors flew thick and fast Dick tried to mask his growing impatience with his assigned duties: "I don't do anything but sit around and chew the rag with the girls and play cards all night long." His letters during July are filled with references to trips to the San Francisco zoo, pin-busting at downtown bowling alleys, attending his first professional baseball games and dinner with friends. By late July he had had enough, witness his letter of the 21st: "I'm getting so soft I don't even feel well. I haven't done a thing but sit around and sleep since they put me to work in San Francisco. All the exercise I get is walking and bowling and not much of that. I sure wish they would get me out of this Interception Center and back on flying status entirely. I'll go nuts if I stay grounded much longer."

As it happened the grounding order was lifted soon after, so Dick could report on the 26th: "Well I finally got up for an hour's flight today. Sure felt good to push one of those P-38s around the sky again. I guess I'll get some more tomorrow and next day. I go out and fly at 11:00 in the morning and go to work down here (at the Intercept Center) at 4 p.m. until midnight.

"I don't know how much longer they are going to keep me down here but I hear they are splitting the squadron again. So I imagine that I'll soon be in another squadron again. I hear they're going to give us P-39s or P-51s instead of P-38s."

The rumored changes mentioned by Dick proved to be just that, unfounded rumors. However, one welcome change did take place in early August when, in Dick's words, he "finally got out of the doghouse and am now stationed at Oakland Municipal Airport (with the 84th FS, 78th FG). I had a big day in the Interception Center yesterday with generals breathing down my neck watching me intercept planes which were attacking S.F. However, I got them all so we did all right."

Dick's new unit - the 78th FG - was gearing up for overseas deployment. Consequently the group's pilots got in as much flight time as possible, Dick logging over 43 hours in August alone. On August 30, 1942 he recorded his last stateside flight, a brief ten-minute hop in an AT-6. Shortly thereafter he and 13 other 78th FG pilots were alerted for deployment. As per the agreement between Kenney and Arnold, these pilots were to make up part of the contingent of 50 P-38 pilots going to Kenney's new Pacific command.

All during August rumors about impending moves, most centering on Australia, had been rampant as borne out by Dick's letters home. On the 13th he wrote: "You don't know how close I came to going to Australia last night. I got back to the field at 5:00 p.m. and found out I was supposed to be ready to leave at 7:00 p.m. However the order was cancelled for some reason or other so I don't know what's up now. So after the scare, why, I'm still here flying P-38s. I checked out in the A-20 airplane the other night. That is the one I've always wanted to fly and I got a half hour on it. I'd like to fly it some more."

Several days later, amid rumors that Dick was being assigned to a night-fighter outfit in Florida, he was again placed on two-hours notice for foreign duty. Air Force personnel put on notice were expected to have their affairs put in order with all bags packed ready to go in two hours. Baggage was limited to 50 pounds in addition to side arm, helmet and liner, gas mask and first-aid kit. Air crews also carried full flight gear. Although Dick thought that this time he was "definitely going," the alert proved to be another case of hurry up and wait.

Despite this frustrating state of affairs Dick kept his sense of humor. He cautioned his family: "It looks like now I won't see home until the war is over or unless I go over there and become a hero so they send me home for a couple of months." Dick good-naturedly concluded: "I guess that's what I'll have to do!"

On August 27th, Dick noted that it "looks like they don't know what they want to do. I still haven't left and they have me on 12-hour notice now. I've really been flying lately. Just got back from a trip to Reno with my squadron commander. We took off at 8:30 p.m. and got back at 10:20 p.m. That makes about eight hours night time in the last week. I looked up my time today and I now have about 595 hours. Quite a bit, eh? I've got about 90 hours in the P-38 now."

By the first of September Dick was still at Hamilton awaiting his travel orders. Although more rumors were floating around claiming that Dick was now bound for England, Australia or Alaska, Fourth Air Force Fighter Command Order SO No. 241, dated 8-29-42, scotched the rumors once and for all - it was to be Australia. In all 14 pilots, six crew chiefs and 22 mechanics, all from the 78th FG, were processed at Fort Mason before reporting to the Control Officer, Air Transport Command for transportation to the Pacific war zone. Many of these same pilots - such as "Jump" O'Neill, Theron Price, J.C. Mankin, Walter Markey, Fred Sibley and Clayton Barnes - would be squadron mates of Dick's in the Pacific.

Just prior to departure Dick found time to send off one last note, a Western Union telegram that said simply: "So long Mom. I'm off. Goodbye and good luck to all of you. Love, Dick." Second Lieutenant Richard I. Bong was on his way to war.

Chapter 5

Into Combat
(September 1942 - February 1943)

The four-engined LB-30 transport droned monotonously over the waters of the South Pacific on the last leg of a journey that had originated in San Francisco. In a few hours the transport would land somewhere in Australia with its cargo of fighter pilots destined for George Kenney's Fifth Air Force. Crammed inside the slab-sided fuselage, Dick and his fellow companions made themselves as comfortable as possible. Inevitably their thoughts turned to what fate might be awaiting them in the Southwest Pacific Theater. Few could have imagined that, within the space of a few short months, they would be helping turn the tide of the war in the South Pacific.

The young, inexperienced pilots on board the LB-30 would soon be facing the deadly Zero fighters flown by veterans of the China, Java and Phillipines campaigns. By comparison, Dick and his traveling companions had little or no combat training. Walter Markey, who knew Dick at Oakland, recalled: "Our training to use the P-38 in a combat mission was nil. Before going into combat, I had never fired the guns on a P-38 and I'm sure it was about the same with Dick. Our group had an A-20 target-towing ship, but with maintenance and scheduling problems we never saw it. Dick might have had some aerial target gunnery while he was over in Hamilton. If he did, it couldn't have been more than a mission or two." At the time of his assignment to the Fifth Air Force Dick had a little over 100 hours in the P-38.

Despite such handicaps, many of those on board the LB-30 would master the nimble Zero fighters. John O'Neill, another Golden Gate bad boy, claimed eight kills by war's end. J. C. Mankin served with the 49th and 475th Fighter Groups, being credited with five kills in all. Jay Robbins, destined for the 80th FS, knocked down 22, yet others would not be as lucky. Art Bauhof and Fred Sibley, for example, would die in action.

By September 1942 the Allies had successfully blunted Japanese plans of conquest. The long series of Japanese victories that started at Pearl Harbor had ended with the Coral Sea battle followed by the debacle at Midway in June 1942. The Japanese, however, still held three-quarters of New Guinea and continued to pose a serious threat to Australia. While ground fighting raged in the New Guinea jungles Japanese bombers escorted by Zero fighters pounded Darwin and other Australian targets. Helping protect Australia was the 49th Fighter Group, the ultimate destination of many of the pilots aboard the LB-30.

The flight to Australia was described by Walter Markey, who recalled: "We flew over in an LB-30, a converted B-24, which could carry personnel. Some of us were up in the nose, some in the bomb bay, some back in the waist. Seemed like we would never get to see the other group that was aboard the plane.

"The flight to Australia was about three layover stops. In Australia we were stationed at an RAAF field called Amberly Field. For a week or two we lived in tents and almost froze to death each night. We were in bed at dark and up at daybreak. After that we lived in the nearby town of Ipswich.

"We did little flying at Amberly. The Ninth Squadron (49th Fighter Group) was to come down from Darwin and check out the pilots who, at that time, were converting from P-40s. We spent more time with the screwdriver than anything else. One of the fuel cells had to be changed on the P-38 as the result of chemical reaction between the self-sealed fuel tanks and the new aero fuels which were coming out at that time.

"Our leisure time in the evenings was mostly spent at the local town movies twice a week and an occasional trip to Brisbane. Time went heavy waiting for our squadron to arrive . . ."

Technical difficulties with the P-38 such as the fuel tank problem described by Markey helped delay the Lightning's introduction to combat. From the time he had assumed command of the Fifth Air Force, Kenney had championed the big, twin-engined Lockheed, believing it was the best fighter available for the Southwest Pacific Theater. The first P-38s began arriving in September 1942. One month later Fifth Air Force had about 60 P-38s on strength but the mechanical bugs seemed endless. Leaking fuel tanks compounded by trouble with the aircraft's inter-coolers, invertors, superchargers and armament dogged the Lightning.

Meanwhile, at Amberly the inactivity chafed at Dick and the other young pilots eager to join the shooting war up north and prove themselves - and the P-38 - to the veterans of the Fifth Air Force. Some of the veteran pilots already at Amberly soon tired of the youngster's fighting talk and boasts concerning the P-38. They readily conceded that the Lightning was fast, had a terrific rate of climb and heavy firepower, but felt it lacked maneuverability. Having battled the nimble Zero fighters over Darwin they felt the big, bulky P-38 would be hard-pressed to best the Zero. As boasts and denials rang out at Amberly, battle lines were drawn. To settle the argument a duel was arranged, an aerial contest pitting two P-38s against a pair of P-40s. Bob McMahon and Frank Adkins, both 39th FS pilots, flew the Curtiss fighters. Dick piloted one of the P-38s.

McMahon couldn't recall "just how it started but word got out to the old timers that Bong could outfly anybody in the bunch. It was a challenge that couldn't be ignored for long. The combat veterans had but an hour or so in the P-38, knew it was fast and had a terrific rate of climb but seemingly it lacked maneuverability. We were trying to point out the futility of a tight turn maneuver with a large twin-engine plane against the fantastic maneuverability of the Zero, which had to be seen to be believed. But by then it was usually too late for many neophytes.

"Frank Adkins and myself decided we could show 'em with a couple P-40s. We borrowed these from the Fair Dinkum Flying Circus, a test section at the field. We were careful to remove the ammo from the wings and about half the fuel to give us the maximum turn advantage possible.

"Then we met Bong and a wingman at a prearranged altitude of 9,000 feet. After the first couple breaks it was apparent that we were in for real trouble (if mock combat could be called that.) We broke off, individually scissoring back and forth, pulling Split-S dives out of half rolls and everything we would think of where the P-40 might have the advantage but the '38s held all the cards. Those guys were doing things with it we didn't know it would do.

"Once when a '38 came boring in from a high tight wingover turn I skidded into him and cut my throttle, a trick that had caught a couple unwary Zeros but the big '38 stood on its tail as it passed me shooting up at an angle that would have snapped me into a spin had I tried to follow. We wound up on the deck practically blowing dust from under the shade of the coolibar trees but the '38s had us.

"Frank and myself rejoined in a tight protective circle on the deck with wing tips practically dragging thru the bush. While one P-38 circled above, the other Lightning dove in, almost ramming his guns up my tail. Even though I knew that he was friendly, to say I was uncomfortable is an understatement. I was too close to the ground to look back over my shoulder but I knew it was Bong. As Frank tried to close the circle to get on his tail, the P-38 bounced back up at an off angle that at best would have given Frank a snap deflection shot while the other '38 was now coming in on him. We'd been waxed. That was it. Frank waggled his wings and we all went back to the field."

The result of this friendly dogfight illustrates why General Kenney was so adamant in obtaining P-38s for the Fifth Air Force. The Lightning offered a tremendous performance advantage over the Curtiss P-40s and Bell P-39s and -400s equipping Fifth Air Force fighter units in the fall of 1942. The Curtiss and Bell machines, in the hands of competent pilots, could be steady performers but a brief comparison of the three demonstrates the P-38's clear superiority.

	P-39D	P-40E	P-38F
SPEED	368 mph at 13,800 feet	354 mph at 15,000 feet	395 mph at 25,000 feet
CEILING	32,100 feet	29,000 feet	39,000 feet

	P-39D	P-40E	P-38F
CLIMB	15,000 feet in 5.7 minutes	15,000 feet in 6.4 minutes	20,000 feet in 8.8 minutes
RANGE	800 miles/with 500 lb. bomb	1,150 miles at 195 mph	1,925 miles at 195 mph

Initially the P-38's main opponents in the SWPA Theater were Mitsubishi A6M Zero fighters (also known as Zekes) and Nakajima Ki-43 Oscars.[1] The Zero had a reputation of being unbeatable. Yet tests pitting a P-38F against a captured Zero Model 21 in December 1942 showed the superiority of the P-38 over the vaunted Zero. In straight level flight the P-38 easily outdistanced the Mitsubishi. The Zero was slightly superior in climbs to 10,000 feet, but at 20,000 feet and above the P-38 was master. Below 300 mph the Zero was much more maneuverable, but American pilots knew it was suicide to try and dogfight a Zero. In terms of armament and ruggedness there was no comparison between the two.

Regrettably, Kenney would never have enough of these prized aircraft. In the fall of 1942 he had enough on hand to equip only one squadron and chose Major George Prentice's 39th FS. Since Dick's assigned unit - the 9th FS, 49th FG - had yet to receive its complement of Lightnings, Dick and several other P-38 pilots at Amberly were temporarily attached to the 39th FS to gain combat experience. On November 15, 1942 Dick flew up to New Guinea to join the 39th FS, 35th FG.

The 39th Squadron was based at Schwimmer airdrome, one of a series of fields extending in an arc around Port Moresby on New Guinea's southeastern coast. Locally the field was known as 14-Mile (its distance from Moresby) or Laloki (for the nearby Laloki River). When the 9th FS converted to P-38s in early 1943, they too would be based at Schwimmer. Grouped administratively under the designation Fifth Air Force, Advanced Echelon (ADVON) the units ringing Moresby were commanded by General Ennis Whitehead. Whitehead, incidentally, had been the commandant at Luke Field when Dick's class of 42A passed through the course.

Schwimmer was typical of combat zone airfields. Taxiways were rough, parking facilities inadequate and the field was subject to Japanese air raids. Dick described Schwimmer as being "plenty rough. We camped in the jungle - utilizing it as camouflage - our camp was a poor one at best. We didn't have fresh meat for nearly four months and after that only on rare occasions."

Dick's letters to his family provided other details of life at Schwimmer. In a letter dated November 27th he wrote that he was "still in good health in spite of mosquitos and Japs. Going for a little trip in the country today to a waterfall and try to go swimming. I've also learned to play contract bridge since I last wrote so you'd better get everybody to learn how to play.

"I've finally seen a little action but I'm not overly impressed by it. My flight leader is from Detroit so we speak more or less the same language and get along fine together.

"Got bombed last night but everybody okay. These enemies of ours play rough and somebody is liable to get hurt if they keep it up. Oh well, it's a lot of fun anyway."

In a letter written on December 4th Dick complained: "I don't think I get enough sleep. The doggone Nips come over at night and cause an air raid alarm and so we have to crawl out of bed and jump in a slit trench. Sure was a job digging the trench, too. The sweat runs off worse than it did pitching hay back home or pitching baseball too."

The reference to slit trenches brings to mind an anecdote related by Walter Markey who recalled that "while with the 39th Dick, 'Sneezy' Hyland and myself lived together in a tent . . . on top of the hill, above the main camp area. We were never enthused about digging slit trenches and Dick was a great deal more casual than the rest of us. We would scratch the ground and never get it very deep.

"Washing-Machine Charley would come over only during the full moon at 20,000 or 30,000 feet. The ack-ack would have at him but never could hit a thing. At that point we didn't realize that between full moons the AA people must have decided to move one of their 105s. They placed it over the hill behind our tent.

"The next full moon raid 'Sneezy' and I dutifully put on our hardhats and sat in the trench. Dick stayed in bed as usual. Shortly after that, all hell broke loose - you would have thought there was a war on. Dick, mosquito netting, bedding and all came in on top of us. After the all-clear was sounded we realized that the noise was our new ack-ack neighbors and not the bombs from Washing-Machine Charley!"

The last months of 1942 were quiet ones for the 39th FS. Dick's logbook records uneventful patrols to the

Buna area on the 22nd of November and the 18th, 19th, 20th, 21st, and 25th of December. During this time period the Japanese were attempting to reinforce Buna by sea, a move met by repeated Fifth Air Force air attacks. To support these reinforcement operations the Japanese moved several air units into the Rabaul airfield complex, among them the 11th *Sentai* and the 582nd *Kokutai*. The 11th was an Army Air Force unit equipped with Nakajima Oscars. The 582nd, a Naval Air Group, flew Mitsubishi Zekes and Aichi Val dive-bombers. Dick's first combat would involve these two units.

At approximately 11:30 a.m., on December 27, 1942, Wewoka fighter control picked up an incoming raid of enemy aircraft. The 39th FS responded by vectoring 12 P-38s against the Japanese, Dick's flight being the first to make contact. On the 27th Dick was flying as wingman for Captain Tom Lynch. Lynch, a highly regarded fighter leader, was a veteran of the group's P-39 era, having scored three kills while flying the Bell machine. Leading the second element of Red Flight was Lieutenant Ken Sparks, destined to score 11 victories before being killed in a flying accident in 1944. Flying his wing was Lieutenant Dick Magnas who would die during the Lae convoy battles in January 1943.

Dick later reported: "We took off just before noon and Lynch led us up to about 25,000 feet. He always liked to start trouble from a high altitude. He liked to locate his trouble from up there because it made him the master of the situation.

"We crossed the Owen Stanley Mountains of New Guinea and we were just coming into the area we were supposed to cover when the ground station at Buna crackled over the radio with the news. There were around 40 enemy planes in the area. That sounded like the start of something and Lynch called back for a check on the Nips' altitude. The ground station said look for them at 14,000 feet. Meanwhile, Buna apparently called Moresby and eight more ships of our squadron were sent to join us.

"We didn't have any trouble finding the Japs - they were right below us and they had already decided we weren't exactly friends. I'm not sure they knew definitely what we were, though - they hadn't seen our P-38s in combat yet. Lynch didn't give them any time to consider the matter either. He took us down into a really screaming dive and we let go of our belly tanks on the way.

"It was a major problem trying to stay with Lynch - he was all over the place and I finally gave up and concentrated on a war of my own. There were Zeros all over the sky and a flock of dive bombers underneath them when we came tearing down and went through the Nips for our first pass.

"I tried to remember everything I had ever learned about keeping calm, aiming right, watching my flight leader, checking the element behind and not letting the enemy pull any counter-tactics that might end up with one of them on my tail and me going in the wrong direction for a successful fighter pilot. Maybe I was trying too hard to remember - anyway, the first four I shot at was a total waste of lead. I didn't hit a thing. About all I succeeded in doing was to scare one Jap off Lynch's tail. There were too many Nips for too few Lightnings right about then.

"Finally I gave myself a mental kick in the ribs and decided I better make some contribution besides conspicuous flubbing of the interception dub. It was somewhere between 12:10 and 12:15 that I finally got into the groove. While I was getting the Nip off Lynch's tail, another one parked himself on mine. We were at about 10,000 feet and I decided my best move would be to dive and dive in a hurry.

"That's how I got my first Nip. As I leveled off about two inches about the shortest tree in the Buna area, there was a Jap dive-bomber sitting right ahead of me. It was a perfect setup and one even I couldn't miss. I gave him a short burst and he blew higher than a kite. Well, I wasn't feeling any too bad about that so I waited to enjoy it for a minute or two. He - or rather what was left of him - crashed into the water off Sanananda Point.

"I pulled up in a vertical turn and that's how I ran into my second Jap of the day. Out of the corner of my eye I saw a Zero coming in a vertical turn that would conveniently put him right in the line of my fire. I started shooting an impressive assemblage of .50-caliber dynamite, and it takes a lot more than a Zero to get through a solid burst of it in one piece. This particular Zero expired right in the middle of my sights and he never fired a single shot at me. He just rolled over on his back and went straight down.

"By this time I was beginning to think combat was a lot easier than everyone seemed to suppose. I swung around and got back into the main brawl again - this time pretty well convinced I could take on the whole crowd if I had to. I got in a good series of hits on another Zero but I never saw what happened to him. Then I chased after a Jap dive-bomber but in the middle of that my ammunition gave out.

"Meanwhile Steve Gallup had come steaming over the range hell bent for election and his two flights were keeping the griddle warm for the Nips. Lynch got us together to go home and I noticed Sparks was missing. I looked all over for him. Finally I saw a P-38 landing on the Dobodura strip. It was Sparks all right. He was okay except that a Jap had tried to ram him and had almost torn his whole right wing off. Well, that was combat No. 1."

Back at Schwimmer the rest of the squadron followed the action over the radio. One of those listening with special interest was Lieutenant John "Shady" Lane. On December 27th Dick was flying the aircraft regularly assigned to Lane-number 15, a P-38F nicknamed *Thumper*. As the squadron returned to Schwimmer, Lane recalled that Dick "came in and did two beautiful slow rolls so we knew that he had done well that day. Lots of excitement as this was the first fight the P-38 had been in and they did so well without a single loss. From that day on the Japanese were fighting a losing battle."

The jubilant pilots had unexpected guests show up on the flight line. Kenney and General Paul Wurtsmith, commander of Fifth Fighter Command (V FC), dropped over to offer congratulations. Pleased with their victory, Kenney, himself a former fighter pilot, donated three bottles of Scotch to ensure a proper celebration. Wurtsmith followed up his comments with a commendation the following day citing "the pilots as well as the members of the ground echelon for the impressive showing of your squadron in combat December 27."

Total claims on the 27th ran to eight Zeros, two Vals and two Oscars. Dick was credited with a Zero fighter and a Val dive bomber, a performance that won him a Silver Star. Tom Lynch added two Oscars to his score, becoming the 39th's first ace. Ken Sparks flamed one Zero only to be bounced in turn by five others who shot up his right engine. Limping back to Dobodura, he ran into two Vals and chopped the wing off one. Lieutenant Hoyt Eason knocked down two Zeros with singles going to Lieutenants Stanley Andrews, Carl Planck, Charles Gallup and Ralph Bills.

Based upon postwar research by aviation historian Osamu Tagaya, the 39th FS engaged a mixed formation of Navy Zeros and Vals with Army Oscars. The Oscars, 31 in all, came from the 11th *Sentai* along with an unknown number of Zeros and Vals from the 582nd *Kokutai*. Although Japanese records are incomplete, it appears the inexperienced Americans overclaimed somewhat on December 27th. The 11th *Sentai* lost two Oscars in the Dobodura/Buna area on that date while losses for the 582nd are unknown. By contrast, the Japanese claimed four P-38s destroyed whereas only Ken Sparks' aircraft was damaged. Whatever the true score on December 27th, the P-38 had been properly blooded.

The actual outcome of this first combat is illustrative of the difficulties the authors encountered in attempting to confirm Dick's true score from official Japanese records. During the war many Japanese air units had little time to keep detailed records of losses and victories. Often such records were lost or destroyed as units retreated. At war's end many such records were deliberately destroyed, making confirmation of American victory claims difficult, if not impossible.

Interestingly enough, Dick filed two separate combat reports on this mission. His initial report, found in the 35th Fighter Group history, reported that his flight "dived on a Zeke. I dropped my belly tank, took pass at Zekes without firing, dived away from four Zekes which jumped my tail, taking shot at one Zeke on the way down without observed result. Reversed direction in dive and took shot at one Val near Buna, missed, turned left and went out to sea at 500 feet. Saw Val and fired long burst at range of 350 yards. Val blew up as a result of direct hit from cannon and crashed in water. Zekes on my tail, so I headed out to sea. Three Vals ahead of me. Right Val pulled off to right. Zekes still behind me, so took short burst at center Val without observed result, so made shallow turn to right, found one lone Val, took pass without firing and went home. Out of ammo."

In this initial report Dick made no claim against a Zero, having taken only a snap shot at one without seeing any result. Apparently another 39th FS pilot saw this Zero crash and later talked Dick into claiming it. Hence a second claim, submitted on RAAF Form A.108 (A), was written up which reported that Dick "saw P-38 No. 36 on transport strip, Dobodura, on nose. Fired at range of 350 yards at Val which blew up and crashed into water. Fired short burst at Zeke which passed in front of me. Zeke crashed in water."

The pride Dick felt in his first victories was evident in his next letter home when he crowed: "Well I've done it at last. Saw the Nips at close range and shot down two airplanes on December 27th. If you watch the newspapers and *Life* and *Time* you might read about it. We were congratulated by General Kenney and

General Wurtsmith. General Kenney is the one who grounded me in Frisco, remember? I don't know if all this will go through the censor or not. Don't know if it is o.k. to say it or not but I'll hear about it if it isn't. Shot down two of them in my first encounter and got one bullet in my plane. Not bad at all I would say.

"I expect to join the 9th FS pretty soon but it will be o.k. to keep on writing to the 39th until I send you a different address. The two squadrons are close together.

"Had an American candy bar the other day and it sure tasted good. Drank a scotch and soda on the night after my victory to celebrate. You'll probably read or have read in the paper where we shot down 19 airplanes in one day and that is the day I had my fun."

Although Dick's time with the 39th FS was drawing to a close, his remaining missions with the squadron would be eventful ones. As December waned the Japanese position in Papua grew steadily worse. No further reinforcements were routed to Buna after December 15th, resistance ending in Papua by January 22nd. With the impending loss of the Buna area, Lae and Salamaua, on the Huon Gulf, assumed greater importance to the Japanese war effort. Fifth Air Force intelligence began uncovering signs of a major Japanese effort to reinforce these two by convoy. Rabaul Harbor had the largest concentration of warships and merchantmen yet seen. Antisubmarine activity, which often heralded convoy sailings, was noted near Lae. Finally, renewed air activity was seen on nearby Japanese airfields.

In the meantime, on December 31st, the 39th Squadron put up 11 P-38s as top cover for a mixed force of B-25s, B-26s and A-20s hitting the Lae airdrome. Arriving over Lae at 12:10 p.m. the Americans spotted some 12-15 Zekes in the target area. The three flights of P-38s promptly peeled off and dove on the Japanese, Dick's flight taking on six Zekes. The Japanese turned into their attackers and the fight was on. Although the Americans claimed some nine kills in all, Dick could only claim a probable, reporting that he "shot at six Zekes in succession, all head-on attacks by Zekes. On the sixth pass I saw either a part of the engine or the cowl fly off the ship as I shot. The Zeke then went off in a shallow dive towards the land." Dick noted in passing that the Japanese pilots had been first-rate, terming them "aggressive, high grade pilots."

During this period, Dick's original unit - the 9th FS, 49th FG - began moving up to Schwimmer. The squadron had received official word on December 24th that they were changing bases and that they would be re-equipping with Lockheed Lightnings, becoming the second P-38 squadron in the Fifth Air Force. The first days of January 1943 were busy ones for the "Flying Knights" Squadron. The unit history recorded on January 1st: "The Squadron was split—some leaving for 14-Mile Strip (Schwimmer) by plane and others staying behind to break camp. Lots of new pilots now joining the squadron. Fourteen of our pilots trfd. to the (P-40 equipped) 7th and 8th (Squadrons)." By January 5th the 9th had five P-38s on strength and the pilots hurriedly began checking out in the aircraft. The unit history noted that "everyone was happy about the new airplanes," but that happiness was short-lived. The entry for January 6th recorded that the squadron's P-38s "were turned over to the 39th Squadron because they are using them for some special missions."

The special missions mentioned in the 9th FS history were part of the all-out effort launched by Fifth Air Force to destroy the long-awaited Lae reinforcement convoy. In the early morning hours of January 6th, Fifth Air Force spotted a convoy east of Gasmata, New Britain heading for Lae. The convoy, made up of transports guarded by destroyers and a cruiser, had a heavy fighter cover overhead. Kenney sent his bombers and fighters against the convoy beginning on January 7th.

During the Lae convoy battles of January 7th and 8th, the 39th FS flew mixed formations of bomb-carrying P-38s protected by top-cover Lightnings. On January 7th Dick recalled that "when the first big convoy was spotted we all went out during the late afternoon to try a dive bombing job on the ships.

"It didn't work out as well as we had hoped, principally because we were tied up in dogfights most of the time. We were going so fast we could never get lined up right on the ships. Captain Tom Lynch was the only one who did some good, as far as we could see. He made a direct hit with a thousand-pounder on one of their biggest ships - it was a beautiful run and he received credit for sinking the ship.

"But I remember that day best because it was the first time I ever tangled with a Nip head-on. That's when you get down to fundamentals all over again - it's either you or the Nip and the one who has the most firepower is the one who flies home. Well, I had it.

"Some Zeros jumped a squadron of Australian Beaufighters which we were covering in between our own dive-bombing runs. I made a pass at one Zero and ended the pass by zooming practically straight up. I decided that was no place for me and kicked the plane down again. That's when I met the Jap face to face.

"We had quite an argument - he started it. His tracer shots were scooting past me when I opened fire. We closed in on each other that way. I thought this clown was trying to pull a repeat performance of the ramming trick one of them tried to pull on my friend Ken Sparks. So I ducked low under him about one second before we would have gotten slightly mangled up.

"It was a good thing I did that - he exploded right over my head and if I'd gone over instead of under him the blast concussion might have ended combat flying for me right there and then."

In all, 39th FS pilots claimed seven fighters over the Huon Gulf convoy. By day's end Dick had boosted his score to four, downing single Oscars during the course of two missions against the convoy.

The first Oscar was destroyed over Huon Gulf at 1:15 p.m., Dick reporting that "a flight of four P-38s was sent as top cover for Beaufighters attacking an enemy convoy in the Huon gulf near Lae, New Guinea. Our flight took off at approximately 11:50 a.m. and arrived over the target area at 1:15 p.m. Our formation was at an altitude of approximately 10,000 feet. Our formation sighted three to five Type 1 enemy fighter aircraft below us and we dived to the attack. In the ensuing combat I shot down one Type 1 aircraft which crashed in flames into the ocean after a long burst from all my guns at a range of 20 to 75 yards."

Two hours later Dick was one of six Lightning pilots covering eight P-38s dive-bombing the convoy, reporting "our formation arrived over the convoy at about 3:30 p.m. When our formation was at an altitude of 11,000 feet we sighted the convoy but did not sight the enemy aircraft until our aircraft were making the bombing run. Our formation sighted 15 to 20 Type 1 single-seater fighters slightly below us, and we made a head on pass at the enemy aircraft. In the ensuing combat I shot down one Type 1 aircraft which crashed in the water after a long burst from my guns from a distance of approximately 40 to 60 yards."[2]

Dick's logbook added several details to the official report, cryptically recording that he "shot down Oscar in flames off Gasmata. Crashed in water. Five Zeros. Shot down Oscar in Lae Harbor. Smoking, crashed in water. Probably shot down Oscar at Lae. 20mm exploded in right wing. Top cover for Beaufighters and P-38s."

The reference to Zeros and Oscars helps identify the Japanese units involved, specifically the 11th *Sentai* and 582nd *Kokutai*. Eight Oscars from the 11th intercepted over the convoy along with an undetermined number of Navy Zeros. Four Oscars were lost, including one flown by a *Chutai* (squadron) leader. Navy losses are unknown.

Despite the best efforts of the Fifth Air Force, the Japanese reinforcement convoy reached Lae Harbor on the 8th and began unloading. The 39th FS flew three missions on the 8th, all of them escort missions covering the A-20s, B-17s, -25s, -26s and RAAF Beaufighters hammering at the convoy in Lae Harbor. Dick flew on the third mission, one of eight P-38s escorting a late afternoon strike by B-17s.

In the hours before the mission launched, Dick found time to get off a letter home, writing with typical understatement that he "got two more Jap airplanes yesterday so that makes four. Also got per diem money from Australia so at the end of this month I'll send about $400.00 home again. Probably by money order.

"I have over 200 hours in Pursuit now. Time is mounting up. Tomorrow I will have 20 months service in and still a 2nd Lieutenant. Been running in bad luck about that. However I still have my hopes. There are about three of my classmates or more over here that are 2nd Lieutenants also. Hard to get promotions on this side of the ocean.

"Been away from the States over four months already but it doesn't seem like it. Time goes pretty fast over here and for that I'm thankful. I'm losing quite a bit of weight up here and getting in pretty good shape again.

"If you want to, you can send my clarinet over here and about ten new reeds to go along with it. Maybe I won't know how to play it after not touching one for over a year. Can't get one in Australia because so many American soldiers bought instruments after they got over here."

Several hours after posting this letter Dick was over Lae, orbiting along with seven other P-38s as B-17s bombed the convoy in Lae Harbor. The Japanese met this attack in force, scrambling some 20-plus fighters. In the combat that followed the Lightings claimed seven kills, Dick destroying an Oscar for which he was awarded the Distinguished Flying Cross. The D.F.C. citation read as follows:

"For extraordinary achievement while participating in an aerial flight over Lae Harbor, New Guinea, on

January 8, 1943. While escorting a bomber formation this officer and seven accompanying pilots attacked approximately twenty enemy fighters. In the ensuing engagement, Lieutenant Bong shot down one enemy aircraft with a long burst from a distance of 200 yards. This plane was the fifth hostile aircraft destroyed by Lieutenant Bong in aerial combat. His achievement is worthy of commendation."

When first spotted, the Japanese fighters had been in scattered flights of two to eight aircraft in line astern formation directly in front of the American fighters. As the P-38s mixed it up with the Japanese Dick noticed one Oscar attacking the aircraft flown by Lieutenant Dick Suehr. Coming to Suehr's aid, he made two passes at the Oscar, the first from head-on about 30° deflection. After Dick's second pass the Oscar started spinning down out of control and pancaked in Huon Gulf about five miles off the coast.

Seven kills were claimed by the Americans who suffered one loss. Records for the 11th *Sentai* reveal only one loss on January 8th, that of the 2nd *Chutai* Leader, Captain Tojo. The Zeros of the 582nd *Kokutai* were also involved in this scrap but their losses are not known. Two transports were sunk but the Japanese managed to land about 4,000 fresh troops at Lae. Some 50 enemy fighters were claimed by Fifth Air Force fighter pilots.

The mission on the 8th was the last one Dick would fly with the 39th Squadron. Hearing of Dick's fifth kill General Kenney decided some rest and relaxation was called for. In his words: "I gave him and Captain Tommy Lynch, who had boosted his score to six during those two days, a couple of weeks' leave in Australia where they could rest, get some decent food, and forget about the war for a while." When he returned to Schwimmer in early February Dick would report to the 9th FS, his original duty assignment.

Dick had flown with the 39th Squadron for slightly over a month and received credit for five enemy aircraft destroyed and one probable.[3] Stanley Andrews, who scored six victories with the 39th FS, summarized Dick's short stay with the squadron. Andrews had known Dick "as a 2nd Lieutenant and flew with him, sat alerts with him and, if I am not mistaken, both of us got our first victory on the 27th of December '42 in the same fight.

"Dick was a quiet fellow and I'm sorry that I never became close friends with him. We respected his smooth flying and accurate gunnery. Whenever I flew with him, he always seemed to be thinking ahead of the immediate situation so as not to get the flight involved in a hopeless situation.

"I recall a couple of times that he mentioned his deflection shots needed to improve and he was spending a lot of time trying to improve them. He said that he had made most of his kills from a tail or quartering tail position (as I had). We were in absolute agreement on the P-38 tactics as far as the Zeros were concerned - never try to dogfight or turn with them, just use fast shallow dives and climbs in passes. That was the rule of the day."

An early family portrait featuring Nelda, Dick and the proud parents.

Dick received his Primary training at Tex Rankin's Aeronautical Academy in Tulare, California from June to August 1941. Dick is pictured here standing next to one of the Stearman biplanes he trained on.

Dick, then an instructor at Luke Field, pictured over the Grand Canyon, March 1942. He tried a loop while flying inside the Canyon, marvelling that he "never got to the top of the wall on the whole loop."

A lineup of 39th FS pilots with whom Dick flew in December 1942 and January 1943. Front row: Charles Sullivan (5 victories), Tommy Lynch (20) and Ken Sparks (11). Back row: Dick Suehr (5), John "Shady" Lane (6) and Stanley Andrews (6). When Dick scored his first two kills on December 27 he was flying as Lynch's wingman. (Stanaway)

During his brief service with the 39th FS Dick flew No. 15, a P-38F named Thumper, claiming three of his first five victories in this aircraft. Dick flew Thumper, normally assigned to Lieutenant John Lane, on December 27, 1942 and January 8, 1943. In this photo Tom Lynch stands third from left. Next to him is Richard Suehr and behind him, looking to the right, is John Lane. (Stanaway)

A poor quality but rare photo of 9th FS pilots in early 1943. Jerry Johnson (22 kills) is at extreme left, second row. Dick, under the "85," is flanked by "Jump" O'Neill (8) and Ralph Wire (5). Others include Wally Jordan (6 kills, eighth from right), Ralph Wandrey (6 kills, fourth from right) and Theron Price (3 kills, second from right).

Mitsubishi's superlative A6M Zero fighter, which equipped units of the Japanese Navy Air Force, ruled the skies for the first months of the Pacific War. Introduction of the P-38, P-47, F4U and F6F models ended its reign. Dick rated Japanese naval fliers as being far more dangerous than their Army Air Force counterparts.

The 49th FG settled into Dobodura in early March 1943 where Dick took this photo, a good illustration of the rather primitive conditions the Americans had to work under. Dick scored at least one kill while flying No. 73; an Oscar destroyed on July 28, 1943 over Rein Bay.

Following the Japanese strike on Dobodura on March 11, 1943 an AAF photographer snapped this photo of successful 9th FS pilots, Dick showing his normal enthusiasm for such matters. Left to right: Lieutenant Tom Fowler (one Zero confirmed), Captain Sidney Woods (one Betty), Lieutenant Jack Mankin (one Zero) and Dick (two Zeros confirmed.)

In all, Dick destroyed 18 Nakajima Ki-43s, the Oscar being the most numerous fighter operated by the Japanese Army Air Force in the early war years. Although outclassed by the P-38 Lightning, the Oscar could be a dangerous opponent. Both Neel Kearby and Tom McGuire were killed in scraps with Oscars.

Ninth Squadron pilots unwind at Dobodura. Seated (L-R) are: Sid Woods, Clay Tice and John Landers. Dick is immediately behind Landers. Woods, Tice and Landers all flew combat in Europe as well as the Pacific. (Ehrmann)

Colonel Neel Kearby's 348th FG, a P-47 outfit, joined the Fifth Air Force during June 1943. In time Kearby, a fierce champion of the Thunderbolt, would demonstrate how potent a warplane the P-47 was, and challenged Dick for top ace honors. (Stanaway)

Dick's latest P-38, an H-1 model, displays his score as of late July 1943. Dick scored five victories in July, boosting his score to 16 kills.

When first introduced into frontline service in April 1943 the Kawasaki Ki-61 Tony was mistakenly identified as a Japanese copy of the German Messerschmitt Me-109. On July 26, 1943 Dick had his first combat with the Ki-61 over the Markham Valley, downing two Tonys along with two Zeros. During his career Dick also scored ten doubles and a single triple.

Dick shares a smoke with two of Kenney's ablest commanders, Ennis Whitehead and Paul Wurtsmith. Whitehead had been the commandant of Luke Field when Dick had passed through in late 1941. Wurtsmith was the 49th FG's first wartime commander.

Gun-camera photos taken during the spring and summer of 1943 show various Oscars under attack.

Gun-camera footage from Dick's P-38 shows a Betty bomber under attack. Exact date of this mission is unknown but may have been taken on September 6, 1943 when Dick claimed two Betty probables.

In November 1943, shortly before returning home on leave, Dick was the ranking ace with 21 kills. He posed with his ground crew, Corporal Bill Finkel and Sergeant Elwood Barden, with No. 79, a P-38H-5.

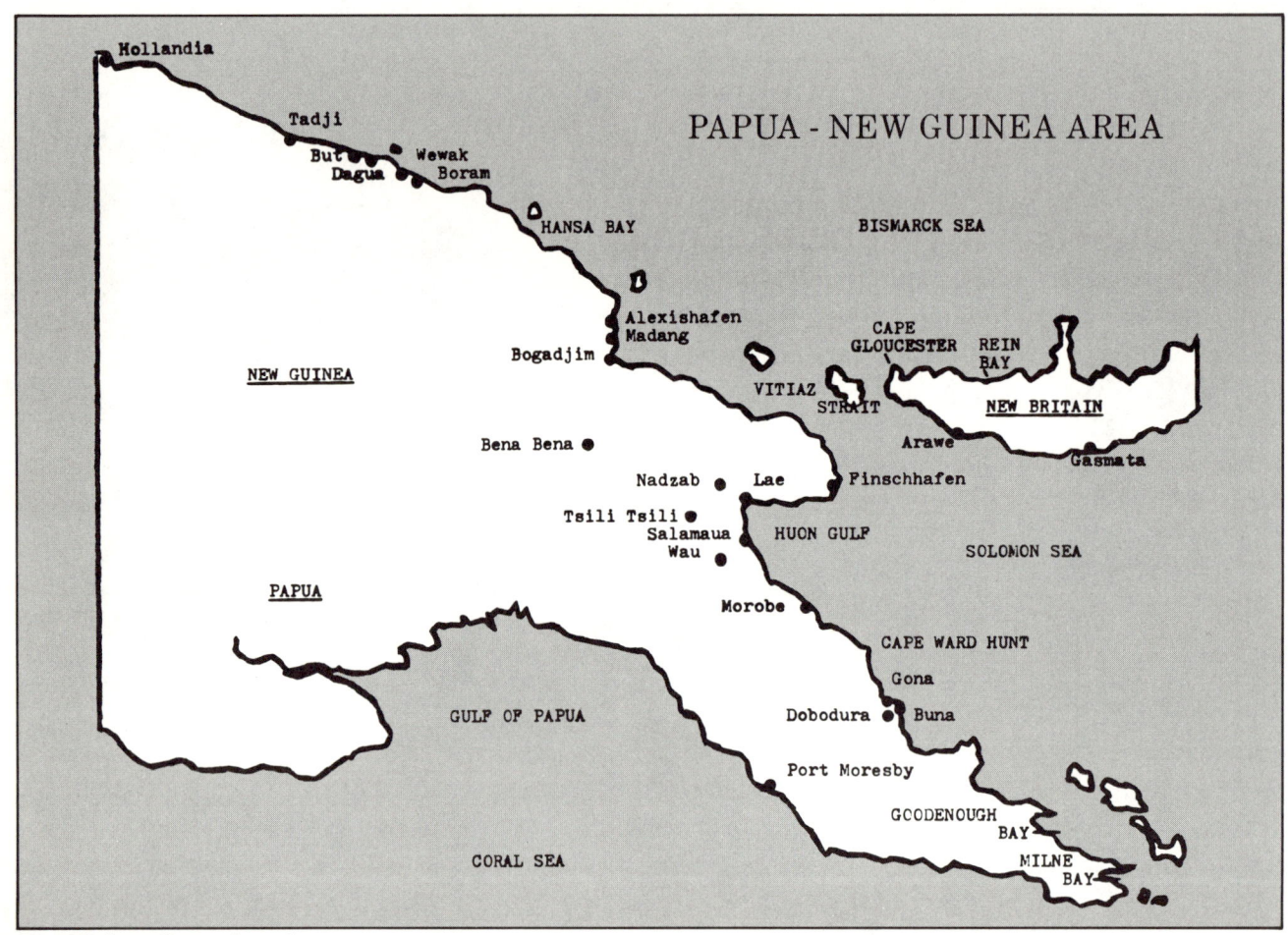
New Guinea Operations Area

Chapter 6

With The Flying Knights
(February - March 1943)

When Dick returned to Schwimmer on February 3, 1943 he reported to the 9th Fighter Squadron commanded by Major Jesse Peaslee. At that time the 9th was second only to the Lightning-equipped 39th FS in aerial victories. By VJ-Day the unit nicknamed the "Flying Knights" would claim some 261 air kills, topping all other Army Air Force squadrons in the SWPA Theater. Only one other squadron would top that score, that being the 353rd FS, 354th FG operating in Europe with 289½ confirmed kills.[1] The 9th FS was one of Kenney's premier fighter squadrons!

The 49th Fighter Group had been activated on January 15, 1941 at Selfridge Field, Michigan. Initially the "Forty-Niners" had flown Seversky P-35s before re-equipping with Curtiss P-40s. In early 1942 the group, under the command of Lieutenant Colonel Paul Wurtsmith, shipped out to Australia. Here they were equipped with P-40 Kittyhawks and assigned to the defense of Australia's North-Western Area. From March to August 1942 the 49th FG claimed 64 victories while losing only 16 aircraft, a remarkable record considering the quality of the opposition facing them.

The 9th Squadron had scored its first victory on March 22, 1942 when Lieutenants Clyde Harvey and Steve Poleschuk downed a Nakajima 97 reconnaissance aircraft over Darwin. Before the group's other two squadrons - the 7th and 8th - joined the 9th at Darwin in April, the "Flying Knights" had several successful scraps with the Japanese. On March 28th four P-40s had knocked four Japanese bombers out of an unescorted formation hitting Darwin. The squadron lost two P-40s on April 4th but decimated a Japanese formation, claiming seven Mitsubishi bombers and two Zero fighters. Lieutenants John Landers, Andy Reynolds and John Sauber were each credited with two kills apiece in this scrap.

By the time Dick joined the 9th FS at Schwimmer in February 1943, Reynolds had become the leading ace in the theater, claiming ten kills. John Landers had steadily increased his score after April 4th and was credited with six victories by year's end. Dick's five kills thus made him the third-ranking ace in the 9th Squadron.

Dick's new CO, Jesse Peaslee, described Dick as "a very quiet, modest young man. He came to the 9th Fighter Squadron after having been in combat with another outfit. He was an ace when he joined my squadron in New Guinea and a flight leader. At that time you had to work at it to get Dick to tell you anything about his combat experience. As I recall he did not smoke or drink at the time and I don't remember him playing poker. He was in no sense a prankster or show-off. The human interest stories on Dick Bong are hard to get because he simply was not a very colorful character, just a good pilot who loved flying and did his job very well. This leaves me with very little to say about the guy except how much he was liked and respected."

Other 49th FG pilots, asked for their first impressions upon meeting Dick, expressed sentiments similar to Colonel Peaslee's. Sammy Pierce, a P-40 pilot with the 8th FS, felt that Dick was "just about the reverse of what the public normally thought about fighter pilots. Instead of a very aggressive, loud, hell-raiser type (which most of us were not) he was a very quiet, reserved, shy type of person. He had a good sense of humor which again was very quiet. He appeared not to cultivate many very close friends but preferred to spend a good bit of time to himself. He would answer questions but wouldn't volunteer much information. I guess you would class him as a master of understatement."

James Harvey first met Dick when they were tent mates in New Guinea. Harvey felt Dick "was a very quiet person but one who was very sincere and always willing to pitch in and help others when needed. With all the notoriety attributed to him he was always very modest and did his share so that all of us could get home sooner. Even though he was a leading ace of WWII he never had any desire to harm anyone, regarding his missions as strictly jobs assigned to him. Many evenings I went to sleep listening to Dick playing his clarinet. Though he was no Benny Goodman, it was good music."

If Dick did not fit the traditional fighter pilot mold he nevertheless had no trouble fitting into his new unit, for the 9th FS was truly a cosmopolitan mixture. According to Ralph Wandrey, pilots like Andy Reynolds and John Landers were "the old boys and called the Darwin crowd. (A second) bunch who had trained in P-38s and, I believe, had been in Hawaii were called the Pineapple Boys. My bunch (which arrived in March 1943) were the P-38 specialists. It wasn't long before I joined the squadron that four other pilots were assigned who had been up in Alaska flying. These were Gerald R. Johnson, Wallace Jordan, Tom McGuire and, I believe, Charles Jager - the Eskimos." Interestingly enough, three of the last four pilots mentioned - Johnson, McGuire and Jordan - went on to become aces and squadron commanders. Both Jordan and Johnson would also eventually command the 49th FG itself.

As previously mentioned, the 9th Squadron had received its first P-38s on January 5th. Twenty pilots had departed for Townsville on the 14th to check out on Lightnings. By January 19th the squadron had sufficient aircraft to fly its first combat mission, an uneventful escort mission to Wau southwest of Salamaua. By February 14th the 9th FS had 25 Lightnings on strength, mainly F and early G models.

Aside from a single victory scored over Wau on February 6th by Lieutenant Dave Harbour, the first two months of the new year were quiet ones of the squadron. Wau was the scene of bitter fighting as Japanese forces -the same ones brought in by the Lae reinforcement convoy - sought to destroy the Australian force there. Dick logged three missions to Wau, escorting C-47s bringing in desperately needed men and material, but missed the action when the Japanese committed their aircraft to the Wau struggle on February 6th.

With time hanging heavy, Dick found time to catch up on his correspondence, writing home: "According to all the letters I've got, why, I must have made just about every paper in the States for a while there. Made the papers even if it took a war to put me there. However I would much rather be home with no publicity whatsoever.

"(So) Bud wants me to hurry home with my airplane. Boy, I just wish I could get home with (the) one I'm flying now and I'd sure give you a going over. How about 500 miles an hour 20 feet above the roof? You'd break your neck trying to follow me. I've gone faster than that and lower than that more than once. Wouldn't be much like chasing the horses over the field in Poplar and 15 seconds later I could be home. That's moving right along. Don't expect I ever would but I sure would enjoy it.

"The 39th FS mail reaches me almost immediately because we're not far apart. I'm definitely assigned to the 9th FS now unless some other calamity besets me. I've sure been having bad luck on the promotion deal. This squadron is already overloaded with First Lieutenants, so I can't be promoted until some of them are Captains. Just plain bad luck ever since I left Luke Field."

Beginning on February 17th, flights of 9th FS P-38s began flying to the Dobodura airstrip some 15 miles south of Buna to stand alert. Work on the Dobodura strip had begun in November 1942. In the coming months Dobodura would become one of the major Allied air bases in new Guinea and the new home of the "Forty-Niners." To service the 9th FS aircraft that flew up to Dobo every morning, a detail from the squadron was stationed at the strip. Dick logged uneventful alerts at Dobodura in late February and early March before getting some action on March 3rd.

In early March action broke out as the Japanese tried to reinforce Lae once again. Kenney had advance warning of the convoy and decided to smash it through a series of coordinated, around-the-clock strikes by all of Fifth Air Force. Pending the convoy's sailing Kenney had husbanded his aircraft and staged rehearsals of the upcoming mission using aircraft from each squadron involved.

On March 1st Fifth Air Force reconnaissance aircraft located the long-awaited convoy - eight destroyers and eight transports bearing the 51st Infantry Division - in the Vitiaz Strait. Contact was lost, only to be regained on the 2nd. Kenney launched his squadrons against the convoy. And the Battle of the Bismark Sea was on!

Due to weather conditions the attacks on March 2nd were only partially successful. Crews of Flying Fortresses claimed to have sunk at least two transports and damaged others. Escorting P-38s from the 39th and 9th Squadrons downed seven Oscars.

Kenney's knock-out punch came on March 3rd. In the early morning hours 109 Allied aircraft rendezvoused over Cape Ward Hunt and set course for the convoy. P-38s from the 39th and 9th Squadrons provided fighter cover for the coordinated strike force, which combined medium-altitude bombing by B-17s with wave-hopping bombing and strafing runs by A-20s, B-25s and Australian Beaufighters.

While still some 30 miles from the target Dick and the other Lightning pilots spotted 25 Zekes, Oscars and clipped-wing Hamps orbiting between them and the convoy.[2] The Japanese, obviously believing the B-17s were the main threat, had decided to concentrate on them. Major George Prentice, leading the 39th FS formation, decided to break up the Japanese before they could intercept the bombers. Banging their throttles forward, the Lightnings forged ahead of their charges and tore into the largest gaggle of enemy aircraft. As the B-17s settled into their bomb runs individual combats broke out all over the sky. An additional 15 enemy fighters were spotted low over the convoy and part of the P-38 escort dived down to handle these newcomers.

Both P-38 squadrons scored heavily on this mission. The 39th claimed ten kills but lost three pilots, including Hoyt Eason and Bob Faurot. Lieutenant Eason had six kills to his credit at the time of his death. Captain Faurot had achieved some notoriety the previous November when he claimed the first Fifth Air Force P-38 kill. Faurot had been dive-bombing Lae on November 26, 1942 when the blast from his bomb caught a Zero taking off and knocked it into the sea.

The 9th Squadron was officially credited with seven kills on the 3rd. Lieutenant Edgar Ball opened the scoring by the squadron when he turned into a Zeke and smoked him in a head-on pass at 9:00 a.m. Dick was credited with one fighter destroyed over the Huon Gulf at 10:15 and reported: "While on cover flight for bombers, our flight was intercepted by seven Oscar type Zeros. In the ensuing engagement I made a 45-degree deflection shot from above and behind and he started smoking. I made another pass at him just before he hit the water and crashed. While pulling up I saw another smoking Zero hit the water about a mile to my right. Made two more passes at another Zero and started his gas tank leaking but he kept going and I came home. Claim one certain and one probable."

The smoking Zero Dick reported may have been the aircraft destroyed by Lieutenant LeRoy Donnell, who downed a Zero fighter at 10:30. Captain Clay Tice also destroyed a Zero over the Huon Gulf convoy. Additionally, four probables were claimed and three subsequently upgraded to confirmed kills, one each going to Lieutenants Clayton Barnes, Bill Gersch and Bill Haney.

Although the Lightnings scored heavily against the Japanese, the main event was played out far below. The Bismarck Sea battle saw the first use of heavily-armed "gunships" employing low-level skip-bombing tactics. The combination was devastating. Some confusion exists as to how many ships Fifth Air Force destroyed in the Huon Gulf, but at least four destroyers and all eight transports were definitely sunk. The 51st Infantry Division suffered over 50% casualties with most of the survivors being returned to Rabaul. Lae had been promised some 7,000 reinforcements. It received fewer than 800. In short, Fifth Air Force had annihilated an entire convoy, smashing the Japanese attempt at reinforcing Lae at a cost of one B-17 and three P-38s!

Kenney's units had scored a tremendous victory, a fact Kenney acknowledged in a signal he sent to Whitehead on March 4th commending them on a "stupendous success. Air power has written some important history in the past three days. Tell the whole gang that I am so proud of them I am about to blow a fuse."

In looking back at the Bismarck Sea battle, Dick commented that he "wouldn't give two cents to be in the Jap navy after seeing what the army air forces could do once they get started. They weren't only started but they were pounding like a steamroller that day and they didn't run out of steam until the Japs ran out of airplanes and stopped bringing their big ships down within range of our land-based planes.

"The Bismarck Sea battle was the best show I've ever seen in the Southwest Pacific. It certainly was decisive enough on our part, anyway. It was the first coordinated mission against enemy shipping that

Lightnings ever escorted and was plenty rough for everyone concerned. But it was 'school' again, the way Darwin had been 'school' the year before.

"We took the Mitchells in for the first true low-level shipping assault they ever made and we were mixed up in combat right then and through the whole show. The only thing I saw were eight transports burning at one time - but that was enough to convince me that joining the air force was the best thing I ever did. Anyway, we learned close escort right there and although it cost us two of our best Lightning pilots - Captain Bob Faurot and Lieutenant Hoyt Eason - we came out of it knowing what we had to do the next time."

Twenty-four hours after its lopsided victory over the Bismarck Sea convoy, the 9th FS began moving up to Dobodura, its new base in New Guinea. Kenney planned to move the 49th FG to Dobo in order to ensure fighter cover over the Bismarck Sea. Initially the "Forty-Niners" were not impressed with their new home. Ralph Wandrey, who had joined the 9th Squadron in early March, recalled: "Our camp area was situated in a rain forest about four miles from the airstrip. The airstrip was a level dirt plane that had been chopped out of the jungle on the edge of a plantation. It was about 11,000 feet long but usually was a mess after the first plane or two had taken off because of the dust that was kicked up. The end of the strip had a few tents around it to carry our equipment. The planes were scattered around the edge of the strip in horseshoe-shaped revetments to protect them in case of a bomb raid.

"The pilots would be called out in time to get out to the airstrip before dawn so we would be ready to take off at first light. There was a field telephone connected back to headquarters where, after a few months, we finally had a radar set. When the radar detected any unidentified aircraft they would holler 'scramble!' and the Ninth pilots would run to their planes and take off.

"Our missions at this time were primarily defensive missions. We waited for the Japs to come over and either hit at our air base or Oro Bay, Milne Bay or Port Moresby, and we tried to intercept them. We passed our time between raids waiting for the phone to ring in the alert shack by playing baseball or throwing knives, playing cards or things on this order.

"At night when we'd sit around in the camp and talk and visit, we'd compare notes on how to survive and how to shoot down planes, types of attacks and so on. Dick's theory was to get in as close as you could and, like he says, 'Get in so close ya can't miss, shove the guns up their butt and pull the trigger.' The only part that I disagreed on in this was that when you got that close you usually ended up with pieces of Japanese plane flying in the air around you. So I preferred to start shooting from a little further back with my 20mm cannon, and usually I could tear them up before I got in too close so that I didn't have to fly through the debris."

Wandrey's comments on Dobodura are mirrored in the official 49th FG history and Dick's letters home. The group history recorded that initially Dobodura was a hardship. Aircraft servicing was rated as not good, with refueling facilities being especially bad. The supply dumps were inaccessible. Units lacked transportation equipment and spare parts. The 9th FS, for example, had to strip its out-of-commission Lightnings in order to keep 16 aircraft operational for the daily alert. Another major problem was the lack of reliable communications with Whitehead's ADVON command at Port Moresby. Finally, the group suffered a high incidence of malaria which sometimes ran as much as 20%.

The "Forty-Niners" had scarcely settled into their new home before the Japanese sent a welcoming committee. The enemy high command had been shocked by the decimation of the Bismarck Sea convoy and realized the implications of that disaster. Increasingly concerned with the deteriorating situation in Huon Gulf, the Japanese responded with a series of air attacks against Allied air bases beginning in early March. On the 9th the airstrip at Wau was the target. Two days later Dobodura was visited by 27 Mitsubishi G4M Betty bombers and a like number of Zero fighters. One flight of P-40s from the 8th Squadron was in the air on patrol. Two additional flights from the 8th and three from the 9th scrambled to stop the oncoming Japanese.

Lieutenant Tom Fowler, a Darwin veteran, was among the first to intercept the Japanese and reported: "I was the leader of a flight of P-38s that scrambled to intercept an unknown radar target. Dick was not in my flight but was in another flight that was on alert. After take-off we were instructed to climb to altitude. Shortly after gaining altitude I was informed that 27 Betty bombers escorted by a like number of Zeros were bombing our airfield. My flight turned back toward the field and saw the enemy formation making a turn heading out to sea. We were above the formation. We attacked the Japs and in the ensuing engagement I shot a Zero down. My element leader, Bill Hanning, was rammed by a Zero and bailed out, landing in the water off Oro Bay. Dick's flight was scrambled and took off as the bombs were falling on the field."

Dick's flight of three P-38s roared down the Dobodura runway at 10:20 a.m., taking off, as he later reported, "just ahead of the bombs and climbed up to 24,000 feet. We intercepted the bombers on their way home. I made a 20-degree pass from ahead and above and put a good burst in the last bomber. There were no observed results. Nine Zeros dove on me and I had to dive to 475 mph indicated to get away. I tried to go back for another pass at the bombers but was intercepted by Zeros and chased down to water level.

"We were headed towards Gasmata. I flew straight until I could see only one Zero behind me. I made a 180-degree turn and put a long burst into the Zero head-on. Instead of only one Zero, there were nine or more and I turned five degrees left and put a short burst into another Zero head-on. Both of these had their belly tanks on. Turned ten degrees right and put a long burst into another Zero from 20-degrees deflection, then I turned 20 degrees left to observe the results.

"The first two Zeros were burning all around the cockpit and the third one was trailing a long column of smoke. Three Zeros split-Sed down on me and shot up my left engine and wing while I was running for home. I feathered the left engine and landed at home field safely. I claim two certains and one probable."

The scrap on the 11th was the roughest mission Dick had yet flown. As he made his one-man pass against the nine Zeros the Japanese pilots had almost gotten the range. At one point Dick saw three separate lines of tracer shells going by him. Although he had the reputation of being cool in battle, Dick later confided that he came "too close to getting knocked down myself" on March 11th.

The action on the ground was no less violent. The 9th FS history reported that "Dobodura happenings were very rough. Twenty-four enemy bombers came over and bombed our planes on the ground. Sergeant Frederick H. Bente, a crew chief, was burned to death while warming up his plane as a bomb hit close to the plane. His assistant crew chief, Sergeant Obert Franklin, tried to get away but caught a lot of shrapnel from waist up. Later in the evening they removed his arm. (Franklin died 24 hours later.) Captain Woods destroyed a bomber, Lieutenant Mankin got one Zero and Lieutenant Hanning destroyed three Zeros but his plane was all shot up so he had to bail out. Lieutenant Bong got two Zeros, two probables, and maybe one bomber. Lieutenant Fowler destroyed one Zero and Lieutenant O'Neill which is nine and there may be ten."

After sorting out the claims the squadron was given credit for seven Zeros and a lone Betty bomber. Dick's score was matched by Lieutenant Bill Hanning. Hanning flamed one Zero and badly damaged a second before hitting a third Zero with a killing burst. This Zero turned into Hanning and rammed him, forcing Hanning to bail out. Lieutenants Tom Fowler, Jack Mankin and Carl Planck received credit for single Zeros while Captain Sidney Woods destroyed the Betty. The 8th FS notched up four kills while losing one P-40. Three aircraft were destroyed on the ground by Japanese bombs.

Oro Bay was bombed on the night of the 14th and Porlock Harbor on the 17th. The last major combat of the month came on March 28th when over 30 Val dive-bombers with a large escort of Zeros and Hamps pounded Oro Bay again. Sixteen 8th FS P-40s and 15 9th FS P-38s intercepted over Oro Bay, claiming 13 victories in exchange for one P-40 lost. "Jump" O'Neill and Walter Markey were among the 9th FS pilots claiming on the 28th.

Although Dick missed the action on the 28th, he did score the next day when the "Flying Knights" scrambled four P-38s to check out an unidentified radar plot. East of Oro Bay Lieutenant Clayton Barnes, Dick's wingman, called in a lone Mitsubishi Ki-46 Dinah reconnaissance aircraft. Dick's combat report summarized the action:

"Lieutenant Barnes saw one plane at ten o'clock high. He and I started after him and dropped our tanks. The bomber observed us catching up to him and started to dive but we caught up any way. I was on the left and Lieutenant Barnes on the right. I dove on him in a 30-degree deflection shot from behind.

"I opened fire at long range and fired right on into him. I hit his left wing and left engine on my first pass. The left engine started to smoke immediately. Lieutenant Barnes made a pass from the right and the bomber started diving. I made another pass from the right, hitting his tail. I then made another pass from the left but with no hits.

"On my fourth pass from the right I stayed on his tail until he blew up in mid-air. He dove straight down and crashed in the sea. We made contact at 11:45 a.m. from about 40 miles out to sea. The bomber was either type Dinah or type Doris apparently. I claim one bomber definite, witnessed by Lieutenant Barnes, Lieutenant McComsey and Lieutenant Donnell." Dick's logbook contains the wry comment that there had been "no Zeros to interrupt my fun."

Dick's victory on the 29th - his ninth confirmed kill - capped the 9th Squadron's first year in combat. During that time the squadron claimed 76 kills. Thirty-four had been added in the first three months of 1943, almost matching the previous **year's** total! Dick contributed nine kills - six Oscars, one Zeke, one Val and one Dinah. New Guinea was the operational responsibility of the Japanese Army Air Force, hence the preponderance of Oscar claims.

Within three short months, Dick was within one kill of becoming the squadron's top ace. The JAAF fighter units in New Guinea were top-notch. Some of them, like the 24th and 33rd *Sentais*, had fought in China. How then to explain Dick's success?

Although Dick was still a newcomer, his fellow pilots felt he had the makings of a very successful pilot. Wally Jordan remarked that "one outstanding thing about Dick's combat tour was his phenomenal luck at making contact with the enemy. It almost seemed as though he couldn't go on a mission without getting into a scrap, which was what all the pilots longed for. Also significant though was the fact that Dick was skillful enough to take full advantage of the opportunities afforded him. By contrast to Dick's experience in making many contacts, we had some pilots who flew their missions every other day like clockwork, for as long as a year and a half, yet never once made contact with the enemy - very frustrating.

"I flew on Dick's wing a few times when I first joined the squadron. This didn't last long, though, because I soon had my own flight. Jerry Johnson and I had previous combat in the Aleutians so were promoted earlier than some others. Nevertheless, I flew enough with Dick to see that he was an excellent pilot, as his record proves. He was always volunteering for extra missions and had many approved. We had to be careful not to overdo this because there were many other pilots, just as eager, anxious to get their chance at the enemy and establish or increase their score."

Part of Dick's success obviously can be attributed to the aircraft he flew, a point also touched upon by Jordan. Prior to joining the 9th FS Jordan "had flown the P-40 but not in combat. I flew the P-39 in the Aleutians (Adak) early in the war and the P-38 and P-47 in New Guinea. Overall, I feel the P-38 was the best all-around fighter in the Pacific. We flew over long distances of jungle and water. Many of us owe our lives to that extra engine. As with the others (P-39, P-40, P-47) the P-38 could not turn with the Nip planes. We got around that by using our superior speed. We could move in, shoot, move out and turn back in. We did not attempt to dogfight the Japanese fighters . . . this was the best way in the world to get shot down. We would never follow a Nip into a turn for more than 90-degrees. The Nip fighters were so light, lacking armor for the pilot or self-sealing gas tanks, that they could immediately get on your tail if you attempted to turn with them."

Walter Markey felt Dick's success was due to his being "cool and calculating yet impulsive. I'm sure he always figured the odds before he ever made any move and then he acted with lightning swiftness. He became bored without action and would do something sometimes to liven things up. I remember on one occasion we sat up over a transport drop for hours behind Salamaua up near Lae, New Guinea. After the last drop, when we were clear to leave the area, Dick signalled the flight into a trail position, dropped from 10,000 feet in a sharp dive. We made a strafing pass down the Jap Salamaua airstrip at 400 or 500 miles an hour. We made such a low pass that I remember having to lift my wing to get over a flag pole on top of a hangar in the middle of the field."

The 8th and 9th Squadrons, as Sammy Pierce pointed out, "flew from different strips . . . but we did work much closer together flying since both squadrons would normally be scrambled together for intercepts. This is the period (April - May) that the 9th started to really score since they had the range to get to the targets that we in the 8th could not get to with the P-40, plus the fact that they could reach altitudes that we could not.

"Dick was a fairly conservative pilot under normal conditions. Not what was back then referred to as a 'rine-shiner.' He did not pull the spectacular type of thing the way several of the fellows did, but had an uncanny ability to get the plane in the right place at the right time. He always contended that he was a poor shot and that he got scores by flying right up their backside. This was part of his ability to understate. Granted, he was not a George Welch or Ernie Harris at deflection, but he was far from being the world's worst, too."

In looking over Dick's combat reports Nelson Flack remarked: "After reading Dick's combat reports I understand him better. He was far more mature and personally organized than the great majority. He understood his role unemotionally. It was business and a lesser regard for his own well being... that went well beyond most. He was consistent. His combat reports reflect truth and use of good judgment in my opinion. Most pilots, especially the self-appointed heroes, wouldn't admit temporarily fleeing or diving out to gain advantage."

Dick was subsequently asked the very same question regarding the reasons for his success and he came up with four. First, Dick felt he'd "been lucky in getting the breaks of frequent contact with the Nip and contact with him in a really top-notch fighter plane.

"Secondly, I was fortunate enough to get in a great deal of gunnery training in flying school. I still think I am an inferior shot to pilots like Major George Welch.

"The third point is more or less inherent. I have always had a real respect for planes and I don't think I've ever needlessly asked for more than they were made to deliver. If you take them that way your chances of coming home in one piece are way above even.

"The fourth point is linked with the last two. Before getting my first combat assignment, I was given an assignment I hated at the time but now realize it was the best thing that ever happened to me. When I was graduated from flight school they made me an instructor - that hurt my pride and I didn't like the assignment at all. But about the second week I began learning how very little I really knew about flying. The fastest way to recognize your own shortcomings is to try to teach someone else."

Perhaps understandably, Dick omitted one factor in his makeup that, in large part, accounted for his success. By nature Dick was a very competitive person. As mentioned previously, when he was growing up in Poplar Dick threw himself into whatever sports activities were available. Childhood friends used the terms "extremely competitive" and "very tenacious" in describing Dick's love of sports. Piloting a fighter aircraft against a Japanese opponent was probably the ultimate form of competition for someone like Dick. Although the Army Air Force preached the concept of leader-wingman, combat still boiled down to one pilot pitting his skills and aircraft against another. Time and again Dick stressed that he wanted to fly combat missions as long as possible. This desire wasn't based upon the fact that Dick worried that someone would surpass his score, but rather that combat flying, although scary as hell, appealed to his competitive nature.

Chapter 7

Dobodura Days
(April - June 1943)

Following Dick's victory on the 29th a brief lull in Japanese air operations over New Guinea ensued. The lull was deceptive, as the Japanese were occupied elsewhere, hurriedly building up Rabaul's Eleventh Air Fleet by flying in reinforcements from their aircraft carriers *Hiyo*, *Junyo*, *Zuiho* and *Zuikaku*. With these additional aircraft Rabaul could field better than 182 Zeros, 92 Vals, 72 Bettys and assorted torpedo planes. Using this force Admiral Isoruku Yamamoto hoped to inflict crippling losses on Allied shipping and airpower in the Solomons and New Guinea, thus delaying the impending U.S. invasion of New Georgia.

The first phase of Yamamoto's plan - codenamed "I Operation" - consisted of two strikes against the Solomons on April 1st and April 7th. A fighter sweep on the 1st by 58 Zeros cost the Japanese 20 fighters while netting them only six kills. The attack on the 7th was more successful. Sixty-seven Vals covered by 110 Zeros broke through an Allied screen of Air Force, Navy, Marine Corps and New Zealand fighters to sink a destroyer, a corvette and a tanker. The Japanese aircrews wildly overclaimed on the 7th, reporting that they sank 25 transports, two destroyers and one cruiser! In the air they claimed the destruction of 175 Allied aircraft. Actual losses were seven Allied aircraft and one pilot lost! The Japanese lost 12 Vals and 27 Zeros.

Yamamoto, deluded by the wild claims made by his pilots, shifted the point of attack to New Guinea. Oro Bay was the scene of a bitter battle on April 11th as 45 Zeros and Val dive-bombers hit Allied shipping. The "Forty-Niners" were among the units intercepting, which claimed over a dozen kills. Lieutenant Theron Price, as related below, scored the only victory credited to the 9th FS. Although Dick was Price's element leader, he missed all the action.

Dick had taken off at 11:30 a.m. with Price and two other P-38s on a scheduled patrol. Half an hour later radar began vectoring the flight - and others - to an incoming raid. As the flight circled over Oro Bay, just prior to interception, Dick's right engine suffered a cracked piston, forcing him to abort. Shortly after Dick turned back 12 to 15 Oscar-type Zeros were sighted below. Price quickly flamed one, only to be bounced himself and shot up by three other Zeros. Wounded in the face and arms, he nevertheless finished the patrol and landed safely at Dobo at 1:20 p.m.

The 80th FS, 8th FG also intercepted the Japanese over Oro Bay. The "Headhunters" knocked down four aircraft, two of which fell to Captain Danny Roberts. The 80th had recently converted from P-39s to P-38s, giving Kenney three full squadrons of Lightnings.

Twenty-four hours later Port Moresby was the target of 45 bombers covered by 60 fighters. The 39th FS, now under Tom Lynch's command, had first crack at the Japanese, making several head-on passes that disrupted the Japanese formation. Hard on their heels came several flights of P-39s from the 40th and 41st Squadrons, P-40s from the 8th FS and a lone flight from the 9th. Final claims ran to 17 bombers and 10 fighters destroyed, Lieutenant Grover Fanning being high man with two bombers and a fighter confirmed. Fanning, a P-38 driver from the 9th, had to pursue his last victim all the way back to Lae before downing it! The Japanese, however, were able to hit the 7-Mile, Wards and Kila airfields, torching several fuel dumps and destroying three B-25s and a RAAF Beaufighter. Two American fighters were lost in the raid.

Having missed two lucrative missions, Dick finally connected on April 14th during the last Japanese strike of the "I Operation" series. On the 14th Milne Bay was the target of 80-plus Bettys, Vals and Zeros. The "Flying Knights" put up two flights which intercepted the Japanese off Cape Frere, Dick leading Green Flight off at 11:30 a.m. He later reported: "Fighter Control said enemy bombers and fighters (were) approaching Milne Bay at 25,000 feet. Two members of my flight turned back and Lieutenant Planck and myself intercepted three waves of Betty bombers at 26,000 feet. Lieutenant Planck had trouble with his engines and failed to get a shot.

"I made a pass from above and behind the last wave and shot one Betty on (the) left flank and set it on fire as witnessed by Lieutenant Planck. I hit another bomber in the second wave and saw no results. Passed under the first wave as they dropped their bombs. I had to leave with six black Zeros chasing me.

"I left them and turned back to make a pass at three Betty bombers. I hit the left wing area and started his left engine smoking. He left formation and started down. Two Zeros jumped me and I had to dive to 5,000 feet to get away and come home. Last Zero put a 20mm cannon shell in my elevator. There were about 27 Betty bombers and 18 or 20 black Zeros that I saw."

Although the Japanese were hounded as far as Goodenough Island only one other 9th FS pilot scored, Lieutenant Ed Howes disposing of a Zero. In return Lieutenant Bill Sells, one of the Squadron's "old hands," was killed while trying to crashland his crippled P-38 at Milne Bay. One other Allied fighter was lost in contrast to claims of ten bombers and three to five fighters destroyed. Known Japanese losses on April 14th amounted to three Bettys, three Vals and a Zero.

Following the largely abortive strike on the 14th, Yamamoto ended "I Operation" believing he had won a great victory. In reality, the raids had failed, a fact Yamamoto would never learn. On April 18th, while on an inspection flight to Bougainville, Yamamoto's formation was ambushed by P-38s from Guadalcanal. Japan's greatest admiral died in the wreckage of his Betty bomber.

After the 14th, contact with the Japanese resumed its spordic nature, as borne out by entries in the 9th FS history. April 27th: "Things are very quiet as far as raids are concerned. The men are working on their tents putting in floors." May 2nd: "Seems like the Japs have decided to leave us alone now." Dick logged routine alerts, patrols and test flights on the 15th, 17th, 21st, 25th, 27th and 29th before drawing some well-earned leave in early May.

On May 3rd Dick left for a week's leave in Sydney. During World War II Sydney was rated as "the pilot's haven" by Fifth Air Force crews since it teamed with, in Nelson Flack's words, "extremely attractive and receptive young Aussie girls." Flack, who went on leave with Dick, also recalled that Dick didn't seem to need "any of the wine, women and song routine." Walter Markey agreed with Flack, remembering that drinking and carousing wasn't Dick's bag. "I suppose we would be what the kids now might call square," Markey said. "Dick and I didn't enjoy Sydney as much as we did the area around Brisbane. We usually went to a beach about 50 miles south of Brisbane callled Southport. There was a Red Cross rest area at Southport - ice cream, thick shakes, sun and swimming! Occasionally we'd get a steak thrown in. It was a great place to stay!"

Dick did not return to the squadron until May 17th, and as a result missed some action. Having been absent from New Guinea skies for a month, the Japanese staged a night raid on May 13th followed by a daytime strike on the 14th. Twenty-plus bombers and 25 fighters hit Dobodura successfully but suffered heavy losses at the hands of the "Forty-Niners." The group scrambled some 43 P-38s and -40s which tore the Japanese formation apart. Air Force records credit the 49th FG with 22 victories on the 14th. The 8th PS (P-40s) topped the list with 13 claims. The 9th scored four kills but lost a P-38 and its pilot. In any case, Dick was back on the job on the 17th with the squadron history reporting: "Lieutenant Bong and Lieutenant Planck returned from leave today. Lieutenant Bong, being an eager beaver, went out and stood alert, getting a couple of box tops for alerts."

The night raid staged by the Japanese on May 13th was followed by a series of such attacks beginning on the 18th and continuing into June. Although these nocturnal raiders ("Washing-Machine Charlies") were little more than nuisances, they did rob the Americans of needed sleep. Plans were put into effect to intercept these raiders using a stock P-38. Walter Markey recalled that it took "a great deal of persuasion on Dick's part (before) we got permission to attempt a night interception." Although Dick logged several night missions he never scored against the raiders. "Charlie" continued his nightly visits, hitting Dobo, Oro Bay, Wau and Bena

Bena in June. On the 12th he made himself very unpopular by hitting Dobodura in the middle of the showing of "Arsenic and Old Lace." Little damage was done but everyone was upset with the interruption!

By early June the "Forty-Niners" had pretty well tamed Dobodura, having overcome the initial problems of lack of equipment and facilities although malaria was still a problem. With time on their hands Dick and the other pilots turned to various pursuits. Wally Jordan remembered that "every once in a while we would have a sing-sing where the entire bunch at the officers club would join in to roar particularly ribald songs into the jungle darkness, the dirtier the better. I believe the ribald aspect of the sing-sing provided an effective psychological outlet in that they could be sung there with no consequence of offending anyone. Such outlet was needed because everyone was always under a certain amount of wartime tension."

Generally, evening activities revolved around the officers' club whether it be singing, reading, listening to records, writing home or having a drink. In a letter home Dick talked about these late night sessions, commenting: "We sit around here at night and sometimes the day and argue and discuss what we are going to do after the war. Very interesting, lots of different views expressed. Some want to stay in the army and raise kids and some want to buy a farm and raise kids. They all want to raise kids, though. Probably be a great boom in marriage ceremonies after the war is over."

Many nights Dick would bring out his clarinet and run through popular numbers. Opinions of his playing varied. Jim Harvey, who bunked with Dick, recalled that "many nights I went to sleep listening to Dick playing his clarinet. Though he was no Benny Goodman, it was good music." Walter Markey felt otherwise, flatly declaring: "Dick was about the world's worst clarinet player. He had rigged up (that particular clarinet) with rubber bands so that the keys would return to the seated position. One night Dick had brought a quart of gin back from leave down in Australia. And he decided he would learn to drink that gin one night during one of his clarinet concerts. It's a toss-up as to which was the sourest - Dick's notes on the clarinet or his face after he'd taken a swig of gin!"

In the midst of uneventful alerts and escort missions came a brief moment of drama. On June 2nd while returning to Dobo from a scramble with 15 other P-38s, Lieutenant Paul Yeager was forced to bail out when his aircraft caught fire. While a rescue party was hastily formed Dick took off in a P-38, flew to the area where Yeager had jumped and soon spotted him hanging in a tree about 100 feet off the ground. The rescue party, headed by the 9th's new CO, Sid Woods, reached Yeager on the 3rd and brought him back to camp two days later. Ralph Wandrey reported that Dick played a larger part in Yeager's rescue than is known. According to Wandrey, Dick was flying cover for the rescue party as it crossed Embi Lake in a rubber raft when he spotted a large crocodile (!) tailing the raft. Dick reportedly rolled in, killed the croc with a strafing run and scared the hell out of the men in the raft. An interesting story perhaps, but . . .

On a more serious level, May and June 1943 were marked by a major buildup in both men and material in the Fifth Air Force. Due to a command reorganization the 9th FS lost several pilots to the newly-created 475th Fighter Group. The 475th was Kenney's dream unit, the first all Lightning-equipped group in the theater. Under an agreement with "Hap" Arnold, Kenney supplied the personnel for the 475th while Arnold provided the aircraft. Consequently, Kenney raided his existing fighter units for a core of experienced pilots. This resulted in the "Flying Knights" losing Frank Nichols, Harry Brown and Tom McGuire. Likewise, the 80th FS lost Danny Roberts, Jim Ince and John Loisel. The 475th's Commander was Lieutenant Colonel George Prentice, Dick's old squadron CO in the 39th FS. Kenney expected great things from the 475th and they would not disappoint him!

The second fighter group to join the Fifth Air Force, the 348th, was greeted with mixed reactions. Fifth Air Force veterans fixed a jaundiced eye on the aircraft the group flew-Republic's P-47 Thunderbolt. New to the Southwest Pacific Theater, the P-47 was viewed with much the same skepticism that had accompanied the P-38's introduction to the region. Similarly, Lieutenant Colonel Neel Kearby and his pilots, much like Dick and the pilots of the old 39th FS, were eager to show the Fifth Air Force what a devastating fighter their aircraft really was!

By July Kenney had, on paper, a fighter strength of over 500 aircraft. He had the equivalent of two full P-38 groups made up of the newly formed 475th FG plus the 9th, 39th and 80th Squadrons.

The Japanese were also busy during this period, deploying new units and new aircraft to various airfields.

The 68th *Sentai*, the first JAAF *Sentai* equipped with the Kawasaki Ki-61 Tony, moved up to Wewak. A second Ki-61 unit, the 78th *Sentai*, simultaneously deployed to Rabaul in New Britain. In part, the introduction of aircraft such as the Tony was due to Allied successes in Papua and Guadalcanal and the enemy's refusal to yield the air to the Allies. Dick would soon be meeting this new fighter in combat.

The increase in Kenney's strength was mirrored in increasing offensive operations by the Allies in the SWPA Theater. Much of this activity was concerned with establishing a beachhead on the Huon Peninsula, a necessary preliminary to the conquest of New Ireland and New Britain. A second less immediate goal was the reduction of the Japanese bastion at Rabaul.

To extend Fifth Air Force fighter coverage over Lae and Salamaua on the Huon Gulf Kenney had his engineers develop a site some 50 miles west of Lae. Initially known as Tsili Tsili (for a nearby village) Kenney renamed the airfield Marilinan. As a diversion, Kenney had natives prepare crude emergency strips at several sites, one of them being Bena Bena. After two months of uneventful escorts, test hops and alerts Dick drew action on an escort mission to Bena Bena on June 12th.

Dick was one of a dozen 9th FS pilots detailed to cover C-47s ferrying in equipment and personnel. He later reported that he "took off from Jackson Field at 9:15 a.m. as cover for 12 transports. I was element leader of Captain Woods' flight, who was Green Flight Leader.

"We went directly toward Bena Bena. About ten miles southeast of Bena Bena we contacted the enemy at 9:35. Captain Woods and myself were the only two in the flight. I saw eight Oscars. We were at 11,000 feet with the enemy at approximately 14,000 feet. The Oscars were camouflaged, some plain silver and others dark green. The enemy peeled off on the Blue Flight's second element.

"I went into attack against five Oscars which were attacking Blue Flight. I got one 90-degree deflection shot with no observed results, then dove through a layer of clouds to lose three Oscars which were on my tail. I went straight on out and climbed to 12,000 feet, turned back into nine or eight of them. They were below me and about a mile away.

"I picked out one that was flying towards me and attacked him head-on, opening fire at about 400 yards and continued to about 60 yards. I hit him but saw no results. I had to dive out again due to Oscars on my tail. I then climbed back to 3,000 feet and saw three Oscars at same altitude at 12 o'clock. I started another head-on attack. Just before opening fire one made a slight turn to (the) left and I opened fire on him. I made a long burst ten-degree deflection at 100 yards. There were two explosions in his plane. After passing him I looked back over my shoulder and saw him going about vertical down in a slight left turn.

"I looked in front, saw another Oscar coming across my flight path at about 45-degrees. I took a shot at him with no observed results. I looked back at the Oscar, which I claim, and he was still going straight down in a tail spin and only about 1,000 feet from the ground. I rejoined the flight. Upon reaching base I found that they had shot up my right tire. Two holes in each wing and the hydraulic system out. With hand pump I got the wheels down. I landed at Dobodura as I was about to run out of gas." In actual fact Dick's remaining engine ran out of gas before the aircraft had quit rolling. He kept better track of his fuel after that!

Lieutenant Clayton Barnes, a member of Blue Flight, also received credit for destroying an Oscar. After making a head-on pass against one Oscar, Barnes dove on another heading towards Madang. Barnes riddled the hapless Japanese fighter, claiming it as a definite kill since he knew that he had hit the pilot.

Barnes brought back grisly confirmation of his kill. When he landed back at Dobodura the squadron history recorded that there was "blood on his windshield. He was that close to the second one." Despite destroying two fighters, the squadron wasn't satisfied with the results of the Bena Bena scrap. They had gone looking for a fight but most of the pilots hadn't been able to get in a shot as the Oscars rolled in on them. Yet the 9th had lost no aircraft, a poor showing for the Japanese since they had started the scrap with the twin advantage of height and surprise.

The June 12th combat is illustrative of the fighter tactics Dick championed. He always believed that if you were bounced by enemy fighters your best recourse was to dive away to pick up an indicated air speed of at least 350 mph, then level out and make a shallow climb to altitude. Generally Japanese fighters would not follow a Lightning in a high-speed dive since their controls would stiffen up. Dick also used the head-on pass to advantage because he realized the Japanese respected the P-38's heavy armament of cannon and machine guns, often breaking away when a P-38 began heading in. Japanese Army Air Force pilots, like those met on the 12th, did not rate high in Dick's estimate. He felt the Japanese Navy pilots in their Zeros were more dangerous opponents.

In any case, the 9th Squadron had cause to celebrate on the 12th, adding two more kills to its long line of victories. June 12th was also important for it marked the opening of the "Forty-Niner's" baseball season! Colonel Bob Morrissey opened the season in true Air Force style by buzzing the ball diamond in the group's Cub trainer, nicknamed *Betty Boop*, and tossing out the ball. Despite the fact that the ball hit *Betty Boop's* prop and was cut in two, the season was off to a good start. The first game, played between enlisted men teams from the 7th and 9th Squadrons, ended in a disaster for the "Flying Knights." Final score was 15 to 1 in favor of the 7th Squadron.

Dick, an avid sports fan, often pitched for 9th FS teams. George Pegg, attached to 49th HQ, supplied some reminiscences of Dick's love of sports. Pegg recalled one game played "between Headquarters Squadron and the 9th Squadron. Rivalry was always strong where Headquarters was concerned, because of its having no planes of its own and having to borrow one from a squadron if they wanted to go on a mission. Dick, although he had flown a mission up the New Guinea coast that morning, was on the mound for the Ninth, regaled in a rather blousy sweat shirt that would have made a good ad for some soap opera. Whether it was the fact that his flying prowess had our boys in Headquarters stunned or whether he was really a big-leaguer never came to light, but he won the game with little or no trouble — not only on the mound but at the plate.

"Following the game we took advantage of the cool waters of Zamboogie (River) and in the course of conversation one of our boys challenged the 9th Squadron men to a tournament in horseshoes for that evening. With no flourish or show Dick said he would like to play doubles with someone just to show Headquarters how it was done. Well, we in Headquarters, knowing something about the farm, thoroughly whipped the 9th Squadron and retired for the day with a feeling of warmth toward our fellow men."

Pegg also recalled that later on, when the group had moved up to Gusap, Dick frequented the headquarters area "because he could play ping-pong or poker or listen to the radio at the same time. The Signal Corps radio could pick up many of the stations from the States and naturally our programs consisted mostly of music, which we were starved for. Dick had a voice that wasn't bad at all. He would sit by the radio, hum the new tunes, memorize the words and then, still humming, would get up and offer to beat someone in a game of ping-pong."

Since the remainder of June and early July was quiet, Dick's letters to his family during this period often were devoted to sports and local happenings. On June 29th he wrote: "We nearly have our officers' club finished and it certainly is a good one for this country. We have worked pretty hard and it has really put a lot of us in better physical and mental shape. Played a couple of ball games. I pitched three innings in one of them and gave up two hits and no runs. My arm is pretty weak, though, from no throwing. If I play a few more maybe I'll be able to throw a full game again." In a letter dated July 9th Dick wrote that he'd "played another ball game this afternoon and won. I pitched not too well but good enough. 13 - 6 was the score. I got two for four in the hits column and scored twice. Our club is finished and opens tomorrow. Probably be right drunk out for a few hours. We are certainly having our share of rain lately."

During this relatively quiet period the "Flying Knights" began receiving the new improved H model Lightning, Dick flying one such aircraft up from Moresby on July 3rd. The H model was equipped with Allison F-15 engines which gave the aircraft a top speed of 402 mph at 25,000 feet, a gain of seven mph over the F models. Such replacement aircraft would be welcomed, as the 9th FS would see much action in July 1943. In June only two enemy aircraft had been destroyed, one by Dick. In July the squadron would destroy 22 aircraft and Dick would turn in his best performance to date!

Meanwhile, on June 23rd, in a seemingly unrelated occurrence Lockheed Aircraft Corporation was issued a letter contract by the Air Force to develop a new fighter around the English de Havilland Goblin jet engine. Lockheed engineers and mechanics set about designing the aircraft which was given the designation XP-80. In time the XP-80 would become the Shooting Star, America's first successful jet fighter and the aircraft in which Dick would meet his death.

Chapter 8

The Score Mounts
(July - November 1943)

By the beginning of July 1943 the Allies were on the offensive in both New Guinea and the Solomons. In New Guinea landings were made at Nassau Bay on June 26th and on Woodlark and Kiriwina Islands on the 30th, the intent being to extend Kenney's air power that much closer to New Britain and the Solomons. Lae would then be crushed between the Americans at Nassau Bay and an Australian force advancing from Wau. Salamaua would be isolated and left to wither on the vine. Allied aircraft provided ground support for the advancing troops while other air units pounded Lae and Salamaua almost daily. The skies over Lae and Salamaua soon became the scene of bitter air battles in July.

The "Forty-Niners" opened the aerial scoring when 7th FS P-40s caught a Japanese formation between Nassau Bay and Salamaua on July 3rd, claiming six victories without losing an aircraft. On the 8th Lieutenants Fred Sibley and Ralph Hays scored for the 9th FS followed by Captain Tom Fowler on July 11th. The P-39s of the 36th FS were also in action on the 11th and came away with six victories.

The 9th, 39th and 80th Squadrons all scored big victories in late July. On the 21st the 39th and 80th Squadrons were covering B-25s hitting Bogadjim when Zekes and Tonys intercepted. The Americans claimed 22 kills, 11 of which were credited to the 39th FS. These kills boosted its total claims to 104, making the 39th FS the first Fifth Air Force unit to top 100 kills. Lieutenant Jay Robbins of the 80th FS was top man on the 21st with three kills, Robbins having flown over to Australia with Dick back in September 1942. The mission was also significant in that it marked Fifth Air Force's first encounter with the Kawasaki Ki-61 fighter. Initially mistaken for a Japanese version of the German Me-109 fighter, Ki-61s were sometimes referred to as "Type III" or "in-line" fighters by Allied pilots.

Two days later, on the 23rd, both units were in action again. The 39th met Tonys over the Lae area and downed five. The 80th, once again escorting bombers hitting Bogadjim, pounced on 20 Zekes and Tonys. Seven Japanese fighters went down before the guns of the 80th's Lightnings, two being credited to the squadron CO, Major Ed Cragg.

On the 26th the 9th FS ran into a swell scrap during a routine patrol over Lae. The "Flying Knights" put up three flights of P-38s, Dick leading off Blue Flight at 12:30 p.m. After sweeping the target area the squadron turned towards Salamaua, overflew the Markham Valley at 16,000 feet and promptly ran into Japanese fighters. In the hectic action that followed three pilots did all the scoring with Dick, Captain Jim Watkins and Lieutenant Jerry Johnson notching a total of ten kills.

Dick spotted the Japanese first, calling in "airplanes at 12 o'clock and we were intercepted at 1:50 over the Markham Valley. There were about 20 fighters; ten in-line fighters and ten Zeros. I dropped my tanks and shot at an in-line job and missed. I dove out and shot at a Zeke head-on and he burst into flames. I shot at an in-line job 45 degrees from behind and above and knocked pieces off his fuselage. I shot at another in-line job and he burst into flames. I shot at another Zero head-on and knocked pieces out of his canopy and engine cowling or engine. I shot at one more in-line job and missed. I left the area at 2:10 and returned to base and landed."

The Japanese had tried to sandwich the Lightnings between two groups of fighters. Shortly after the initial 20 bandits were called in, 15 more joined the scrap. Finding Zeros and Tonys behind and in front of him, Captain Watkins turned his flight into the threat at his six o'clock position. In a series of head-on passes he flamed three Tonys and then blew apart the cockpit of a fourth Ki-61, killing the pilot instantly. Jerry Johnson, in the meantime, smoked an Oscar and then blew the left wing off a Tony.

Further details on Dick's quartet of kills can be found in his logbook and interviews given to the press. His logbook recorded that he "shot down inline in flames. Shot down Zero in flames. Shot down Zero out of control. Shot down inline out of control. All over Markham Valley about ten miles back of Lae. Saw about 20 Nips but there were about 50 of them." In describing the fight to newsmen, Dick said, "things happened so fast that all I can recall is the sky being full of Jap planes twisting crazily, hot lead whizzing past my face and all hell breaking loose above and below me. I just kept boring in close, trying to get a rising sun in my sights and then firing a burst or two. Couldn't help but hit something under those conditions."

Interestingly enough, the 9th FS historian commented on the brevity of Dick's combat report of the 26th, noting that "this brief report, of a pilot who shot down four enemy aircraft in one engagement, is typical of Lieutenant Bong's reticence. He would describe a major engagement in the same amount of space another man would take to tell of drinking three beers."

Dick's performance on the 26th netted him a Distinguished Service Cross for "extraordinary heroism in action over Markham Valley, New Guinea on July 26, 1943." Dick, however, took it all in stride. His crew chief, Technical Sergeant Elwood Barden, recalled that when Dick landed after his four-in-one mission he was more excited over the fact that he had come back without a single bullet hole in his plane. Normally Dick, who liked to wade right into a scrap, came back with combat damage, but not on the 26th!

Two days later the 9th turned in another fine score, which boosted its total claims to 105, and once again Dick and Jim Watkins were involved. On the 28th nine P-38s flew an escort mission, covering B-25s hitting Rein Bay, New Britain. Jim Watkins led Captive Blue Flight with Dick leading the second element.

Dick's combat report related that the P-38s "were intercepted by about 15 Zeros of the Oscar type. They were above us at 11 o'clock. Two of them dove on me and I dove to lose them. I pulled up an climbed to 8,000 feet and made a 45-degree head-on pass at two Zeros with no observed results.

"Shot once at another one 90-degrees deflection and missed. Peeled off to join five other P-38s and a Zero jumped me from behind and put five shots into my airplane. I dove to lose him and picked up two Zeros about to make a pass at the B-25s. I made a 45-degree deflection shot from the rear and above until he almost turned into me. It was a long burst and he slid off on one wing and crashed northwest of Rein Bay. Two more Zeros chased me as I started home and they finally gave up because they couldn't catch me. I left the area at 9:05 and joined the B-25s. We came home and landed at 9:55."

Jim Watkins was top man on the 28th, claiming three Oscars in all. The first two were downed in head-on passes while the third tried to climb away, took a long burst in the belly and fell straight into the sea. Three other 9th FS pilots - Major Sid Woods, Captain Bill Haney and Lieutenant Ralph Wandrey - also knocked down Oscars to run the mission total to seven kills with no losses.

The Oscar kill was Dick's 16th victory, a fact he commented on in his next letter home. Dick wrote: "Here it is almost the end of July already. Been over here almost 11 months now. I suppose I hit the headlines again with both feet. Got five more in the last three days, makes 16 now. Got a few more bullet holes but not bad." What Dick failed to mention is that his latest kills made him the top ace of the Southwest Pacific Theater! His closest competitors were Captain Tom Lynch with eleven kills, Captain Andy Reynolds with ten and Captain George Welch with nine. Within the 9th FS Jim Watkins was the closest challenger with eight victories, seven of them scored within a two-day period!

On August 2nd Watkins continued his hot streak by downing three Oscars. Watkins was one of 16 P-38 pilots protecting B-25s on a barge hunt along the coast from Heldsback to Bogadjim. Eight other 9th FS pilots claimed kills when the squadron mixed it up with 12 to 15 Oscars off Teliata Point. And what of Dick? In the words of the 49th FG history: "Lieutenant Bong had left on leave the day before, August 1, and so missed the fun."

Regrettably, Jim Watkins' hot streak ended on August 2nd, his next - and last - victory being scored in March 1945. His total of 12 kills, however, made him the third-ranking ace of the 9th FS, behind Dick and

Jerry Johnson. Watkins, who retired from the Air Force as a colonel, recalled his wartime association with Dick in the following words:

"Thirty years have not dulled or dimmed my memories of Dick Bong. In my opinion Dick was a real 'fighter pilot.' When he saw an enemy he went after him until he got him and, as we know, he got quite a few.

"Dick was a fighter and it took fighters of the same caliber to stay up with him. Many a good pilot wished he were good enough to fly wing for Bong. Dick flew that plane like a young boy handles his pet bicycle and fired it like a rifle."

Although Dick missed the August 2nd scrap, his leave-taking proved well-time since, in the words of the 49th FG history: "The next few days offered only routine escort missions to all squadrons of the group. Apparently the Nip had learned that interception was a costly game for him and that discretion was much the better part of valor."

Shortly before he went on leave Dick had a chance to pit his skills against the Republic P-47 Thunderbolt, the newest aircraft in the Fifth Air Force inventory. Although the 348th FG had been operating P-47s since June, most Fifth Air Force veterans still viewed the big, seven-ton fighter with skepticism. In order to convince such skeptics the 348th CO, Lieutenant Colonel Neel Kearby, staged a series of mock dogfights pitting his skills at the controls of a P-47 against veteran P-38 pilots. Wally Jordan recalled: "The mock fight between Kearby and Dick resulted from the constant arguments between P-47 and P-38 pilots relative to the comparative performance of the two airplanes. Although they had not yet been in combat in the theater, the '47 jockeys were quite arrogant while occupying the Dobodura strip with us. However, the first time they observed a 49th formation returning from a successful contact with the enemy, watching the victory rolls in the landing traffic pattern ... they became quite meek and friendly." The actual outcome of the dogfight between Dick and Kearby is still argued by P-38 and -47 pilots although Jordan felt that "Dick had a slight edge on Kearby even though he was a very good pilot."

The Brisbane leave was a welcome break for Dick. He told his family that he "had a pretty good time but it was still pretty cold down there for us who have been in the tropics for so long. I put on about eight or ten pounds while I was down there. You know - ice cream, steaks, liver and onions, roasted chicken and various other good things to eat. I went to all the trouble of carrying back 12 bottles of liquor 2,000 miles and then busted one bottle here in the club taking it out of the bag. Sure was a sad case because we are pretty short of liquor right now. Brought back a couple cases of beer too."

It was during this period that the publicity spotlight began concentrating on Dick. During the months since his first victories his name had appeared in various newspaper articles stateside. Although he was featured prominently in Wisconsin newspapers, most other papers regarded him as just another rising fighter ace. After his victory on July 25th however, he was the leading Army Air Force ace in the SWPA Theater and the newshounds began clamoring for more on Bong, a situation not to Dick's liking. On August 22nd he wrote home: "So you think I was going to come home and sell bonds, eh? Boy I hope I never have to do anything like that. They want me to be on a broadcast next time I'm on leave but I hope they forget it by the time I get down there. They never gave me any kind of choice or anything else but I wouldn't have if they had." In a subsequent letter he commented that he "had no desire whatsoever to come home to make speeches to any hero-worshipping public. Not that I don't want to get home but I don't want it under those circumstances. I would rather get home without anyone knowing about it." Unfortunately, as Dick's score mounted in the coming months the media demands on him and his family in Poplar increased that much more!

One other passage from Dick's letter of August 22nd also bears repeating because it reveals his feelings about the honors that had come his way. In answering a question from his mother regarding the medals he had been awarded, Dick replied that he had received "the Distinguished Service Cross for the four in one day you were talking about. So I have everything but the Purple Heart and the Congressional Medal of Honor. You have to get wounded to get the one and really do something to get the other so I don't want the one and probably wouldn't do anything to deserve the other. I've got too many to know what to do with already, anyway."

The remainder of August and early September gave Dick little opportunity to "really do something" as the missions yielded no contact with the Japanese. Dick's logbook recorded uneventful escort missions on the 14th to New Britain and Finschhafen, night tracking missions on the 17th, 19th and 22nd and so on into September.

Interestingly enough, on August 21st Dick, who had a fondness for twin-engined aircraft, checked out as co-pilot in a PBY-5 Catalina! Although the lumbering amphibian seems a strange contrast to the sleek fighters Dick was used to flying, the PBY flight time was perhaps another indication Dick was planning a postwar career in aviation and trying to widen his background.

The routine of uneventful missions and equally dreary camp life was sometimes broken by unexpected moments of humor. Ralph Wandrey related an experience he and Dick were involved in, which might be best described as gallows humor. During this period the 49th FG had been experiencing some problems with guns jamming during high-G maneuvers. An armament officer wanted to motorize the ammunition feeds and since Wandrey's aircraft was in maintenance for a 200-hour overhaul, Wandrey volunteered his P-38. The modifications and overhaul complete, Wandrey decided to test the aircraft since a big mission was upcoming.

Wandrey had his P-38, nicknamed *The Beast*, about halfway down the runway and 30-feet off the ground when both engines died! Engine restart failing, *The Beast* went tearing down the runway, shedding its gear. Narrowly missing a line of bombed-up B-26s, the Lightning tore off the runway, skidded along a drainage ditch, hit a culvert, bounced over the road and smashed head-on into the other side of the ditch. Wandrey got clear as the aircraft went up in flames.

Dick had been watching all this with other personnel. Since no-one had seen Wandrey escape, they assumed their friend had perished and took appropriate action. Wandrey related that later when he "walked into the mess hall, Dick was sitting at a table facing me. You never saw a face go so white in such a hurry as his. He said 'Wandrey, what in the hell are you doing here? We saw you hit and I jumped in a jeep and ran over to the tower and asked the guy in the tower whether the pilot got out. He said that he was watching through binoculars and no one got out of that plane alive.'" Once he heard Wandrey's version of the events Dick sheepishly asked if he wanted his flight jacket and Aussie boots back. Dick and the other pilots had already begun to split up Wandrey's effects! And Wandrey remembers it took him "almost four days to round all of it up again and get it back in my tent. I never did get my good sheets back!"

In mid-August both the Americans and the Japanese were occupied with constructing new airfields and improving existing ones. The Tsili Tsili field west of Lae was able to handle Fifth Air Force fighters by mid-August. Meanwhile, the Japanese complex at Wewak received additional reinforcements. Since fighters staging out of Tsili Tsili could now cover bombers hitting the Wewak complex, the scene of combat shifted to Wewak.

On August 17th five squadrons of B-25s, covered by P-38s, swept over the Wewak complex and claimed to have damaged or destroyed over 100 Japanese aircraft. The next day a combined strike by B-24s and -25s met with fierce resistance and the escorts from the 475th FG piled into the Japanese. In all, the P-38s downed 15 enemy aircraft while losing two. Lieutenant Tom McGuire, formerly with the 49th FG, notched up his first aerial kills by downing two Zekes and a Tony. In time McGuire would become Dick's closest rival in the aerial scoring race. On the 20th the Japanese intercepted a Wewak mission yet again. Among the P-38 pilots scoring was Captain George Welch who claimed three kills, boosting his total to nine. The final mission on 21 August, which completed the destruction of the Wewak complex, saw 35 enemy aircraft downed by the Americans.

Having gutted Japanese air strength in the Wewak area, the Allies felt confident in launching amphibious attacks on Lae and airborne assaults at Nadzab. On September 4th American and Australian infantrymen began wading ashore near Lae covered by naval forces and Fifth Air Force. The Japanese did not commit their air units until early afternoon when a large formation of bombers and fighters was tracked by radar, approaching from the north. About 60 P-38s and P-47s intercepted the Japanese and claimed 15 fighters and four bombers. The 80th FS was among the first to engage the Japanese and came away with 11 kills, four of which fell to Lieutenant Jay Robbins. The 9th Squadron had been covering the landings earlier in the day and Dick could only note ruefully in his logbook that he "missed big fight by 45 minutes."

Two days later, as the Nadzab area was being secured, the 8th and 9th Squadrons did the honors as they tackled a formation of Bettys covered by Zekes and Tonys. The Japanese were intent on striking Hopoi when they were intercepted over the Huon Gulf by P-40s of the 8th FS. The 8th scored four kills, three of them going to Lieutenant Bob White. Then the "Flying Knights" got into the act. Sixteen Lightnings from the 9th FS were patrolling the Morobe area when they were diverted on to the Betty formation. At 1:45 p.m., over Huon Gulf, they sighted the enemy. The Bettys were in two groups, the first group of nine being unescorted. The second group, also of nine aircraft, was flying 15 miles behind the first but had escorts. In the ensuing combat Captain Ralph Wire downed a pair of Zekes and Lieutenant Theron Price a Betty. Dick had an eventful mission, dropping at least two Bettys from the enemy formation and then crash-landing at Marilinan after being hit by fire from the bombers. For all his troubles, however, Dick's claims - for two Bettys destroyed - were downgraded to probables!

Dick did not return to base until September 8th, at which time he submitted his combat report. In it he stated: "The bombers were sighted at one o'clock low and we caught up to them with Red Flight on the right and Blue Flight (which Dick was leading) on the left. I made my first pass from the left and behind the bombers, drawing the Zeros from the right over to me. I shot up the element leader of the flight of three on the left side of the bomber formation and pulled off to the left. This bomber dropped out of formation.

"I made another pass from the left front quarter with no observed results. I made one more pass from the stern on the left man in the formation and observed hits along his fuselage and wings. I pulled off to the left and looking back over my right shoulder, I saw my right engine smoking heavily. Pulled out of combat and feathered the engine and flew to Marilinan where I landed and ran the ship into a gully. Landing time was 2:00. I claim two Betty bombers definitely destroyed. Lieutenant Price saw them going down smoking."

Price confirmed that he had seen "Captain Bong make his passes on the bombers (and) one fell out of formation on his first pass.[1] Both engines were smoking badly and it lost altitude rapidly. On his last pass another bomber fell out of formation with both engines smoking badly and it was also losing altitude rapidly. Both bombers lost about 9,000 feet in less than five minutes and were only 500 feet above a broken layer of cumulus clouds which were about 1,000 feet high. For that reason and as badly as they were smoking, I am sure they crashed into the water before they reached land or an air field."

Despite Price's statement the score for the September 6th mission remained three confirmed kills for one loss, Lieutenant Jim Fagan being lost on his first mission. Dick amended his logbook for the 6th to read "probably shot down two Betty bombers between Hopoi and Finschhafen ... not accepted, not seen to hit." He did feel, however, he had downed the two since his next letter home contains the statements that he "got two more on the 6th and collected a few more ventilation holes in my airplane." As usual, Dick was downplaying the dangers of combat for the sake of his family.

Dick borrowed various P-38s for missions on the 8th and 10th before journeying down to Eagle Farm to pick up a new Lightning. Returning on the 27th he flew a mission the same day, being assigned Red Flight Leader in a formation of 16 P-38s covering B-25s to Wewak.

Near Boram at 11:00 a single camouflaged Tony was spotted coming from the west. Dick reported: "We dropped our belly tanks and dived to the attack. We dove and he chandelled over us. I followed suit and gave him one long burst as he was sliding off the top of his chandelle. No damage observed on this pass. Four other pilots of our squadron shot at him and the enemy pilot bailed out and his plane was seen to crash into the water, east of Boram about one mile offshore." Lieutenant Bill Bleecker was credited with the kill.

By the end of September 1943 the Allied drive in New Guinea was gaining momentum. The rapidity with which Lae and Salamaua fell accelerated plans to take Finschhafen on the upper side of the Huon Peninsula. By October 2nd Finschhafen was in Allied hands, only ten days after troops waded ashore. The advance bases at Lae, Finschhafen and Nadzab were rapidly developed and would soon be joined by a site to the north known as Gusap. The Japanese complex at Wewak had been pounded by the August strikes, although enemy air units were still being fed into the area. Nevertheless, the Allies were in good position to finish off Wewak before turning to more lucrative targets. The invasion of Bougainville was scheduled for mid-October and that meant Fifth Air Force would have its turn at the great Japanese bastion at Rabaul, New Britain.

Meanwhile, on October 2nd, Dick was back in action. Mission 524 called for 14 P-38s of the 9th FS to fly cover for B-25s and -26s hitting Cape Hoskins, New Britain. Dick, commanding Green Flight, took off at 8:05 a.m. The flight in was uneventful until 9:25 when, Dick's words: "West of Gasmata, while our flight was at 15,000 feet, we observed a single enemy airplane, Type 100, R/F, Dinah. It was flying at 15,000 feet and when first observed was coming from the north. The Dinah was dark in color and camouflaged with brown. It had red roundels on the wings.

"I made a gentle turn to the right which brought me right in on his tail. I shot about four bursts and he started smoking and burning and fell off into a vertical dive in flames. Apparently he never saw our formation of P-38s." This was the only kill scored by the 9th FS on October 2nd.

On the 6th Dick left for two weeks leave in Australia, therein missing several healthy scraps with the Japanese. On October 11th Colonel Neel Kearby led a quartet of 348th FG P-47s over Wewak and came back with six kills to his credit, earning himself a Medal of Honor. Rabaul was the target 24 hours later as Fifth Air Force B-24s and -25s pounded Rabaul's airfields and harbor installations. The Japanese responded with a raid on Oro Bay on the 15th by 25 Vals with Oscar and Zeke escorts. The "Forty-Niners" and the 475th Group massacred the Japanese, downing all the Vals and 18 escorts. Jerry Johnson destroyed two Vals and an Oscar. Two days later the Japanese were back once more and again were mauled by the 49th, 475th and 35th Groups. Tom McGuire flamed three Zekes before being forced to bail out of his crippled aircraft. The 475th scored again on the 23rd during a B-24 strike on Rabaul, claiming an even dozen kills.

Dick returned to combat on the 24th flying cover for B-25s hitting Rabaul. Some 40 to 50 Hamps and Zekes were waiting over the target and a terrific scrap broke out. The 80th FS came away with 12 kills, four of which fell to Jay Robbins. The 9th Squadron downed six with "Jump" O'Neill accounting for two. Although Dick was in action he could only report that he "shot at three Zeros with no luck." Near Tobera Airdrome three grey-black Zekes had been spotted above Dick's Red Flight. The flight dropped belly tanks and climbed to the attack. Dick later reported having "shot one burst at Zeke at 2,000 feet high, no results. Shot one burst at Zeke 11 o'clock high, no results. Shot one burst at Zeke ten o'clock high, no results." These particular Zekes had no stomach for fighting, preferring to avoid combat by climbing into cloud cover. Total claims for October 24th came to 40 kills with no P-38s lost.

A repeat mission to Rabaul on the 25th was only partially successful due to bad weather conditions. A recall order was sent which most of the escorting fighters heard and obeyed. Due to radio problems the bombers did not turn back and flew the mission with only eight 475th FG P-38s as escort. Although the mission was uneventful for the 9th Squadron, Ralph Wandrey felt it was memorable for several reasons. Wandrey remembered that "since Dick had all the (victory) flags painted on his plane, Fifth Air Force decreed that he should not fly this plane because he was too valuable a property. So the order came down that he was to trade planes for that day. Since we had no spare planes the squadron CO advised me that Dick and I would swap planes for the day. I wasn't too happy about being the pigeon for that day." Fortunately, as previously mentioned, the fighters turned back due to bad weather and landed at Kiriwini Island.

As Wandrey shut down his engines an enlisted man drove up in a jeep, got out and asked the dumbfounded Wandrey for his autograph! As Wandrey was trying to figure this out he happened to glance over and spotted the 17 victory flags on the nose of the Lightning. Turning to the soldier he directed him to Dick who had just landed and was still sitting in his aircraft. Wandrey then "hopped off the wing of the plane and trotted around to the other side where Dick couldn't see me and stood there listening to the conversation. The corporal saluted again and Dick stood there wondering what was coming off. Then the corporal said 'Captain, can I have your autograph please, sir?' Dick looked at him and said, 'My autograph?' About that time I couldn't hold it any longer and started snorting and snickering. Dick looked over his shoulder, spotted me and said, 'Aw, Shit!' However, I finally convinced him that he was a celebrity and that he should sign the corporal's book. After which the corporal decided that maybe he should get my signature too. So he got both of us that day."

Rabaul's airfields took another pasting on the 29th and this time Dick was in fine form, downing two Zekes. The Japanese put up between 30 and 40 fighters to break up the bomber attack but failed miserably, losing 17 aircraft. Ten victories fell to the 9th Squadron with Dick and "Jump" O'Neill getting two apiece.

The "Flying Knights" put up 13 Lightnings on October 29th, with Dick leading Red Flight. The squadron arrived over Rabaul at 1230 hours where, as Dick later reported: "We observed approximately eight enemy airplanes consisting of all fighters. They were in string formation and about 22,000 feet high. When first observed they were going straight down thru the bombers.

"We dropped our belly tanks and dived to the attack. Zekes attacked from directly above and I made a pass on one below me after it had gone through the bombers. Two Zekes jumped on my tail and I was driven down to 3,000 feet with my wing man. I made two shots at Zekes on the way down with no observed results. I made a

The Score Mounts 63

head-on attack at one Zeke at 1,000 feet and he crashed out of control. I chased two more Zekes toward Open Bay and shot one down in flames and damaged the other one. Broke off engagement due to lack of ammunition." Lieutenant George Haniotis confirmed Dick's claims, which raised his score to 19 victories.

Dick's latest victories drew a passing comment in his next letter home: "Well I did it again. Got two more so that makes nineteen. That puts me three up on anyone over here. Have over 1,000 hours flying time in army airplanes now. About 500 in the airplane I'm flying.

"Let's see, I guess it's been about two years today or tomorrow since I was home last. Does the place still look the same? I suppose the trees must almost hide the house from the road now. Trees out against the pasture ought to be high enough to see by now, too.

"Boy am I going to eat when I get home. Chicken, venison, pork, apple pie and anything else I can get my hooks in that is good. We were talking about eating last night and it seemed I was in good position because I lived on the farm. Of course I agreed with them profusely. Then I had the advantage in having an excellent cook in my mother."

The Fifth Air Force attacks on Rabaul had cost the Japanese dearly. In order to build up Rabaul's Eleventh Air Fleet, reinforcements were flown off the Imperial Fleet carriers *Shokaku*, *Zuikaku* and *Zuiho* -some 170 Kates, Vals and Zekes in all. These aircraft began arriving in Rabaul on November 1st, boosting its inventory to almost 400 fighters and bombers. The Japanese planned to use these planes in "Operation RO" to halt Allied advances in the Solomons and head off the upcoming invasion of Bougainville. As it turned out, Bougainville was invaded even as the first Japanese carrier planes were landing at Rabaul.

Bad weather kept Fifth Air Force away from Rabaul on November 1st but on the 2nd Kenney sent his B-25s and P-38s back in to hit Lakunai airfield and shipping in Simpson Harbor. It was to be the roughest Rabaul strike of all, costing eight B-25s and nine P-38s. The Americans claimed to have destroyed 94 aircraft in the air and on the ground and sunk three destroyers, eight merchantmen and four coastal vessels.

Warrant Officer Takeo Tanimizu, a Zero pilot with the 253rd *Kokutai*, claimed his first victories - two P-38s - on November 2nd over Rabaul. Tanimizu commented: "It was difficult to make the American planes burn in the air. You could tell by the way they smoked if it was one of our Zeroes or an enemy plane. I think the Grumman F6F was the toughest opponent we had. They could maneuver and roll, whereas planes such as the P-38 and F4U made hit-and-run attacks. They were not maneuverable. The P-38 at low altitudes were easy prey. They were not very fast. They usually stayed at highter altitudes. The weakest part of the P-38 was its tail. One 20mm shell there and its tail would snap off."

On November 5, 1943 Fifth Air Force hit Rabaul in conjunction with units from Task Force 38. Twenty-seven B-24s from the 43rd BG pounded the wharf area while the naval units worked over the shipping in the harbor. Fifty-eight P-38s covered the Liberators. The 9th put up 11 Lightnings, Dick once again leading Red Flight. Although Japanese aircraft were seen in the target area only one P-38 pilot scored that day, Dick claiming numbers 20 and 21. He described the mission as follows:

"We proceeded to Rabaul flying at 12 to 20,000 feet. At Rabaul, about 2:15, while our flight was at 20,000 feet, we observed approximately 15 enemy fighters. When first observed they were coming from the northwest. The Zekes were black in color and camouflaged with brown. They appeared to be old planes.

"We dropped our tanks and dived to the attack. I came down on two from the rear and fired a short burst into the last one from 100 yards and he blew up. I fired a long burst at another and he split S'ed but never pulled out. He blew up about 5,000 feet above the ground. Fired at two more with no apparent results. Broke off combat for lack of gas and ammunition."

Lieutenant George Haniotis, Dick's wingman, disappeared during the scrap and was not seen again. It appears at least one other P-38, that from the 39th FS, was also lost on November 5th.

Two days later Kenney had his bombers hitting Rapopo airfield. Sixteen aircraft were claimed destroyed on the ground while P-38 claims added 23 more, all air kills, to the pot. Five Lightnings were lost, including one flown by Dick's wingman, Lieutenant Stanley Johnson.

The 9th FS had put up two flights of ten P-38s for the November 7th mission, Dick leading Red Flight. Over Rabaul, at 12:30, 40 Zekes were called in below, flying in scattered groups between 15,000 and 30,000 feet. The squadron dropped tanks and rolled in on the Japanese fighters. Dick's combat report picked up the action:

"I made several passes at different Zekes with no results. Finally my wingman and I observed about eight-ten Zeros above one P-38 so we dove through them to break them up. My wingman disappeared on this pass and is missing. On the way home I engaged four Zeros that were attacking P-38 No. 91, who was flying with one engine. He got away and I finally shook off the Zeros. The enemy was last seen heading back towards Rabaul."

As Dick shut down his engines after the November 7th mission he had no idea that he had just flown his last combat mission. Dick had heard some rumors in late October that he would be home by Christmas or early January, but now the rumor was reality. After slightly more than a year in the war zone Dick was on his way home!

During that year Dick had flown 158 missions, running up a string of victories that merited the Distinguished Flying Cross, Distinguished Service Cross, Silver Star and numerous Air Medals. He received confirmation for 21 kills, as follows: eight Oscars, seven Zekes, two Tonys, two Dinahs, one Betty and one Val. In return his aircraft was damaged seven times by enemy fire, three of which were serious in nature. On five occasions he downed two aircraft on one mission. On July 26, 1943 he downed four enemy aircraft on one mission. Dick scored five victories in the P-38F, 11 in the G model and five more in the P-38H.

Since the end of the war various statements and criticisms, some bordering on slander, have been made regarding Dick's military career. Dick was not the sole target of controversy. Tom McGuire, Dick's wartime rival, has also had his share of detractors. The statements made about Dick need to be examined as thoroughly as possible in order to clear the air.

One charge claimed that Dick received special treatment while assigned to the Fifth Air Force because of General Kenney's personal interest in him. This matter will also be discussed further in Chapter 10. As regards Dick's first tour, however, such a charge cannot be proven. The record shows that Dick received no special consideration while assigned to the 9th Squadron. He was assigned missions on the same rotational basis that applied to all pilots. Generally, he flew every other day although he had a reputation of being an eager beaver ready to take any additional flight time that came along. He flew his share of rough missions but, at the same time, missed out on some good scraps because he was not scheduled to fly that day or was on leave.

It took Dick 12 months to score 21 victories. He scored two kills in December 1942, three in January 1943, four in March, single kills in April and June, five in July, three in October and two more in November. If anything, his score represents the cyclic nature of the Pacific air war where months might go by with no Japanese sighting followed by heavy action.

Given the same opportunities, other pilots turned in better scores than Dick. Jim Watkins, for example, ran up ten kills in just three missions. Jay Robbins of the 80th FS downed 11 Japanese during the same number of missions while George Welch of the 36th FS racked up 16 kills during five air battles. The deciding factor in such victories was not favoritism but a combination of frequent contacts with the Japanese, aggressiveness and skillful use of the superlative P-38 fighter.

Few Fifth Air Force personnel queried by the authors were able to supply any specific information - pro or con - on this matter. General Kenney may have felt Dick would produce the best combat record, but, as regards Dick's first tour, there is no evidence to support claims that Kenney took any action to help Dick build up a score.

Over the years statements have been made that Dick lost an excessive number of wingmen in combat. Various unidentified sources have quoted different figures, one even claiming that Dick lost seven wingmen! Others have said that Tom McGuire, Dick's chief rival, never lost a wingman in combat. Such claims imply that Dick was a poor combat leader, one more interested in scoring kills than in watching out for his wingman. This issue needs to be examine at some length.

For the record, Dick began leading two-ship elements and four-ship flights as early as March 1943. From March 1943 to the end of his first tour in November Dick scored all his victories while serving as either a flight or element leader. Two kills were scored while leading elements. Thirteen victories were recorded while commanding flights. Thus, of Dick's initial score of 21 kills, 15 were scored while serving in leadership positions.

The factual basis for the wingmen claim rests on two Rabaul missions, those flown on November 5th and

November 7th. On the 5th Lieutenant George Haniotis, while flying Dick's wing, was posted missing in action after the 9th Squadron tangled with 15-plus Zeros over Rabaul. Two days later Lieutenant Stanley Johnson disappeared after he and Dick bounced a formation of Zeros.

The circumstances of Johnson's loss on the 7th are fairly well known. Over Simpson Harbor the 9th FS met 40 Zeros in scattered groups between 15,000 and 30,000 feet. Diving to the attack, Dick made passes at different aircraft without success. Finally he and Johnson sighted eight or ten Zeros below who were ganging up on a single P-38. In Dick's words: "We dove through them to break them up. My wingman disappeared on this pass and is missing."

It is difficult to fault the decision to bounce the Zeros. Both Dick and Johnson were experienced combat pilots, Johnson having two kills to his credit. The two Lightning pilots had the advantages of altitude and surprise. Certainly Lieutenant Del Moore, the pilot of the trapped P-38, welcomed their decision. Since other eyewitnesses are lacking, it seems likely that Johnson fell victim to a snap shot taken by one of the Zeros as the Lightnings flashed through their formation.

Haniotis was lost on November 5, 1943. The squadron, 11 P-38s in all, escorted B-24s to Rabaul when 15 Zeros were sighted below. Dick's flight dove on one group of Zeros and he flamed two enemy fighters. Interestingly enough, he commented that the Zeros "appeared to be old planes" flown in combat by pilots who were "inexperienced and unwilling to engage in combat." Haniotis was apparently lost in the course of this action. In truth **no one in the squadron** witnessed his loss.

Charles McElroy, who flew as Red Four in Dick's flight on November 5th, elaborated on the mission, commenting: "Nobody knew why or how Haniotis was lost. He was sighted the next day off the coast in his life raft. The returning 9th planes were low on gas and could not remain over him until the rescue plane arrived. He was never found."

McElroy also recalled that the Rabaul missions "were considered some of the most 'hairy' in the war. The distance and weather were unfavorable. We did not know how to conserve fuel in those days as later on after Lindbergh flew with us. From a military standpoint it was considered a stronghold because of heavy fighter opposition and anti-aircraft from both land and sea."

According to Ralph Wandrey the loss of Haniotis was "directly due to the inability of the rescue teams to get to the area we were operating in." He also felt the wingmen were lost due to "their inability to stay with Dick in combat."

In an attempt to resolve this controversy the authors solicited comments from former 49th FG personnel, feeling that such men were the best judges of Dick's actions. Their uncensored comments are given below.

William Bleeker recalled: "Regarding Dick's losing wingmen, he did have a reputation for being rough on them, particularly the new guys. He jumped into a fight so fast it was damn near impossible to stay with him. Of course he was sticking his neck out by this, but he was so good I guess he didn't need protection."

Wally Jordan "at one time or another (had) heard comments relative to his losing wingmen, the implication being that he was at fault, somehow failing to care for his wingman. These comments and their implications have always infuriated me. I feel they are completely without foundation. Dick always effectively used our two-ship element mutual support tactics. Whoever of his wingmen may have been lost were undoubtedly lost through their own fault. My comment when I first heard of these contentions was that the thing was probably generated by someone jealous of Dick's score - sour grapes."

Charles McElroy, who was heard from previously, commented that he could not "imagine Bong being at fault for the loss of this wingman (Haniotis). There was some gossip about his loss of wingmen but I did not know of any bitter feelings. Possibly his superior ability as a pilot made it difficult for some to stay with him."

Walter Markey felt that "a wingman's responsibility is always to stay with his flight or element leader. There are situations that would cause him to become detached but that can't be blamed on the leader. In my time I knew of no one who would not fly with Dick. I would guarantee that anyone who had flown with him would never be the source of such comments."

Jim Watkins had "heard that Dick lost wingmen. So what! Dick was a fighter and it took fighters of the same caliber to stay up with him. Now, to be honest about it Dick, was not as good a flight leader as he was a fighter. He didn't want to be! I have never been concerned about the men who were lost when they tried to stay with Dick."

A closing comment on the subject was received from William Hess, Secretary of the American Fighter Aces Association. Hess, a widely respected aviation historian, queried AFAA members over the years on this same issue. None of the responses he received supported the criticisms levelled at Dick. In a letter to the authors Hess summarized his findings by stating that he "had never heard a bad word about Dick Bong from anyone that flew with him and that is the important thing. His record speaks for itself."

Chapter 9

Stateside Leave
(November 1943 - February 1944)

News of Dick's imminent arrival in the States brought a flurry of activity in the Bong household in Poplar. Hopes that Dick might have a quiet leave in the company of his family and friends soon evaporated. In downing 21 Japanese aircraft Dick had not only become the leading ace of the Fifth Air Force but also one of America's top three aces, the others being Joe Foss and "Pappy" Boyington of the Marines. Consequently, Dick's homecoming became a media event.

Bud Bong remembered Dick's arrival in Poplar and the reception that awaited him: "The fall of 1943 had seen heavy snowfall in northern Wisconsin, burying Poplar in a heavy snowfall of around 12 inches in mid-November. We were snowed in for three days and on the 16th word came through that Dick was on his way home. On the 17th Butch Kemp, a cat skinner driving for Jondreau's of Brule, came down the driveway clearing away the 12 inches of wet snow. There was a relatively large area at the back of the house that was used for parking. This was all cleared, and as it turned out it was a good thing that there was a lot of room.

"That night there was an aura of excitement throughout the house as the whole family waited in anticipation of the arrival of our very own war hero. A car drove up. All flocked to see if it was Dick but no, it turned out to be some news photographers from the *Superior Telegram*. We gathered around the piano and sang many songs but none with more gusto than the Air Corps song. More cars, more newsmen! About eight o'clock some representatives from the Superior Legion Post arrived, followed by several professors from Superior State Teachers College. Finally the R.O.T.C. Band with 27 souls drove up. They joined in with the singing and added some of their own. The house soon filled up.

"Finally, sometime after midnight, another car came down the driveway and this time it's the Captain. So many people! You hardly got a chance to greet him. Now many more pictures. The Legion presented Captain Bong, Carl Bong and Dick's younger brother Bud with boots for the coming hunting season as a gesture of appreciation for a job well done. The college profs offered some ammunition for the deer rifles, a scarce item with the war going into its third year. The band played the Air Corps song. More pictures. Finally Mrs. Bong said 'all out,' as Dick was very tired from his long trip home. It was 2:45 a.m.

"The next day more turmoil, more newsmen, more pictures, beef steaks and T-bones presented by the Peterson Brothers Market. Final plans were made for the deer hunt and rifles were sighted in.

"The first morning of the hunt a 12-point buck came down the trail that Carl Bong was watching. He did not miss. A short time later Roy Bong wounded an eight-pointer. We met back at the house at 8:30 a.m. It is decided to get after the wounded buck. I took up the track along with Warren Jones and Roy Bong jumped the buck. A snap-shot dropped him.

"While this was going on a conspiracy was hatching. Carl suggested to Dick that we report this buck as being shot by Captain Bong so that the waiting news people would leave us in peace." The press fell for the deception, dutifully reporting that Dick had been successful in bagging his buck. As events turned out, Dick wasn't quite as successful against the Wisconsin deer as he had been in combat with the Japanese. The second day of deer hunting he pumped four shells at an eight-pointer only to discover the screws holding the telescopic sight on his rifle had loosened.

Despite such minor mishaps Bud remembered: "It was a good hunt, all the tags were filled. After the day's hunt there was the customary stop at the Gravel Pit Tavern. Dick would have a glass of sherry wine. In the background the juke box would be playing *There's a Star-Spangled Banner Waving Somewhere* and other current hits. The hunt over, the next order of business was a trip to the Superior Airport where all members of the family, aunts and uncles included, were treated to their very first flight in Jules Bernt's Piper Cub."

The time Dick could spend with his family was limited by the fact he was a celebrity. Soon after Dick's arrival home Superior celebrated "Dick Bong Day." Following a brief parade in which Dick was driven through Superior in an open-air coupe - in 15 below zero weather - he was feted at a luncheon at the American Legion. A ship launching at the Globe Ship Yards was capped off by Dick's being declared the "Number One Pin-Up" by the female workers at the Ship Yards, an honor that embarrassed Dick no end. At each event Dick would say a few appropriate words and quickly sit down. Having little use for all the hoopla, he good-naturedly cautioned one roomful of well-wishers: "Don't ever do anything that'll get your name on the front page of the papers."

Even with his family or close friends like Marvin Peterson, Dick rarely spoke of his life as a fighter pilot. When people tried to draw him out he usually passed off his exploits as luck, stating that "a lot of Nips happened to get in my way. I couldn't have missed them." When a close friend asked about his decorations he characteristically replied: "Somebody just pinned those things on me from time to time and I keep on wearing them." In one interview he did allow that the medals were "fine but I'd just as soon miss the Purple Heart." Now and then, however, comments would slip out that revealed the grimmer side of fighter combat. One night, while bowling with friends, he mentioned that "we used to have a ball game going out there in New Guinea on the runways waiting for the Japs to come over but, after a while, we didn't have enough fellows for a whole team."

Being the local celebrity was a two-edged sword. In part it meant giving up precious time spent with family and friends in order to fill the demands made by the news media. *Collier's* magazine sent a team up to Poplar to do a feature on America's ranking ace, perhaps expecting to find the typical hell-raising, glory-seeking fighter jock made famous by Hollywood. Instead, what *Collier's* found - and reported in its February 26, 1944 issue - was that "probably no quieter man has ever flown a fighting plane, and in all the world, it would be hard to find a man who looked and acted less like a hot pilot. Bong is a blond, chunky fellow of twenty-three, with a turned-up nose and rosy cheeks that puff out in a cherubic sort of way... Looking at him in the setting of his home town, it is utterly impossible to think of him as a fighter pilot or a killer of Japanese."[1]

Yet Dick's notoriety also brought pleasant - and unexpected - changes as well. The Wisconsin State Teachers College in Superior celebrated its annual homecoming shortly after Dick arrived home on leave. A delegation of students from the college asked Dick to help crown the new homecoming king and queen and, after some thought, Dick "guessed he would do the job." He asked the name of the outgoing queen and was told it was Majorie Vattendahl. To most people, however, she was "Marge."

Marge and Dick met face-to-face for the first time the night of the prom. Marge recalled: "The crowning was to take place at 10 p.m. Dick must have been half an hour late. We were nearly in hysterics, including most of the faculty, when the door burst open and in walked the most fascinating man I have ever seen. He stood there smiling until someone recovered his equilibrium sufficiently to go over and rescue him and escort him to the platform.

"Well, when it came time to crown the king, Dick did a perfect job. But when it was my turn to crown the queen my faculties refused to function. So Dick picked up the crown which I held and smilingly placed it on the bashful girl.

"Dancing followed the crowning ceremonies and there was keen rivalry among the admiring co-eds for Dick's attention. What a let-down for most of them when he announced timidly that he didn't know how to dance. Yet it didn't surprise me. Somehow dancing didn't seem to belong to Dick. That shortcoming seemed to fit him. Some of the girls begged to teach him the minimum essentials but no go. He preferred to sit on the sidelines and watch the kids jitterbug."[2]

After the dance Marge and a friend decided to walk to a nearby ice cream shop. As they entered they saw

Stateside Leave

Dick, Nelda, Jerry and Marvin Peterson occupying a corner table. Dick motioned them over and asked them to join their group. He soon put them at ease, although Marge admitted to being in "sort of a dreamy daze" for several days after. Dick asked Marge out on a date soon after and, in Marge's words: "It wasn't long before we were seeing each other every evening."

Some time after Dick and Marge began seeing each other, Dick decided to treat her to an impromptu air show. With Bud in tow Dick drove out to the Superior airport, borrowed a radial-engined Monocoupe and set course for Poplar. It turned out to be a memorable flight, as Bud related:

"We took off and headed for Poplar. Our altitude was 200 to 500 feet when we arrived over Poplar. We circled until a number of people gathered on the sidewalk, including Marge. We then did a series of chandelles at a maximum altitude of 500 to 600 feet. After about a dozen of these maneuvers Marvin Peterson (a close friend of Dick's), Marge and Dick's sister got into a car and headed for Superior. Dick turned the stick over to me and said 'take us up to 3,000 feet.' Dick was watching the car below. When we reached altitude he took over the stick, pulled us up into a stall and kicked us over into a tail spin! It seemed to me that we were getting kind of close to the ground, but I figured he knew what he was doing. As it was, we pulled out right over a field and I can remember we were below the tree tops along the edge of the field. It wasn't until some time later that I found out we nearly crashed that day. It seems Dick was so busy showing off for Marge that he didn't watch where he was going!"

As their relationship deepened, Marge saw a side of Dick few others were permitted to see. Stanley Johnson's widow happened to be visiting Superior. Johnson had been lost flying Dick's wing over Rabaul on November 7th. After Dick visited with Mrs. Johnson, Marge recalled his anguish over the sad meeting and his admiration over how bravely Mrs. Johnson had withstood her grief. In the course of this conversation Dick, perhaps influenced by his meeting with Mrs. Johnson, commented that he didn't think "anyone should rush into marriage until this war is over. The future is too uncertain and there is too much misery in store for those left behind."

In mid-December Dick was ordered to Washington for public relations duties. His letter of the 13th summed up the type of duties Dick was assigned while in Washington. He wrote home that he "had just about every important newspaper in the country today listening to my press conference. Also had a newsreel made by Fox Studios. I go up to New York on Sunday and Columbia Broadcasting Studios has a room reserved for me in the Waldorf Astoria so I'm going to be in high society. I broadcast next Tuesday night on the *Report to the Nation* program from 9:30 to 10:00. I have lunch with Senator Wylie tomorrow and (Congressman) O'Konski is supposed to call me tonight. He wants to have me up and see the House in session and I may go bowling with him tonight a little later."

With much of his time taken up by such duties, Dick's leave quickly drew to a close. On January 29, 1944 most of Poplar turned out to see Dick as he left for the war zone. Few of the people who stood in the frigid Wisconsin air waiting for one last handshake or hearty thump on the back could have realized what was in store for Dick. Within three short months he would topple the Army Air Force record which had stood unbroken since World War I, Eddie Rickenbacker's record of 26 victories. In doing so he took over the mantle of America's ace of aces, a position he would never relinquish.

Chapter 10

Return To Combat
(February - April 1944)

In early February 1944 Dick reported back to the Southwest Pacific Theater and Fifth Air Force. During the preceding two months Fifth Air Force had continued its aerial campaign against the Japanese fortress of Rabaul, plus incessant strikes against Saidor, the Wewak airfield complex, and Cape Gloucester. In December 1943 and January 1944 landings had been made on New Britain's Arawe Peninsula, Cape Gloucester, and Saidor opposite Cape Gloucester. These landings, coupled with American air strikes, helped reduce Rabaul to impotence by early February 1944.

Along with all the action, Fifth Air Force had undergone some changes. Dick's old outfit, the 9th FS, was now flying out of Gusap but in a far different aircraft than the Lightnings Dick was accustomed to. In late November 1943, due to a lack of P-38s, the 9th Squadron had reluctantly converted to the Republic P-47 Thunderbolt, an aircraft most P-38 drivers had little use for.

Somewhat surprisingly, when Dick was given his duty assignment after reporting to Fifth Fighter Command at Nadzab, he found he was going to be attached to Fighter Command Headquarters rather than one of the other P-38 squadrons. Although this assignment would eventually prove very advantageous, Dick initially bemoaned his fate, thinking he would spend the duration "flying a desk" as the assistant operations officer (A-3) in charge of replacement aircraft! Events would prove otherwise.

Dick was assigned to Fifth Fighter Command by General Kenney, a move that some have interpreted as favoritism towards Dick by Kenney. With regard to the Nadzab posting, several points need to be made. First, we have little hard information as to why Kenney assigned Dick to Nadzab rather than one of the P-38 units. In a letter to the authors, Kenney stated that he "had assigned Dick to General Wurtsmith in Fifth Fighter Command with instructions to let him and Tommy Lynch free-lance together as a team but not to bother them with paper work as I didn't think either of them would be any good at it." Kenney's whimsical comments ignore the fact that Lynch, having previously been the CO of the 39th FS, was well equipped to handle a staff position.

Lynch's assignment to Nadzab raises another issue. In the spring of 1944 Kenney had his top three aces -Dick, Lynch and Neel Kearby - holding down headquarters positions at Nadzab. Kearby, former CO of the 348th FG, was Wurtsmith's chief of staff at Nadzab. Lynch, who had returned from stateside leave in January, was Kearby's operations officer. Such an arrangement seems more than coincidental.

Although it is only speculation, it appears Kenney had an ulterior motive in assigning Dick, Lynch and Kearby to Nadzab. For some months Dick had been the leading Army Air Force ace in both Europe and the Pacific. Kenney, by all accounts a very practical officer, must have realized the publicity value in having such a pilot in his command and having that pilot retain his status as AAF "top gun." Viewed in this light, the Nadzab posting seems less a case of favoritism than the best possible utilization of proven talent.

Much has been made about the fact that Dick and Lynch were not weighed down by command responsibilities. Yet command is a two-edged sword. Command of a squadron or group brings with it responsibility but also the power to pick and choose which missions to fly. Interestingly enough, almost all of the top aces in Fifth Air Force were either squadron or group commanders. This phenomenon is by no means limited to Fifth Air Force. This is not meant to disparage the achievements of those aces but to point out a fact of life. Command brought with it advantages as well as burdens.

Before closing this discussion one final point needs to be made. If Kenney had some grand scheme to help Dick keep his "top gun" status, Tom Lynch's presence at Nadzab may have been an indication Kenney was hedging his bet. Although Lynch trailed Dick in the scoring race, his Nadzab assignment gave him the same advantages as Dick enjoyed - and in the ensuing weeks Lynch and Dick would match each other kill for kill. If Lynch had surpassed Dick and become "top gun" would Kenney have given the matter a second thought? Probably not. Kenney was a practical commander and what mattered was having the top ace in your command, whomever that individual might be.

As previously mentioned, Dick was not pleased with the Nadzab posting, both he and Lynch feeling their fighting days were over. Dick later stated: "Neither of us liked desk work. So we went to General Wurtsmith and asked permission to start flying again. To our considerable surprise he told us that as long as we kept operations running smoothly we could fly all we wanted to."

To the two aces the set-up was heaven-sent. "We could fly wherever and whenever we wanted to," Dick recalled. "Some days we would hook on with other squadrons escorting bombers to Kavieng or Wewak or Tadji. Some days we went out on sweeps by ourselves. Often we took the early morning weather reconnaissance job over Wewak in the hope we would pick up some Jap stragglers. We also figured out a dusk patrol that gave us some victories and some probables. We had our own stripped-down Lightning fighters." Dick and Lynch promptly christened their two-man air force the "Flying Circus."

Dick's partner in the "Circus" - Tom Lynch - has never received the credit due him. Lynch was one of Kenney's best, a proven combat leader, fighter ace and tactician. His final total of 20 victories does not adequately reflect the contribution Lynch made to the success enjoyed by his unit - the 39th FS - and to the larger war effort. Charles King, himself an ace who served with and eventually commanded the 39th FS, recalled that when Lynch assumed command of the squadron: "We were pleased. I think everyone liked and respected Tommy. The enlisted men loved him and would do anything for him. He studied each kind of airplane and knew more about the performance of the P-38 than any other combat pilot I knew.

"After Tommy took command of the squadron he did a good job of picking his flight leaders and handling all personnel. It was quite evident that the people at HQ recognized him as a top combat leader. His opinions were sought out and he was always ready to contribute. From the very beginning his contribution to the successful tactical use of the P-38 was most important.

"Tommy was also a personal friend. Living with men for two years you get to know very well their virtues as well as their vices. We had many fine people over the two-and-a-half years that I was in the outfit, but Tommy was the one I admired most as a man."

Dick also held Lynch in high esteem. He respected him as a fighter pilot and called him friend. In fact, Tom Lynch was probably the closest friend Dick had in Fifth Air Force. For three weeks he and Lynch ran their "Flying Circus" against the Japanese in New Guinea and New Britain. Dick later remembered that those three weeks were "the most real fun I have ever had as a fighter pilot."

The Circus made its first killing on February 10th during a sweep of the Tadji airfield southwest of Hollandia, New Guinea. Spotting activity on the field the two Americans circled, waiting for further developments. In short order six single-engined fighters and a twin-engined bomber were seen taking off. Lynch and Dick punched off their drop tanks and dove on the bomber, a Kawasaki Ki-48 Lily. Roaring down from 15,000 feet, the two Lightnings effortlessly caught up with the Japanese craft. Lynch, who was leading the element that day, pulled in behind the bomber and fired a short burst. The Lily's right wing burst into flames and the aircraft dove straight into the waters of the Bismarck Sea.

Less than a week later it was Dick's turn to notch up another kill. On February 15th he and Lynch attached themselves to an A-20 strike hitting Kavieng, New Ireland. The Havocs' assigned escorts were 18 P-38s from the "Headhunters" of the 80th FS. No enemy aircraft were sighted until the return flight home. At 10:50 a.m. Dick spotted a lone Ki-61 Tony fighter flying at 12,000 feet over Cape Hoskins, heading for Rabaul. Making a 180º turn to the left, Dick "started after him. In a few minutes I caught up with him and closed in on his tail. At about 75 yards I opened fire and observed the enemy plane to blow up in midair and crash into the water, about ten miles north of Cape Hoskins."

Although Dick had a reputation for closing to point-blank range, on this occasion he almost came too close, later admitting that he was "so close I had to fly right through a ball of fire, which was all that was left of him. I couldn't have been in the flames one-hundredth of a second, yet my cockpit was so hot then and for some minutes afterward that I nearly burned up myself."

Interestingly enough, when he wrote home describing this kill Dick minimized the danger, reassuring his family: "Well another day, another dollar and all is going well. I feel good and am losing weight I think. Get lots of sleep and rest, fly about every other day with Major Lynch. He got number 17 and I got number 22 the other day. All very interesting without sticking our necks out."

Having top fighter aces on the Fifth Fighter Command staff proved handy in late February. On February 28th Fifth Air Force decoders intercepted a Japanese radio message stating that a transport aircraft carrying VIPs would soon be landing at Wewak in New Guinea.

Dick and Tom Lynch were called in, hurriedly briefed and scrambled to make the intercept. With their throttles wide open the two Lightnings raced to the Wewak area only to discover that the transport, ahead of schedule, was already in the landing pattern! The after-action report filed by Dick and Lynch reported what transpired.

"At 6:10 p.m. sighted a Betty landing on Wewak Drome. Both planes dove down from 9,000 feet and made a pass. The flight leader made his pass while the plane was still taxiing down the runway with unobserved results. The wingman, Captain Bong, strafed the plane after it stopped, causing it to burst into flames. No one was seen to leave the plane before or after it caught fire. The Betty appeared to be unarmed as no rear turret was visible. 60 - 70 Japs, who were believed to be a reception committee for high officials arriving on the Betty, were seen running for cover as the planes came down to make their pass. A/A intense, medium, accurate as to altitude - bursts behind the plane."

The statement about high-ranking officials on board the Betty proved correct. Subsequent radio messages between Wewak and Tokyo confirmed that the Betty had been ferrying a major general, a brigadier and various staff officers.

The intercept on the 28th had an interesting - and illuminating - conclusion. During the debriefing following the mission's end Kenney pressed Dick to claim a kill. Unlike the Eighth Air Force in Europe, Kenney's Fifth Air Force did not give official credit for enemy aircraft destroyed on the ground. Only kills against airborne aircraft were allowed. Dick had reported that the Betty had been on the ground when it exploded. Kenney, who wanted the kill for Dick, suggested that perhaps the Betty "had been just an inch or so above the runway" or that it may have "bounced back into the air temporarily." After hearing Kenney out Dick matter-of-factly reiterated that the Betty "was on the ground all right. He had even stopped rolling." Dick thus passed up the chance to get an easy kill.

The Tadji area yielded more victories for the "Flying Circus" on March 3, 1944. Dick and Lynch had taken off at 4:10 p.m. on yet another two-man sweep. Arriving over Tadji at 5:40 the two fliers promptly ran into action. In a series of running engagements Dick and Lynch hammered two Sally bombers and two Tony fighters into the ground. Dick's combat report summarized the action thusly:

"Sighted one Sally headed east by Tadji Strip and dove down for a tail attack when he was about two miles east of strip. Major Lynch damaged this Sally and I followed in on it and shot him down into the trees. Went back over the strip at 6,000 feet and sighted five fighters about 12 o'clock same level about a mile offshore. Made a tail attack on a Tony and damaged him. Dove away from other Zeros and saw pilot bail out of Major Lynch's first plane. Pulled up in time to see Major Lynch shoot down the Tony I damaged and joined Major Lynch.

"Sighted two Sallys down below. Major Lynch made a tail attack on one but he ran out of ammunition before he could knock it down. I followed up and fired from close range and his tail blew off. He crashed to the ground, exploded and burned. Both bombers crashed within 100 yards of each other about two miles east of strip. I claim two Sallys definitely destroyed. Left the area due to lack of ammunition and landed at 7:30 p.m."

The Americans had clearly caught the Japanese off-guard. In his report Lynch remarked that "only one of the Sallys attacked took any evasive action, and that consisted merely of making a turn to the right. The enemy fighters did not press their attacks the few times they were in position to do so." In return for destroying four Japanese aircraft, one of the Lightnings had suffered a lone bullet strike in one wing.

The two Sallys boosted Dick's total to 24, edging him that much closer to breaking the Rickenbacker record. Lynch now had 19 to his credit. These latest victories may have been the reason Neel Kearby decided to get back into the scoring game. At the beginning of 1944 Kearby had shared top fighter honors with Dick, both aces having 21 kills. Unfortunately, Kearby's staff duties kept him grounded while Dick and Lynch continued their two-man war. On March 5, 1944 Kearby decided to borrow a leaf from the "Flying Circus" and take a three-man fighter sweep to Wewak, New Guinea. That decision was to net Kearby his 22nd victory and cost him his life.

Kearby's formation was composed of three P-47 Thunderbolts, Kearby leading the flight in his regular aircraft, *Fiery Ginger IV*. His wingmen, Captains Bill Dunham and Sam Blair, were both aces flying with Kearby's old outfit, the 348th FG. The trio set course for Wewak, an area that had yielded many victories in the past.

Over the Dagua strip the Americans bounced a flight of three Mitsubishi G3M Nell bombers, flaming all three in a matter of seconds. Preoccupied with the Nells, Kearby failed to spot a lone Oscar fighter which suddenly appeared on his tail. The Nakajima poured a burst of machine-gun fire into the cockpit of Kearby's aircraft, inflicting fatal damage. Although Bill Dunham flamed the bandit in short order, the damage had been done. Kearby's death was a great loss to the Fifth Air Force, for he had been a talented, energetic leader and tactician.

Coincidentally, Dick and Tom Lynch were also flying that day and ran into action in the same area where Kearby was lost. The two aces took off at 11:20 a.m. on a sweep of the Wewak area. After finding no activity at Boram or Tadji, the pair flew down the coast to Dagua where Lynch called in three Oscars at about 3,000 feet. The P-38s were perched above the Oscars at 17,000 feet.

Lynch subsequently reported: "I dropped my tanks and made a tail attack on the rear plane in the enemy formation. The Oscar burst into flames and fell off flaming from my first burst. I made several more passes with nil results and then sighted six more enemy aircraft approaching. I called Captain Bong to break off and we headed for the overcast at 6,000 feet. We started to return to base and then decided to attack again. I made a head-on pass at an Oscar and observed hits around the engine. A fairly large piece of metal came off his plane and hit behind my left prop, denting the engine cowling. I made two more passes and then called Captain Bong to break off."

Dick was also in the thick of things, claiming one Oscar destroyed, which unfortunately was disallowed. After Lynch had flamed the number three man in the formation, Dick had fired at the lead Oscar and missed. He then "made two more passes at the remaining two but both shots 90° deflection and no hits. Saw one Oscar headed towards the coast and followed him. At about 400 yards I opened up on him as he started to turn. Several hits in the tail section and he fell out of control and crashed and exploded about 1,000 yards off the west end of Dagua strip. This action took place beneath a cloud layer and as Major Lynch was above it he was unable to witness the action.

"Pulled up through the cloud layer and rejoined Major Lynch. We went back and I made a 45° deflection shot at an Oscar and scored some hits but not enough to cause him to go down. Made one more 90° deflection shot and missed. Broke off combat at 1:40 a.m. because about five more Oscars joined in and it got too hot for us. Landed at Gusap at 2:45 a.m. I claim one Oscar definitely destroyed and one damaged."

Fifth Air Force confirmed Lynch's kill but downgraded Dick's Oscar claim to a probable. As Dick stated in his report, Lynch had not witnessed the scrap with the Oscar and hence could not confirm Dick's claim. Both Lightnings were equipped with gun cameras but Dick's malfunctioned, a frustrating development that left the Victory Credits Board with no choice. Final claims for the March 5th mission were one Oscar definitely destroyed (Lynch's 20th kill), one Oscar probable and two Oscars damaged.

Three days later the Bong-Lynch partnership came to an abrupt end. On March 8th Dick and Lynch returned to the Tadji area once more looking for action. The night before Dick had helped Lynch celebrate his promotion to lieutenant colonel. Both men were in good spirits on the 8th and eager to scare up some enemy aircraft. Dick was flying Lynch's wing and later recalled that, finding no Japanese aircraft, the two decided to sweep the coastline for targets of opportunity. Shipping was sighted in Aitape Harbor and the two Lightnings dove to attack, a fateful decision. Here, published for the first time, is the official summary of what happened next.

"Three luggers and three barges were sighted in Aitape Harbor. One lugger was strafed and left afire. Our losses: one P-38, piloted by Lieutenant Colonel Thomas J. Lynch, O-388066, was definitely destroyed by small arms fire from one of the luggers. One P-38 received holes in the left wing, right engine and stabilizer.

"On the second strafing pass over the luggers the P-38 piloted by Lieutenant Colonel Lynch was hit by small-caliber fire from one of the luggers. No explosive shells were seen. The planes were at approximately 20 feet at this time. The whole nose section came off and the right engine caught fire. Colonel Lynch pulled up to 2,500 feet, made a turn to the left and called Captain Bong on the radio and asked if he could see him. Captain Bong called him back and told him his right engine was on fire and to bail out. At this time both planes were about one mile inland.

"Colonel Lynch was seen trying to get out of the left side of the cockpit. Finally at about 100 feet the whole canopy flew off and Colonel Lynch was seen to fall out of the plane. The plane exploded below Colonel Lynch. His parachute came out of the pack but did not have time to open. Captain Bong circled the area but could not see any signs of the parachute in the trees. No enemy airplanes were sighted in the area at this time. Captain Bong was forced to feather his right engine in the vicinity of Gusap in order to make base. Landed, 2:20 p.m."

Within the space of a few minutes Fifth Air Force had lost one of its finest leaders and Dick had lost a close friend. In the short time Dick and Lynch had flown together a deep friendship and respect had grown between the two. Of his friend Tom Lynch Dick would only remark that "losing Tom was just about the worst single blow I ever took while flying combat."

It appears that one of the luggers may have been a flak ship judging from the punishment meted out to Lynch and Dick. Corporal Herman Ladner, Dick's crew chief at Nadzab, remembered that Dick's P-38 returned with 87 bullet holes in one engine and a blown oil line in the other. Ladner also made the revealing comment that March 8th "was the only time I saw (Dick) nervous, that morning that Colonel Lynch was shot down."

General Kenney was concerned that Lynch's death might affect Dick's nerves. Kenney's recollection is that he immediately ordered Dick to Brisbane to ferry a new P-38 back to Nadzab, thus giving Dick time to collect himself. Dick did report to Brisbane but not until the end of March. More importantly he flew **eight** combat missions in the weeks following Lynch's death before reporting to Brisbane, hardly the performance of a pilot coming undone! From Dick's flight records it appears he was in Brisbane for 11 days at best, returning to Nadzab on March 31st.

Several days after Lynch's death, however, perhaps in an attempt to take his mind off his loss, Dick did something out of the ordinary for him. Prior to March 1944 most of Dick's aircraft carried no distinctive personal markings aside from miniature Japanese victory flags on the nose. In fact, Dick once jokingly commented that he had never had "one aircraft long enough to paint anything on it. Too many bullet holes." Now, however, he decided to have his aircraft - a P-38J-15-LO, serial number 42-103993 - decorated in the fashion of other fighter aces. Thus was born *Marge*.

Dick approached Captain Jim Nichols, an intelligence officer at Nadzab, with his ideas. He had Nichols enlarge a small photo Dick had of Marge Vattendahl to a 20x24" print. The print was then tinted and pasted directly on to the nose of 42-103993. Several coats of varnish, Marge's name in stylized black letters and 25 miniature Japanese flags completed the process.[1] Dick wrote home crowing that the finished result "sure looks swell and a hell of a lot better than those naked women painted on most of the airplanes."

While Dick was at Brisbane, other members of Fifth Fighter Command used this aircraft since it was assigned to the Command. On the 22nd Lieutenant Tom Malone, a member of the 421st Night Fighter Squadron temporarily assigned to Fifth Fighter Command, used *Marge* on the morning weather reconnaissance flight over north-central New Guinea. Malone remembers that the ship "was silver, trimmed in red - prop hubs, wing tips and rudder tips were red."

Malone was piloting *Marge* on March 24th when the aircraft was lost. Immediately after takeoff Malone and his wingman, Lieutenant Forrester, ran into heavy overcast and very turbulent winds. The two fliers climbed to 30,000 feet without breaking out of the overcast. About 50 minutes into the mission Malone began having trouble with the left engine's automatic oil cooler shutter. Radio reception and transmission deteriorated and soon after Malone lost contact with Forrester. Malone was ordered to return to base but his problems were just beginning.

In short order Malone lost his radio, the electrical system and the left engine. Unable to feather the engine's prop, Malone rapidly lost altitude. Down to 11,000 feet he decided to bail out since the area, still completely covered in overcast, held mountains over 12,000 feet high! Shooting out of his aircraft "like a cork out of a champagne bottle," Malone quickly pulled the rip cord and floated down through the storm. He was subsequently picked up by a patrol from the 32nd Infantry Division. In discussing the incident with Dick, Malone later recalled that Dick mentioned having had some problems with the aircraft.

In late March 1944 the scene of action shifted to Hollandia. MacArthur's forces were scheduled to launch a three-pronged invasion on April 22nd with landings at Aitape, Humboldt Bay and Tanahmerah Bay. To smash Japanese air power at Hollandia - estimated at 350 aircraft - Kenney brought together over 100 B-24s plus light and medium bomb groups. To facilitate fighter cover he moved the 8th and 475th Fighter Groups up to Nadzab.

The major strikes against Hollandia began on March 30th, shortly before Dick returned to Nadzab. In the first two days of strikes Fifth Air Force claimed the destruction of almost 200 aircraft. The largest strike was mounted on April 3rd when 63 B-24s followed by low-level waves of A-20s and B-25s swept over Hollandia. By day's end Hollandia was finished as a major Japanese air base.

Escorting the A-20 Havocs on April 3rd were 18 P-38s from the 432nd FS, 475th FG. Over Annenberg, enroute to the target, the squadron acquired a 19th member as Dick attached himself to the formation. Just before reaching Hollandia the squadron fought off several attacks by four Tony fighters. Shortly thereafter six Oscars, flying in line astern formation at low altitude over Sentani Lake, were called in. Drop tanks were jettisoned and the 432nd dove to the attack.

The lead flight knocked down two Oscars in short order. Dick meanwhile picked out a third fighter and fired a burst with no apparent result. The Oscar split-S'ed with Dick in hot pursuit. This particular Japanese pilot seemed to lead a charmed life. Dick made two 90° deflection shots and again failed to score. He then turned in behind the Oscar and managed to get in a few hits. A flight of P-38s took their turn at the agile Japanese but were unable to down the Oscar.

The Oscar pilot's luck finally ran out when Dick latched on to his tail for a second time. Framing the Oscar in his reflector sight, Dick took aim and fired, hitting the Oscar "some more and he turned left and down gradually. Caught fire behind the engine on the bottom. Crashed and exploded on the side of a hill about 50 yards from the west side of Sentani Lake."

While Dick was busy disposing of this Oscar the pilots of the 432nd were chopping apart the scattered formations of enemy fighters that rose in opposition. Approximately 20 Japanese fighters were encountered and the 432nd destroyed over half, claiming three Zekes, six Oscars along with single Hamps and Tonys. One P-38 and its pilot was lost. Dick summed up the lopsided victory when he commented that the Japanese pilots "were not as good as they used to be."

The Oscar over Sentani Lake was Dick's 25th victory, putting him within easy reach of establishing a new record for Army Air Force pilots. Thus far two American pilots - Joe Foss and "Pappy" Boyington - had equalled the record set in 1918 by Eddie Rickenbacker of 26 victories.[2] That score had earned Rickenbacker the title of America's ace of aces. Foss and Boyington were Marine pilots. Thus the honor of being the first Air Force pilot to equal or surpass Rickenbacker's record was up for grabs and competition for the prize was fierce. Air Force public relations officers in the European Theater were grooming Captain Don Gentile of the 4th Fighter Group for the honor. Gentile's task was made easier by the fact that the Eighth Air Force counted ground kills as being equal to air kills. Had Fifth Air Force followed this policy, Dick's score as of April 3rd would have been 26, including the Betty kill on February 27th.

Given the pressure that Dick was under at this time his inner thoughts, as revealed in his letters home, are illuminating. In his customary matter-of-fact way he acknowledged the scoring race, stating: "You know that I have 25 confirmed Nips now. Actually have 28 but 3 of them are not confirmed.[3] Oh well this war isn't over yet. They tell me that if I get 27 confirmed they will send me home so fast I won't know what hit me. Good idea I think."

As Dick astutely pointed out, fame brought rewards. By this stage of the game Dick had come to realize that notoriety was also a two-edged sword. As his score rose so did the attendant publicity and hoopla which, in turn, made increasing demands on his time. Initially pleased and somewhat bemused by the media attention he was getting, Dick grew to dislike the attention being focused on him and especially on his family in Poplar. Topping Rickenbacker's record would only serve to increase the media spotlight.

The magic lay not in becoming the top ace but in flying combat. Time and again Dick brought up the fact that he didn't "have to go into action here if I didn't want to but I would go crazy if I didn't go out with the boys and get some excitement now and then." Continuing to fly combat, especially after he broke Rickenbacker's record, was Dick's main concern, not the number of victories he scored. It was "a great game that made life interesting."

Yet if flying - especially combat flying - made his life exciting Dick realized that publicity chores were part and parcel of any successful fighter ace's existence. He also realized the temporary nature of his newly-won fame. So, as he poised on the brink of becoming a national hero, Dick's mind turned to other more meaningful thoughts. After much soul-searching he had decided to ask Marge Vattendahl to marry him.

A Bong family portrait taken during Dick's first leave home in November 1943. Front row: Joyce, Sue and Nelda. Back row: Bud, Carl Sr. (holding Jimmy in his lap), Dick, Dora, Barbara and Geraldine.

Dick and Tom Lynch swap war stories on the wing of Lynch's P-38, early 1944.

The Mitsubishi Ki-21 Sally bomber formed the backbone of the Japanese land-based bomber force along with its stablemate, the G4M Betty bomber. Dick shot down three Sallys, similar to the aircraft in the photo, in March and December 1944. In all, Dick claimed seven victories over Japanese bombers or reconnaissance aircraft.

Marge Vattendahl's graduation picture from Superior's State Teachers College which adorned the nose of Dick's most famous Lightning, a J-15-LO model serial number 42-103993.

The P-38 most closely identified with Dick was Marge, a J-15-LO model named after his fiancee Marge Vattendahl. Dick scored several victories with the aircraft in February and March 1944 before it was lost while being flown by another Fifth Fighter Command pilot.

Dick pictured at Ward's Drome, Port Moresby with the P-38J-15-LO he flew after Marge was lost. Dick had this aircraft's spinners, wing tips, fin and rudder tips painted in red to distinquish it from other P-38s.

Arriving in the Souhwest Pacific with Dick was Jay T. Robbins, who became one of the fastest-scoring pilots in the theater. He finished with 22 victories in the 80th FS, 8th FG, as the fourth-ranked P-38 ace. On April 12, 1944 Dick bagged two Oscars over Hollandia to break Eddie Rickenbacker's WWI record, flying with the "Headhunters" under Robbins' leadership. (Stanaway)

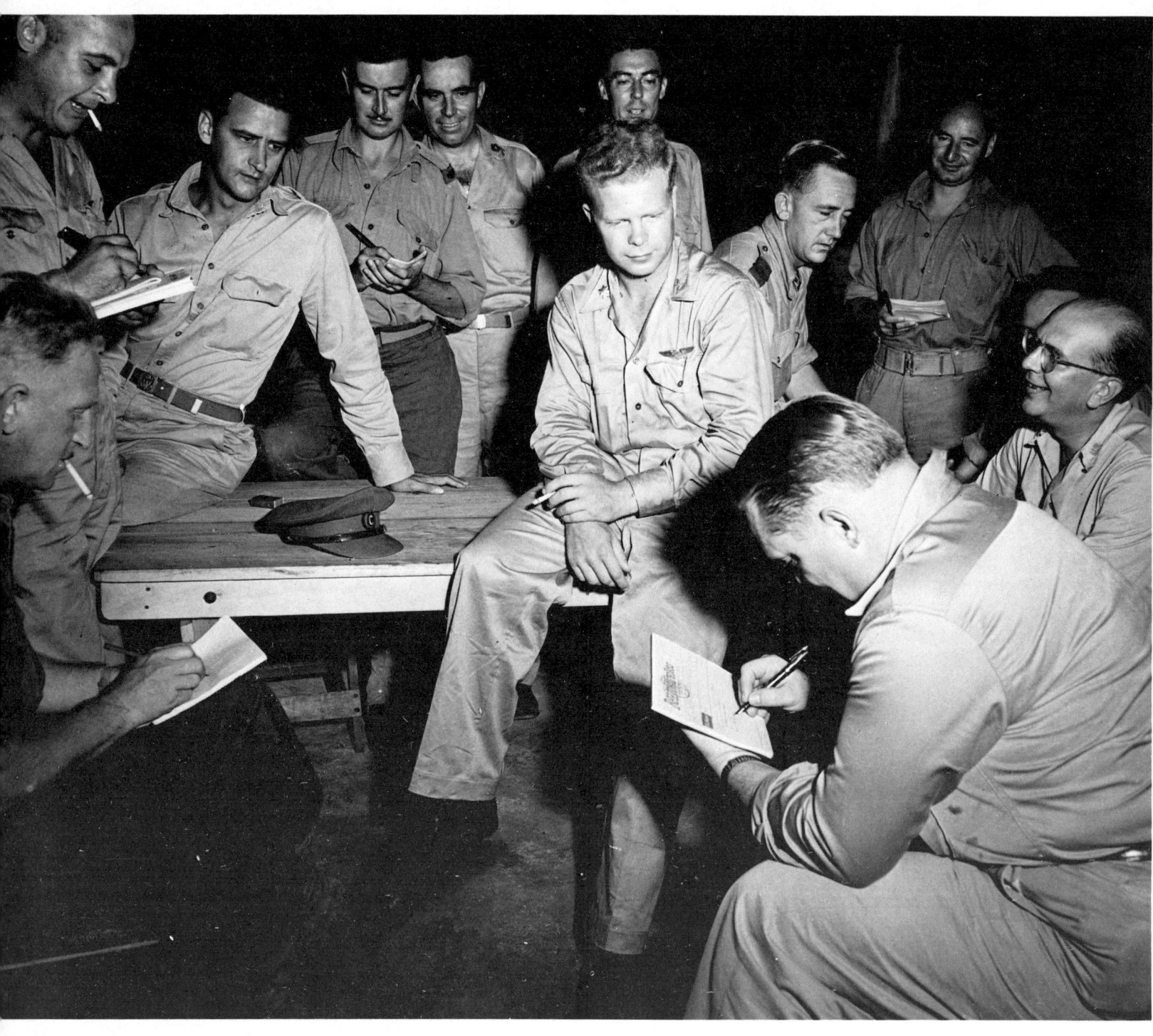

Sessions with the press grew to be a part of Dick's life as his score mounted. Here Dick fields questions after breaking Rickenbacker's record of 26 victories on April 12, 1944.

Dick swaps war stories with Eddie Rickenbacker, the man he deposed as America's Ace of Aces. Rickenbacker received credit for destroying 22 German aircraft and four observation balloons between April and October 1918, a performance that earned him a Medal of Honor. His record of 26 kills stood until April 12, 1944 when Dick destroyed his 27th kill over Hollandia.

Low-level buzz jobs were a passion with Dick, especially exciting when he had a P-38 strapped on his back! Here he treats workers at Superior's Butler Shipyards to a display of low-level flying.

During mid-1944, while Dick was on leave, Charles Lindbergh toured the Southwest Pacific teaching Kenney's fighter pilots how to extend the P-38's range through proper cruise control. Lindbergh is seen here strapping into Dick's 27-victory aircraft prior to a mission. Although a civilian, Lindbergh flew several combat missions and downed one Japanese aircraft.

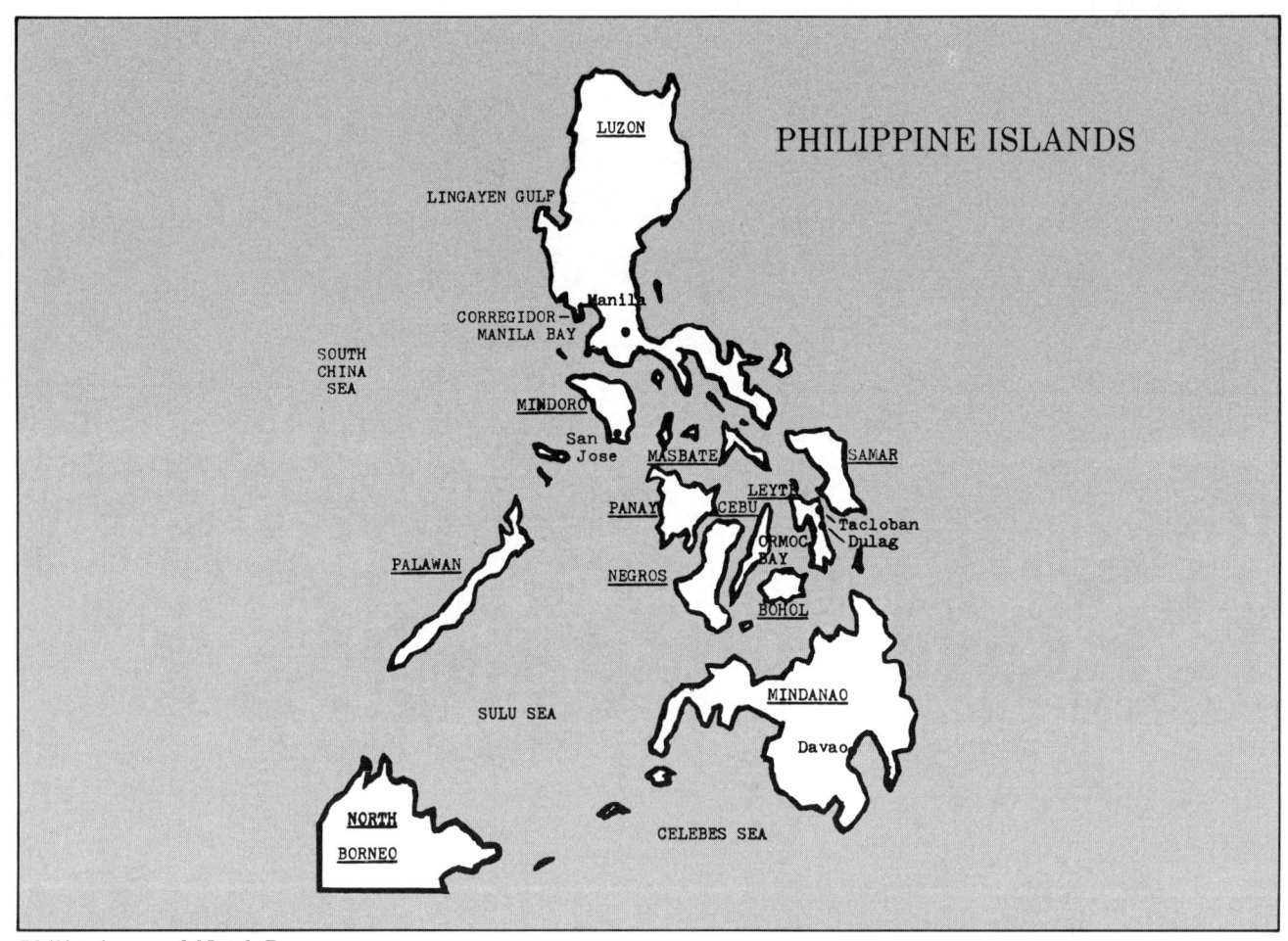
Philippines and North Borneo

Chapter 11

Breaking The Record
(April - October 1944)

On April 12, 1944 the ace race was decided in the skies over New Guinea. While flying cover for Fifth Air Force Liberators hitting the Hollandia airfields Dick claimed two Oscar kills, raising his officially confirmed score to 27 victories. A third Oscar went unconfirmed due to lack of witnessess. In one memorable mission Dick became the first Army Air Force pilot to break Eddie Rickenbacker's World War I record of 26 victories and was now the leading American air ace of the war!

Dick's record-breaking mission resulted from a flare-up of Japanese air activity at Hollandia. Following the devastating attacks on Hollandia in late March and early April 1944, Japanese air activity in the area had been minimal. Then on April 11th a small force of Japanese fighters staged to Wewak, scored three quick kills over P-47s from the 58th FG and flew back to Hollandia. Fifth Air Force responded with a strike on Hollandia the next day. And the stage was set.

Cover for the Liberators on April 12th was furnished by the 80th FS, 8th FG. The "Headhunters" of the 80th put up 20 P-38s on April 12th, two of which aborted. Dick took off with the squadron, flying as "tail-end Charlie" in Captain C. M. Smith's flight. Dick, who flew the mission without a wingman, was using Lieutenant Bill Caldwell's plane, maintained by Staff Sergeant Sam Scher. Caldwell's P-38, a J15-LO model, was nicknamed *Down Beat*. Dick had used the aircraft on at least one other occasion, that being the mission flown on April 1st. Leading the formation was Captain Jay Robbins, squadron CO. Robbins had been on the LB-30 that had ferried Dick over to Australia in September 1942. At that time Robbins had thought of all the pilots on board, Dick was the least likely to become an ace. Now, ironically, Dick was **the** top gun in the Fifth Air Force while Robbins himself had 16 kills to his credit.

When the "Headhunters" arrived over Hollandia at 11:45 a.m., 12 to 15 Oscars and Tonys in scattered groups of threes and fours were waiting for the Americans. The Japanese had hopes of sandwiching the P-38s between two forces, some fighters orbiting at 14,000 feet while others held at 18,000 feet. The "Headhunters" made short work of the Japanese scheme. In short order they destroyed three Oscars and three Tonys. Dick described his kills in the following fashion:

"When we arrived at Hollandia at 11:30 we sighted two SSF (single-seat fighters) at 11 o'clock same level and went after them. The flight leader hit the first one and it fell off burning and on fire. I shot at the second one with no apparent effect. He dove for the clouds and I followed. I shot at him from the stern and he started smoking. We went through a cloud and the Oscar crashed into the sea in Tannemerah Bay. Lieutenant Ince saw me shoot at this plane and the smoke and the resultant crash on the water. At this time we were separated from the rest of the squadron.

"I pulled up and saw two more SSF in an element headed toward a cloud. I closed on their tails and started the wing man smoking and he turned off to the left. I shot at the leader and he started smoking then entered a cloud and I lost him.

"I saw an Oscar on a P-38's tail and took a 50-degree deflection shot at him. His engine conked out and I got more hits in his left wing. He spiralled down and crashed in Tannemerah Bay. No one observed this forced landing.

"Sighted one Oscar below me and dove on him. He split-Sed and I missed. Pulled around and dove after him. He went right down on the deck and as I closed and started shooting he tried to turn and caught his wing in the water and crashed. Lieutenant Adams had also made a pass at this airplane and he saw it crash as I closed and fired. We pulled up and joined some more P-38s.

"I saw another Oscar being chased by P-38s. I turned to cut him off and he split-Sed. Another P-38 shot at him, he started to turn and saw me and split-Sed again. He pulled out two feet above the ground and shot at us coming up. I never saw him again. Sighted no more enemy so left the target area at 12:30 and landed at 1:20."

Dick was jubilant as he climbed down from his P-38 at Nadzab following the mission.[1] He knew several pilots had witnessed two of his kills and counted on his gun camera film confirming his third claim. Even so, Dick later revealed that "the hardest I ever sweated was the night and morning following my last combat mission over Hollandia. You see I had my cameras set wrong so there was no really accurate photographic report of the victories I claimed that day. It depended on whether or not members of the flight could give positive confirmation. The fighter pilots were strung out from one end of New Guinea to the other that night and it wasn't until the next morning that the fighter command could get them together and take a reading on what had happened. Fortunately for me, not one but several pilots witnessed my first two kills - so that put me over the top."

Although he lacked confirmation on the third kill - which would boost his score to 28 - Dick nevertheless claimed it as a definite kill, stating that he knew "the exact spot where he crashed into the water. It's on a kind of coral shelf, not very deep."

Dick expressed some admiration for the enemy pilots he bested on the 12th, commenting: "The last one I snared that day was probably the cagiest I ever tangled with. When he wasn't trying to make tracks toward Tokyo he was engaging in some plain and fancy acrobatics. That made my shots - especially since we were about ten feet off the water most of the time - a little more difficult than usual.

"I really got in one long burst though and it must have raised cane with his right wing. He went down right after that burst. I think that particular Jap was more scared than anything else. He was strictly a third-rate flier although his acrobatics weren't too bad."

Dick's two Oscar kills brought the total claims for April 12th to eight. Credited with two kills apiece were Lieutenant Burnell Adams and Captain Jay Robbins. Lieutenant Ross Roth and Captain "Corky" Smith were credited with single victories. After listening to Dick's description of the mission, General Kenney made an unusual promise to him. Kenney told Dick that after Hollandia was in American hands he would send a diver down in the location Dick mentioned and try to confirm the 28th kill.[2] Kenney also promoted Dick to Major on the spot. And then he dropped the bombshell - effective immediately Dick was forbidden from flying any more combat missions.

The news that Dick had broken the Rickenbacker record was flashed across the world. Congratulations came pouring into Nadzab. MacArthur's wire spoke of the general's "highest admiration for Major Bong's aerial skill and gallantry." General Arnold wrote that "the Army Air Forces are proud of you and your splendid record." And from Eddie Rickenbacker, the following message: "Just received good news that you are the first one to break my record in World War I, by bringing down 27 planes in combat, as well as your promotion, so justly deserved. I hasten to offer my sincere congratulations with the hope you will double or treble this number. But in trying, use the same cool, calculating technique that has brought you results to date for we will need your kind back home after this war is over."

Kenney's grounding order, however, effectively blocked Dick from adding to his score for the present. While Dick was at his prime as a fighter pilot Kenney was taking no chances of losing America's ace of aces in combat. Kenney was already having orders cut sending Dick home at the end of April. In part Kenney's action was brought about by a radio message received from Arnold expressing concern over "the high loss rate of pilots who have shot down many enemy aircraft" (Kearby and Lynch) and requesting Kenney's comments on "the desirability of restricting from action combat flying or return to United States of this type of personnel. A case in point is Captain Bong, who is credited with 27 enemy aircraft."

If Dick was barred from more combat missions he had more than enough action on the ground trying to deal with the wave of publicity that erupted once he topped Rickenbacker's record. Dick summed up the situation for his family in a letter dated April 19th, commenting that he "sent you a telegram yesterday because I haven't written to you since all the big news happened. I've heard that you are having trouble with the reporters back there and I'm certainly having my troubles with them.

"I broke the record and by so doing procured for myself a lot of trouble. Besides that they have grounded me from combat flying. I suppose that doesn't make you mad but it certainly doesn't make me happy. I suppose Marge is catching hell too. I feel kind of sorry for her in this position.

"I wasn't thinking far enough ahead or I would not have put her picture on my airplane and she could have lived in peace. I didn't figure on breaking the record but they got in front of me so I had to shoot them down. Oh well, live and learn, I guess. I suppose they will be sending me home pretty quick and if they do, I'm certainly going to have a life of misery. What I got when I was home last year will be as child's play along side of a giant's labor."

One of the reporters who dogged Dick's trail, Frank Kluckhohn of the *New York Times*, reported on the ingenious ways Dick got back at the newsmen. Kluckhohn swore that Dick took out his frustrations by buzzing the press camp, invariably when some of the reporters were sacking out! Although barred from flying combat missions, Dick was allowed local hops in his P-38. Inevitably, as Kluckhohn reported, "every time he did he came in off the sea at ten feet or so, pulled his plane up a bit and went over our camp, invariably when I was sleeping. Each time there was a whoosh! as the palm trees bent at a hurricane angle and the breeze raised the tent top." Kluckhohn "left his cot horizontally."

Perceptive reporters such as Kluckhohn saw beneath such boyish pranks, recognizing that Dick did not fit the popular concept of a hero. In Kluckhohn's words, Dick was "naturally modest to the point almost of shyness while having deep confidence in his ability to do his job. Most youngsters his age would be bubbling over if they were in his position. But the 23-year-old ace takes it in his stride. He has an inherent sense of balance and proportion on the ground as well as in the air, which this correspondent believes is so well rooted nothing will upset it. He has a touch of iciness in his make-up of truly Arctic proportions. He keeps his mouth clamped because it is his nature to do so, but when he opens it it is to make not merely a pertinent remark but usually a witty one."[3]

While Kluckhohn was busy analyzing Dick, another correspondent, Frank McCarthy from United Press, asked for a first-hand demonstration of Dick's flying skill and barely survived to report the results. After cramming McCarthy into the back of his P-38's cockpit Dick strapped in, fired up the engines and taxied out. As the aircraft lifted off Dick cautioned McCarthy to "hang on by your teeth." McCarthy reported what happened next:

"Major Richard I. Bong glanced at me where I sat crouched on his shoulders and grinned impishly as he gave me that advice. But he wasn't kidding and in the next few minutes I was hanging on by my teeth, my eyeballs and my toenails. With me glued to his shoulders Bong went through the exact combat tactics that he had used in shooting down a record 27 Japanese planes. We had taken off as effortlessly as a feather being kicked into the air by the wind.

"Now Bong zoomed steeply upward for several thousand feet into the cloud-free, sunlit sky. Then America's ace of aces whipped his streamlined P-38 into a power dive on an imaginary target and gave it a short, fierce burst. Executing a sharp bank he made a second run with all guns blazing then simulated a dogfight, going through a complex series of Immelmans, slowrolls, reverse verticals, barrel rolls and old-fashioned loop-the-loops.

"These seemingly uncontrolled gyrations, executed at speeds ranging from 200 to more than 400 miles an hour, left little room for conversation. Bong occasionally shouted up at me to hold on a little tighter for extra special tricks. Among other things he gave me a demonstration of his P-38's airworthiness. Cutting out one motor in mid-air he took his hand off the stick, offered me a cigarette and lighted one himself. We both smoked while the Lightning flew itself.

"Bong asked me if I had blacked out at any stage of the proceedings. I replied 'No, that I had rather enjoyed it although I had a hard time keeping my insides intact.' Bong said to my horror that he had blacked out during the exercises just completed, adding 'In fact, I am very prone to blackout.' While I stared with mouth agape

Bong added: 'You don't have to worry. Even if I am blacked out I know - or rather my hands know - what to do.'."[4]

Several days later America's newest ace of aces got the chance to talk to the man who had held the title for 26 years. The National Broadcasting Company arranged a two-way radio conversation between Dick and Eddie Rickenbacker, Dick flying down to Port Moresby to take part in the broadcast. Dick was worried about speaking on the broadcast, General Kenney describing him as being "as nervous as a stagestruck actor on opening night." Upon arriving at Moresby, however, Dick was handed a script written by Air Force public relations personnel, the "conversation" actually consisting of Dick and Rickenbacker reading the script furnished to both of them. In a few short weeks, however, Dick would have the chance to talk to Eddie Rickenbacker face to face.

Soon after their two-way conversation the two aces found themselves embroiled in a silly controversy. When Rickenbacker had toured the Southwest Pacific in the fall of 1942 he had visited Kenney's command and promised that the first pilot to break his World War record would receive a case of scotch. Kenney kicked in a second case and, after hearing of the prize, MacArthur contributed a case of champagne. Once Dick broke the record - and news of the scotch prize leaked out - various anti-saloon groups in the states hit the roof, taking Rickenbacker to task for "glorifying whisky by publicly offering a prize to the idolized flying hero of the present World War." In retrospect the whole affair seems rather silly, but MacArthur thought enough of the criticisms to withdraw his offer. General Arnold avoided the problem by shipping Dick two cases of Coke, commenting that he understood Dick preferred "this type of refreshment to others." When Rickenbacker's scotch eventually arrived Kenney added his scotch, Arnold's Coke, slipped in a case of champagne and sent the whole works up to New Guinea for a proper celebration.

On May 3rd orders were cut sending Dick back to the states, Kenney giving Dick a personal letter to be delivered to Arnold. In part Kenney's letter requested 30 days leave for Dick "followed by about the same period collecting all the latest information on aerial gunnery and fighter tactics. At the conclusion of this tour of instruction I want him back here to take charge of gunnery training at Nadzab, where I am establishing an advanced combat training center for both the Fifth and Thirteenth Air Forces." Should additional time be needed for publicity or war bond tours Kenney was aggreeable but wanted Dick back by August 1st. So while Dick was on his way home he at least had reason to believe his combat days were not yet over.

During the period from February 15th to April 12th Dick had destroyed seven Japanese aircraft - four Oscars, two Sallys and one Tony plus three probables and two damaged. He also scored one ground kill, the Betty on February 28th. All claims were made while flying the J model P-38.

Dick arrived in Washington, D.C. on May 9th and reported to General Arnold. Arnold promised him three weeks of leave at home followed by gunnery school in Texas, but first Dick had to undertake some public relations tasks for the Air Force! Dick had warned his family that by breaking Rickenbacker's record he had "procured for myself a lot of trouble . . . a life of misery." The misery was about to begin. Dick's first press conference was scheduled for two days later.

On May 11, 1944 Dick met the reporters at a conference held in Secretary of War Henry Stimson's press room at the Pentagon. Dick was accompanied by a public relations colonel who had briefed Dick prior to the conference regarding the sort of answers Dick should give to press questions. Despite promptings from the colonel, Dick handled the conference in his own no-nonsense fashion.

Reporters who had interviewed Dick in December 1943 found little had changed. One reported that Dick seemed "more accustomed to being interviewed and did not blush at every other question as he did in December but he still seemed indifferent to publicity." Another had noticed that Dick entered the press conference room "wearing a new uniform and an air of resignation."

Many of the questions revolved around Dick's score and his gunnery abilities. He recounted his last mission, noting that he had fired so many rounds in that fight that he had warped the barrels of his guns, making accurate shooting very difficult. His 27th kill had "tried to turn but his wing dug into the water. I guess he was scared."

Dick mentioned he was to be assigned to a gunnery course in the coming weeks and then floored the reporters by stating he felt he was "the lousiest shot in the Army Air Forces." When asked to explain his claim

Dick replied: "I'm not a good shot. I have to hit them either straight from behind or from straight ahead - or with a deflection of not more than ten degrees. A good deflection shot should be able to get them from the beam. If I could shoot like Major George Welch I'd have 75 planes. He's been in four or five scrapes and got 16 planes. It took me 25 to get only 27.[5] I consider it a big accident when I hit anything with deflection shooting, but with sufficient practice you can do it. In my own case - well, you've got to hit them once in a while."

If the public relations colonel hadn't been squirming during that exchange, Dick's next comments - about the Air Force's gunnery training schools - proved too much. Dick commented that the gunnery training most pilots received left a lot to be desired, with insufficient attention being given to deflection shooting. Pilot training schools did not devote enough time to gunnery practice. As a result pilots new to combat opened fire at too great a range and made other elementary mistakes. At this point the colonel interrupted Dick, gave an alternative version of what he thought "Major Bong meant" and asked Dick if that was not what he meant to say. Dick eyed the colonel for a minute and then good-naturedly replied: "Oh, I guess that's as good as anything."

Replying to a question about returning to combat and increasing his score, Dick stated: "I'm not worried about my score. I had no intention of going out there and breaking somebody's record but I would like to fly again." He wasn't overly optimistic about getting back into combat, bemoaning the fact that as far as he knew he was out of combat. That comment brought the following memorable exchange:

question: "Do you regret it?"
answer: "Absolutely. I don't think it's a good idea at all."
question: "Whose decision was it?"
answer: "General Kenney's I guess."
question: "Why did he issue such an order?"
answer: (Given with big smile) "Aw, I don't know. Maybe he didn't want me to get killed."

After that the conference pretty much ran down. He was pleased that Captain Bob Johnson of the Eighth Air Force had scored his 27th victory, commenting that "it takes a lot of pressure off me." He hoped to get home to see his family by Mother's Day. When a reporter, in a thinly veiled reference to Marge Vattendahl, asked Dick if he planned to see anyone else besides his mother Dick broke into a wide grin and countered, "What do you think?"

The next day - the 12th - was a memorable one. In the morning Dick met Eddie Rickenbacker at an impromptu meeting at the Pentagon. Rickenbacker offered hearty congratulations to Dick, posed for photographers and then hauled Dick aside to talk shop. The two fliers compared experiences and swapped war stories of flying Spads and P-38s.

At noon Dick was a luncheon guest of Wisconsin Senator Robert La Follette, Jr. Dick, who mercifully was not required to give a speech, was feted by members of the Wisconsin delegation and such Senate powerhouses as Barkley of Kentucky, White of Maine, Russell of Georgia and Taft of Ohio. Later, when Dick entered the Senate gallery to watch the legislators in action, La Follette introduced him to his colleagues who ignored their own rules against demonstrations and gave Dick a boisterous round of applause.

Having finished his initial public relations chores, Dick left Washington on the 13th to meet his parents and Marge in Chicago. Marge and the others, in an attempt to avoid publicity, had registered at different hotels under false names, Marge's being "Margaret Olson." Yet, according to Marge, it seemed she and Dick barely had time to say hello before "people began rushing about and hurried him off for something or other."

Soon after this Dick proposed to Marge, making it official on June 1st by presenting her with a diamond engagement ring. Dick and Marge had driven Bud into Poplar for a high school graduation ceremony that Thursday night, Dick handing out the diplomas to the graduates. Later, after leaving Bud off the two went for a drive in the cool Wisconsin night. Dick pulled over to the side of the road, took the keys out of the ignition and began trying to unlock the glove compartment. Marge thought that was a little strange, since the glove compartment was never locked but Dick refused to acknowledge her questions as to what he was doing. Marge's questions however were "soon answered. The worried look was erased from his face and he had a little grin as he took out a little pink ring case and I opened it. Inside was the most beautiful diamond ring I had ever seen . . . And it was for me!"

As it turned out much of June was devoted to more public relations duties. In early June it was back to

Washington for a press conference featuring Dick and Captain Bob Johnson, the second Air Force pilot to break Rickenbacker's record. Johnson, a P-47 pilot with the Eighth Air Force's 56th Fighter Group, had scored his 27th victory on May 8th over Germany. Johnson remembered: "It was 40 years this coming June 8th that I first met Dick in Washington. We were together off and on for three days and then went our own way.

"Dick had been in Washington for a week or ten days before I got there and was thoroughly fed up with all the public relations and fanfare. About all he would say to anyone was 'It's a hell of a war, ain't it?'

"We had a great visit with General Arnold. The General asked many questions about our combat with the enemy. Part of his interest was to find out if our aircraft were adequate compared to the enemy aircraft and part of his interest was envy that he could not participate as we had. I've met a number of great people but I list General Arnold as number one.

"General Arnold asked what we planned for the future and offered both of us regular commissions in the Air Force. We then separated. I spent a couple of weeks in Oklahoma and then went on a two-month tour around air bases in the U.S. flying a new P-47D-30. Dick was in a P-38 doing the same thing but our paths never crossed again."

From Washington Dick flew back to Poplar in a P-38, the first stop in a 15-state tour to help promote the fifth war bond drive. Dick put on quite a low-level show for the residents of Superior and Poplar, having warned a few friends that when he returned from Washington they had better "duck in their storm cellars or he'd part their hair in the middle" with his P-38. The next day, June 10th, he treated Milwaukee to a buzz-job. After sweeping across the city's business district he banked his P-38 and lined up for another pass. Spectators on the ground, which included a reporter fom the *Milwaukee Journal,* watched as Dick's aircraft raced in, steadily dropping lower and lower. The *Journal* reported: "A moment later the silvery plane was streaking north again, up the river. It banked around the north part of the city, straightened out for another run across the business district and then Major Bong gave the watching thousands the really big thrill of the day.

"He came in, weaving slightly and ever so low. As the plane flashed toward Wisconsin Avenue, Bong banked it moderately and streaked between the Wisconsin Tower Building and the Schroeder Hotel! He came so fast and was gone so fast, racing below the top level of the two buildings, that watchers were left breathless at Bong's daring."[6]

In conjunction with his publicity duties Dick was also assigned to visit a number of Air Force bases "for the purpose of obtaining information on fixed gunnery matters." One of the bases Dick visited was Craig Field where he was introduced to Lieutenant William Coleman. Coleman, who later flew combat with the Fifth Air Force, recalled that "when I first met (Dick) he was a major and I was a lowly second lieutenant. In those days second lieutenants didn't spend much time having conversations with majors.

"Dick was amazed at the method of aerial gunnery we were shooting then; our accuracy and the fact that we were getting a high percent of hits well out on what was called the Pursuit Curve. Dick said he had gotten most of his shoot-downs from the tail position. We were teaching the use of 70 mil and 100 mil sight. (In the 100 mil sight, one mil subtends one foot at 1,000 feet.) Dick had a little trouble getting that at first. But with his outstanding airmanship he conquered the system quickly. We began to hear him say, 'Wait till I get back over there with this new knowledge.'"

One of the last stops on Dick's tour was the Lockheed Aviation Corporation in Santa Monica, California. While at Lockheed Dick learned of the company's revolutionary new jet fighter, the P-80 Shooting Star. The first of the pre-production YP-80A models was in the final stages of construction at this time, not being completed until September 1944. Nevertheless the sleek fighter held great promise for the future. It was at this point that Dick apparently began thinking of a career as a test pilot, subsequently writing to his family that he "discovered a job that I would like to have here in the States. So if I can get it, why I may not go back overseas. If I get it, I'll be stationed out in California someplace probably in the desert."[7] As events transpired, over a year would pass before Dick did get this position, a dream assignment that would end in tragedy!

On July 7th Dick reported to Foster Field, Matagorda, Texas which was his last assigned duty station before returning to the Fifth Air Force. At first the fixed gunnery course at Matagorda was a bit of a challenge, Dick writing home that "this shooting game is quite difficult. Still can't hit anything." The schedule at Matagorda was hectic. Dick flew every day, racking up over 50 hours in July and August. In the midst of this training Dick did find time to fly home for his parents' 25th wedding anniversary. As an anniversary gift Dick paid off the mortgage on the Bong farm, some $2,500 in all. Then it was back to Matagorda where Dick finished the course on August 6th, shipping out immediately after for San Francisco.

In early September Dick reported to Kenney at Hollandia, New Guinea. Kenney was now commander of the Far East Air Forces, which combined the Fifth and Thirteenth Air Forces under one roof. Kenney wanted Dick to serve as an instructor and pass along the gunnery information he had obtained in the states. For the next month Dick was to visit FEAF's fighter units and instruct them on the new gunnery techniques. After that Dick would be allowed to tag along on one or two missions to see how the pilots utilized the new information but Kenney emphasized Dick was not to do "any shooting except in self-defense." Although Dick readily agreed to the conditions, Kenney had his doubts. He knew Dick loved combat flying too much to ever stay on the side-lines for long!

Chapter 12

Balikpapan to Tacloban
(October - November 1944)

Dick returned to the Fifth Air Force in mid-September 1944, arriving in the midst of the campaign against the oil and fuel refineries at Balikpapan, Borneo. Due to its location far from the main battle arena Balikpapan had thus far escaped damage. Capture of Noemfoor Island, which possessed several airfields, finally permitted Kenney to strike at this lucrative target.

The first strikes against Balikpapan had been flown just before Dick's return to the Southwest Pacific. Even though the B-24s staged through Noemfoor the missions still stretched the bombers to their limit, encompassing a staggering distance of 1,000 miles. The strikes on September 30th and October 3rd were flown without fighter escort, losses running to 11 B-24s. Dick and other pilots were anxious to fly cover for the next Balikpapan strike although the range was daunting to even hardened fighter jocks.

Kenney decided that by combining use of underwing fuel tanks with new methods of cruise control championed by Charles Lindbergh, he could put his P-47s and P-38s over the target and have them return safely. Lindbergh had flown with the 475th Fighter Group in the summer of '44 while Dick was in the States, demonstrating to the P-38 pilots that they could increase the range of their aircraft by as much as 50%. Using Lindbergh's methods ten-hour missions were possible, which meant Dick would get a crack at Balikpapan.

Cover for the next Balikpapan mission, scheduled for October 10th, was provided by 16 Thunderbolts from the 40th and 41st Squadrons and 16 Lightnings from Dick's old unit, the 9th Fighter Squadron. Colonel George Walker, 49th FG CO, would command the P-38 formation. While at Fighter Command Headquarters to help plan the mission Walker was collared by Dick who asked to fly the mission with the "Flying Knights." After checking with General Wurtsmith, Walker agreed and assigned Dick to his flight, Dick leading the second element as Red Three. Lieutenant Warren Curton, Walker's wingman on 10 October, described the mission as follows:

"We took off, headed straight toward the target and joined up in flights enroute to conserve fuel. I remember we flew over an occupied island 40 to 50 miles out and were still climbing for our cruise altitude. To conserve fuel we did not detour around the island. The Nips popped away at us with AA, little realizing we were on our way to Balikpapan. It was kind of lonesome on the way to the target because we were observing radio silence. We did meet a couple of B-24s about half way to the target and heard one say to the other 'there go our little friends on the way to the biggie.'

"Just about the time we arrived over Borneo, Dick broke radio silence to say: 'Red One (Walker) from Red Three, we have a bandit following us in.' Colonel Walker replied: 'Red Three from Red One, roger, you lead.' We turned around and flew for what seemed to me to be ten minutes before I spotted the bandit. It wasn't that long but it was a long time before I spotted the Japanese plane which we were now approaching head-on. This was one of Dick's secrets of success - his uncanny eyesight. Dick maneuvered directly astern of the Irving and at about 150 feet opened fire. The Jap plane immediately burst into flames and went out of control. I honestly believe that the tail gunner bailed out before Dick opened fire!

"We proceeded on to the target area and saw numerous Zeros below us frantically climbing for altitude.

Colonel Walker picked out one Zero some 4,000 or 5,000 feet below us and started a diving pass on him. Just about the time Colonel Walker got into firing range the Zero flipped up on a wing and turned right out of his sights. I had dropped back into an attacking tail position and I turned with the Zero about 30 degrees. Our overtaking speed was too high and his turn too tight for me to get any lead so I broke off with Colonel Walker. To my surprise that Zero continued his turn and was firing at me before I was out of range. I was quite relieved to see Red Three (Dick) had anticipated this maneuver and blasted his second Jap plane of the day."

Shortly after Dick's second kill Walker dove on another Zero which also tried to turn inside him. Curton made a head-on pass against this aircraft and scored hits in the engine, wing roots and fuselage. The Zero spun in, trailing a long trail of smoke and flames. The Zero was Curton's second confirmed victory. He would finish the war with five kills to his credit. Lieutenant Ed Howes also claimed a single victory over Balikpapan while Major Wally Jordan, 9th FS CO, knocked down two Japanese fighters to make the final score six kills for no losses.

Interestingly, in his combat report Dick claimed that the Irving's pilot had jumped and not the tail gunner! He reported: "We arrived at the delta just north of Balikpapan at 10:45 a.m. Just beyond that I sighted one Jap twin-engined plane at 12 o'clock low. We were at 14,000 ft. and he was at 7,000 ft. I waited until I was over him then called Captain Baker (Dick's wingman) to cover me as I went down. I caught him and as I started firing he made a turn to the right. I followed and with the next burst he caught fire and rolled over on his back. The pilot bailed out and the plane crashed about a mile off shore and north of Manggar strip."

Soon after this kill the flight dove on a single Oscar, which Baker damaged, after which Dick took a 40⁰ deflection shot at a Zero but failed to score. He then "got on the tail of an Oscar or Zeke and closed to 100 yards and opened fire from 5⁰ to the left. He blew up and went down in flames. I sighted about four more Jap fighters but I had been in action for 15 minutes so I called Colonel Walker and suggested that we remove ourselves from the area. He agreed and we left the target at 11:15."

Eighteen victories were claimed on October 10th, the bulk of them going to the 35th FG Thunderbolt pilots. As previously mentioned the 9th FS claimed six kills: three Oscars, two Irvings and one Zeke. Dick's share of that total was an Oscar and an Irving, boosting his score to an even 30 kills.[1] Loss records for the Japanese units involved - the 309th and 602nd Fighter *Hikotai* (Zekes) and 902nd Fighter *Hikotai* (Irvings) - are incomplete although the 902nd lost at least one Irving over Balikpapan on this date. Gunners on board the B-24s claimed an additional 49 kills, an over-inflated figure that nevertheless indicated the ferocity of the battle waged over Balikpapan on October 10th. Yet Kenney's gamble had paid off, for only four B-24s were lost.

Upon hearing that Dick had boosted his score Kenney had him grounded. Writing home about this unhappy state of affairs Dick groused: "I'm back from the mission none the worse except that I'm tired. Knocked down a couple Nips so now they have grounded me all over again. Looks like it is for good this time. Makes 30 that I have now so I'll probably be grounded until somebody passes me again."

In the meantime Kenney sent a tongue-in-cheek wire to Arnold regarding Dick's action on October 10th, reporting that while Dick was "conducting his observations (of the gunnery tactics he had been preaching since his return from the States) he was forced in self-defense to shoot down two Nip aircraft." Since Dick was a valuable commodity Kenney reassured Arnold that he had "cautioned Bong to be more careful in the future." Arnold wired his "congratulations to Major Bong on his continued mastery of the manly art of self-defense. Feel sure your warning will have desired effect."

The grounding order did not sit well with Dick. Not only did he miss the last Balikpapan mission, flown on October 14th, but he also had to fend off the reporters eager to talk to the first Army Air Force pilot to crack victory number 30. In response to their questions he replied that he didn't "feel a damn bit different except that I'm pretty miffed over all this - especially over all this (interview) business." When asked about his tactics he stressed the fact that "all I do is make a pass at them and try to knock them down. Of course I try to get above them if I can. Wednesday when I got my last two, I must have made 14 passes before I shot one down. If I make a pass and miss I go on away and come back later to try to get him." He also added that he'd "go nuts if I couldn't keep on flying in combat."

As mentioned, due to Kenney's edict, Dick missed out on the last and most effective strike against Balikpapan on October 14th. Over the target 50-plus Oscars, Tojos, Tonys and Hamps had intercepted the Liberators. Two B-24s were lost but at a cost of 35 of the defenders. Tom McGuire, who flew the mission with the 9th FS, scored three kills which put him within six notches of Dick's score. McGuire made no secret of the fact that he wanted to topple Dick from the catbird seat.

An abortive raid on the 18th ended the aerial campaign against Balikpapan. Although the refineries had been hit, bombing accuracy had varied and overall damage was minimal. The Japanese had the installations back in operating order within weeks. The raids, which cost 22 B-24s, six P-47s and three P-38s, ended because the aircraft and crews were needed elsewhere. Douglas MacArthur was about to fulfill his famous pledge to the Philippines!

On October 20, 1944 troops from the American Sixth Army waded ashore on the island of Leyte, quickly establishing two beachheads on Leyte's east coast. Initial resistance to the landings was light although the beachheads were subjected to short but vicious attacks by Japanese aircraft.

MacArthur's plan recognized the vital need for land-based air support and called for the capture of Leyte Valley and the establishment of a complex of air bases to furnish that support. By D+5 MacArthur envisioned that air base facilities for three fighter and bomber groups, along with other units, would be completed. As events turned out, MacArthur's timetable - overly ambitious - was never met.

Two vital airfields - Tacloban and Dulag - were in American hands by October 21st. On D+4 (October 24) Fifth Air Force aviation engineers and crews came ashore to ready **the** airfields for Kenney's fighters. Even as these efforts were underway the Japanese committed all available naval units in an attempt to dislodge the Americans. Although these forces were decisively defeated in the Battle of the Leyte Gulf the American foothold in the Philippines was not yet assured of success!

By October 26th the feverish work at Tacloban was almost completed and two squadrons of the 49th Fighter Group - the 7th and 9th - were put on deployment alert. In a signal to Whitehead, Kenney specifically stated that he wanted "nothing but experts" in this first contingent for they would bear the brunt of air defense duties. Shortly after noon on the 27th, just after the final sections of steel matting were laid on Tacloban's runway, 34 Lightnings swept across the field. Cheers broke out from Fifth Air Force personnel and infantrymen alike as the P-38s touched down, the first U.S. aircraft to land on Philippine soil since April 1942. Among those waiting to greet the "Forty-Niners" at Tacloban were Kenney and MacArthur. Kenney was surprised to see a "short, stocky, towheaded lad" climb down from one of the P-38s. Dick had once again managed to wangle his way into combat!

Colonel George Walker, who led the "Forty-Niners" to Tacloban on that October day, recalled: "Bong wanted to go with the 49th Fighter Group on our move into the Philippines. The 49th was to go in first. I took the first contingent in. Dick and Colonel Robert Morrissey flew in my flight up to Tacloban, Leyte. Since General MacArthur and General Kenney were down there waiting for us to land I sent Colonel Morrissey and Dick in first. I held the first squadron up for about an hour to fly cover till I could arrange the rest of the cover over the airdrome."

Shortly after landing Dick was able to talk Kenney into letting him fly combat. Given the desperate need for experienced fighter pilots, Kenney's decision was the only correct one under the circumstances. As if to underscore that need, three warning shots rang out shortly after Dick talked to Kenney, signalling an incoming raid. Two Zero fighter-bombers angled in and everyone on the strip scrambled for cover. Fortunately anti-aircraft fire drove the Zeros off.

Four hours after he landed Dick was back in action. At 4:15 p.m. the 9th FS scrambled 11 P-38s to patrol Tacloban and strafe enemy positions in the Lapdok area. Dick, Bob Morrissey and Major Jerry Johnson made up Captive Green Flight. Although a ground controller reported enemy aircraft approaching from the northwest, the Americans were unable to make contact. Overhearing a report on their headphones of bogeys in the Tacloban area, the P-38s headed back to base and promptly ran into two Oscar fighters. Dick's combat report described the action that followed:

"I fired one 90° deflection short burst at the lead plane and then Major Johnson got on his tail. Colonel Morrissey got on the other one's tail and I saw both Oscars crash in the water. I spotted another Oscar at ten o'clock and gave chase. I closed in and fired, observing hits all over the airplane. He fell off on the right wing and went right on into the water. He started to burn just before he hit.

"I then saw another Oscar at ten o'clock high and gave chase. He led me through a bunch of clouds and I hit him a couple of times but he finally got away in the clouds. Major Johnson and Colonel Morrissey shot down a Val while I was chasing the second Oscar. The combat took place at 5:20 and 5:45 and was broken off due to lack of targets."

Having destroyed four of five enemy aircraft encountered, Captive Green Flight landed back at base at 6:45. Interestingly enough, the remaining eight P-38s who had scrambled with Captive Green Flight were only able to claim two Vals destroyed between them. Jerry Johnson's pair of victories brought his total to 17. By war's end he would have 22 confirmed kills and been 49th Group commander.

These one-sided victories did not reflect the true state of affairs in the Philippines. By October 25th MacArthur had expected to have two fighter groups plus bomber, night-fighter and patrol units operating from Leyte bases. Typhoon rains coupled with the terrain of Leyte Valley set back MacArthur's plans. Until October 30th (D+10) Dick and the 30-odd fighter pilots of the 49th Group were the only land-based air cover MacArthur possessed.

Conditions for the "Forty-Niners" at Tacloban were primitive, harking back to the early days at Dobodura in 1943. The pilots' camp consisted of a number of 16 x 16 tents situated in a coconut grove some four miles from the Tacloban strip. Each tent, which had dirt floors, held four folding cots. Food varied from cold C-rations to whatever could be cooked up on the small Army-issue gasoline stoves. Rainfall during late October and early November, as previously mentioned, was unusually heavy. The road from the "Forty-Niners" camp became almost impassable, forcing the use of amphibious vehicles to get to the strip. The rains turned camp sites into water-logged swamps in short order. Even more importantly, the rains wrecked havoc on the few available airstrips, causing many accidents that depleted the inventory of available aircraft.

Enemy air raids on the Leyte beachheads, which included kamikaze attacks, came thick and fast. The 49th FG history records "numerous raids by Japanese planes on Tacloban strip and shipping in San Pedro Bay" on October 24th and 25th, "20 separate raids by enemy formations of various sizes" on the 26th and "countless raids and alerts" on the night of October 27th making it "impossible to sleep for more than a few minutes at a time."

On October 28th the 9th FS, to which Dick had attached himself, alternated between base patrols over Tacloban and dive-bombing attacks against the port of Ormoc on Leyte's west coast. At 4 p.m. Dick led Captive Yellow Flight off during a red alert. The flight, which included Morrissey, Johnson and Walker, climbed to 11,000 feet and soon spotted a single Oscar directly ahead. Dick watched as an unidentified "P-38 made a pass at him but did not hurt him. The Nip headed west and I gave chase.

"I caught up with him on the west side of Leyte Island, at 4:15, and closed and fired from directly astern. I observed strikes and he rolled over on his back and started to split-S. I followed and fired into him until he caught fire. Major Johnson followed him down and saw him crash. I climbed and joined Colonel Walker and Colonel Morrissey.

"We searched around point 'L' waiting for Major Johnson to join us. We saw no further enemy airplanes and Major Johnson failed to join us. The three of us started up to Masbate Island at 11,000 feet. We got to the south tip of the island and met one Oscar head-on, at 4:50, at a little above us. I chandelled up toward him and he jettisoned his belly tank and started diving to the west. We followed and I was not quite in range yet when it looked like he tried to drop his bomb. It came back and hit the tail. The whole empennage broke off right behind the trailing edge of the wing and he crashed into the water.

"We climbed back to 10,000 feet and started up towards Masbate Strip when we sighted 17 Oscars from 3-7,000 feet at nine o'clock right over the southern end of Masbate Island headed toward Biliran Straits. Colonel Morrissey turned back for help and Colonel Walker and I shadowed them. They spotted us so I attacked the top man because he was rolling his wings and trying to warn the others. I got strikes on him from a 45-degree deflection shot and he split-essed. I then pulled up and took a 30-degree deflection shot at another one and got some strikes. The whole formation then dropped their tanks and bombs and started after us. I dove out towards home and got hit in the left coolant radiator so I feathered the engine and started for home with Colonel Walker escorting me. At the north tip of Biliran Island a Zero got on Colonel Walker's tail but did not fire a shot. Then the Zero pulled up and went into the clouds. Colonel Walker and I landed at 5:30. I claim two Oscars destroyed and two Oscars damaged."

Colonel Walker subsequently added a humorous footnote to Dick's account of the combat. Walker recalled that Dick called in the Oscar over Masbate Island and Morrissey promptly broke in to encourage Dick to "get him yourself. Walker will miss him anyway." Colonel Walker good-naturedly admitted he "was not the best shot in the world."

It says much for the quality of the Japanese pilots involved that, despite having a great numerical advantage, they failed to destroy either Lightning and failed to complete their original mission of attacking American forces on Leyte. Curiously, when mechanics repaired Dick's aircraft at Tacloban they discovered the round that had damaged his left radiator was an American .50 caliber. Since no other American aircraft had been in the vicinity when Dick's P-38 was hit, he concluded that he had unwittingly flown into one of his own shells!

The abundance of Japanese aircraft over Leyte helped the "Forty-Niners" reach a long sought-after milestone on October 29th. The group's 500th confirmed victory fell to the guns of Lieutenant Milden Mathre from the 7th FS. Mathre was flying dawn patrol with six other P-38s over Tacloban when a lone Oscar was sighted above the Americans. After three other flight members missed shots at the enemy aircraft, Mathre took his turn, flaming the Oscar with a long burst in the cockpit area. It was the first of his five confirmed kills.

Mathre's victory notwithstanding, Dick had good reason to remember the 29th for, on that date, he had yet another narrow escape from Japanese bullets. Dick had been airborne on the 29th but failed to get in on the action. As he landed, however, three Japanese Val dive-bombers, sneaking in under the American radar, roared over Tacloban strip heading directly for Dick's aircraft, strafing and dropping small bombs as they came! Strapped into his aircraft, he watched helplessly as the Vals drew near, later remembering that "the three Jap planes passed right over my head about 200 feet up. A bad experience . . . sure was scared."

Dick's crew chief, Sergeant John Cummings, had a front-row view of the Val's attack and later told a *Chicago Tribune* reporter that even as he dove for cover Dick "just kept taxiing his plane until he had it where he wanted it. Then he left his motors running about 1,500 revolutions and watched until it was all over. Not until then did he shut off his motors and leave the cockpit. I told him he'd better get under the wing because the flak was really coming down but he said he guessed it was all right and walked off!"[2]

Although Dick wasn't hit, the 9th FS CO, Major Bob McGomsey, was injured in the attack. McGomsey, a Darwin veteran on his second tour with the squadron, was subsequently evacuated due to the wounds he suffered on the 29th. Several of the bombs dropped failed to explode, being released too low. None of the Vals survived to relate their success, all three falling to P-38s or anti-aircraft.

As October waned, any hopes that the American situation on Leyte would improve were soon dashed. The Seventh Fleet escort carriers which had helped furnish air cover for the landing withdrew to refuel and replenish. The Third Fleet was engaged elsewhere and could not provide the air support MacArthur needed. Taking advantage of the situation, the Japanese began pouring reinforcements into Ormoc on Leyte's west coast.

As the American advance pressed forward on the ground the number of operational Lightnings steadily fell. By October 30th only 20 P-38s remained of the 34 flown in three days previously.

Kenney funneled in as many reinforcements as Tacloban could hold. The 8th FS arrived on the 30th to bring the "Forty-Niners" up to acceptable levels. Reportedly one of the pilots flying into Tacloban on the 30th was Tom McGuire, Dick's closest aerial rival. McGuire's squadron, the 431st, did not arrive until November 9th. Six P-61 night-fighters from the 421st NFS arrived on the 31st. Two days later the 432nd Squadron, with P-38s, flew in followed by the P-40s of the 110th TRS on November 3rd and so on.

Even as these penny-packet reinforcements were fed into Leyte, the Japanese increased the tempo and intensity of their raids. The 49th FG history noted that November 2nd was "the most hectic day within memory . . . the Japs kept fighters constantly in the air over Ormoc." Darkness brought no respite, for the "Forty-Niners" were on constant alert all that night, enemy aircraft dropping bombs every ten to fifteen minutes. The next night more than 50 separate raids were logged, followed by a surprise strafing attack by 25 Zeros at dawn. These attacks resulted in the destruction of two precious Lightnings and damage to 39 other aircraft.

The fourth of November was almost as bad, although a temporary reprieve was in store for the Americans. Dick used the time to describe the Leyte campaign to his family, explaining: "It has been a long time since I wrote, but oh my gosh have I been busy. Been here for several days now and we get bombed every night and some times in daylight. Everybody flies and as a result I have knocked down three more Nips up here bringing my total up to 33. Nips come over at night and it is just like the 4th of July back home when all of the Roman candles go off all together, lots of noise. I saw the ack-ack shoot down one in flames right near the camp... Have had several more or less close calls and thrills. Things will become much better in the next few days I hope.

"I'm also losing weight I reckon. Plenty warm here. We have had one typhoon already but it was a mild one. I guess the story about the 49th Fighter Group has been released so I can tell you that I'm living with them at the present time. Damn good outfit. Tossed my cookies at noon today. Must have been something I ate because I feel all right except that I'm tired from lack of sleep."

By the 6th Dick could report: "It looks like we are a little better off now because the Nip planes didn't give us much trouble last night and we had a good night's rest. Haven't been flying for a couple days but probably will pretty quick again. The boys are improving their gunnery I believe and at least they are better than the old boys were."

Yet, as always, Dick's thoughts centered on home - and Marge - as revealed in the following passages from the letter of the 6th: "Sometimes I wish I had got married when I was back there last time. Just wishful thinking but I'm sure ready to get myself hitched up to her. Won't take me any longer than the law demands to finish it up when I get back home again. Sure do miss my mail from you and her.

"Guess you had better start my Christmas shopping for me. You ought to be able to pick out something nice for Marge, the kids and you and Dad and Grandma. You've got the money so make them nice and don't slight yourself. Say, if you and Dad can see your way clear why don't you take a trip somewhere this winter on me? I know you will have to go by train but a trip will do you both good."

Although Dick had definite plans concerning Marge, he was less certain about his future in the military. On November 9th he wrote: "The way things look now I may stay in the Army after the war but I'm not at all sold on the idea yet. Things are too damned unsettled to try and plan one way or another. I'm just like Nellie -can't make up my mind as to what I want to do. All I know is that I will continue to fly. I'd really like to fly some fast stuff now and then."

Thoughts of postwar life were put on the back burner on November 10th as Dick went back into action. During the first weeks of November Kenney's squadrons had continued to batter the Japanese reinforcement convoys steaming into the port of Ormoc. On the 10th the 9th Squadron put up five P-38s as escort for P-40s dive-bombing Ormoc Bay shipping. Wally Jordan led the flight, Dick flying as Captive White five. Enroute to the target the Americans ran into opposition.

Dick's combat report recorded that the first enemy aircraft, a lone Oscar, was sighted at 8:15 when "it came out of the clouds and the P-40s jettisoned their bombs so we went down under the clouds to find them. I sighted five Oscars at 8:30 at 7,000 feet over Ormoc Bay. We attacked and I shot a short burst into an Oscar but he pulled back up into the clouds. I pulled over and took a 40-degree deflection shot at another Oscar and he burst into flames and crashed near Ormoc strip. I pulled around to the left and fired another burst at an Oscar but he got into the clouds safely. I saw a few more in the clouds but was unable to close with them for a shot. I counted the ships in the harbor and then returned to base, landing at 9:15." Dick's Oscar claim was confirmed by Major Jordan, who accounted for two Oscar kills of his own. A fourth Oscar was credited to Lieutenant Ishmael Corley.

On the return flight to Tacloban another Oscar was spotted in the distance and Jordan began stalking the Japanese fighter. As he closed on the enemy aircraft Dick came over the radio with an impish warning: "You better not miss this one, Wally!" Unfortunately, the Oscar sighted the approaching Lightnings and escaped by diving into cloud cover.

Jordan felt that the cloud cover cost Captive White Flight several more scalps on the 10th because "the Nips would duck into them after being hit. There was quite a bit of cloud cover over the area. They were fairly large and cost us many scores that day. We could only claim probables even though several pilots had Zeros smoking, pieces flying off, etc.

"One important thing we were able to report from that combat was that it appeared the Nips had begun to attempt to use our two-ship element formation. Heretofore they had usually flown in a bunch with no indication of any formation tactics.

"Dick's kill that day was a piece of very good deflection shooting. I think his shot was a deflection of closer to 90-degrees than the 40-degrees he reported, a really difficult shot which attested to his effective absorption of the gunnery training he received at Foster Field during his return to the States."

Yet not all Fifth Air Force pilots on Leyte were as experienced as Dick or Wally Jordan. The Americans were slowly gaining the advantage, but at a heavy cost. Captain Nelson Flack, operations officer of the 8th Squadron, remembered: "We were outnumbered ten to one upon landing at Tacloban, and almost lost it and the group function. They were wild and wooly days of combat, more action in a week than in three months in New Guinea. Life expectancy at the November 1944 pace of combat was about three months. The 8th Squadron lost 40-50% of its pilots in the November-December period due to one cause or another.

"The worst day I recall the 49th could muster only nine aircraft. On Leyte we were down to a low inventory of pilots, something like 20, and then received a bunch with zero experience and the pace of combat, from 6 a.m. to 7 p.m., so hot that you could barely get their names. They were told to get in there and hang on. The 8th Squadron took about 28 to 30 pilots to Leyte and in six weeks lost 13. We, along with others, cleaned out 800 to 1,000 Jap planes of the P.I. and permitted the ground troops to clean up. Also prevented shipping reinforcements. I guess that's still (a good victory ratio) from the business point of view."

As a roving gunnery instructor Dick spent time with various P-38 squadrons during his tour on Leyte, passing along information to help inexperienced pilots survive the Leyte meatgrinder. On November 11th he flew with the 7th Squadron, attaching himself to a flight escorting a C-47 transport to Homonhon Island. After completing their assigned mission, Pinky Special Flight diverted to Ormoc Bay to see how Fifth Air Force was dealing with the latest Japanese reinforcement convoy.

As Dick later recounted, near Ormoc a ground controller "called us and said there were some bogies south of Ormoc so we climbed to 13,000' and sighted several Navy planes on the way. At 12:30 we sighted seven Zekes at 13,000' about to make an attack on six Navy TBFs. We dropped our tanks and turned to attack. In the ensuing engagement I shot at three Zekes and got two of them smoking without being able to observe the crash. I saw Major Johnson, the flight leader, shoot down his first one in flames and saw where four planes had crashed into the water. We landed at base at 1:00. In later discussions it was found that both of the enemy planes I had started smoking had crashed."

Four Zekes were destroyed on November 11th, split between Dick and Jerry Johnson. The Japanese pilots, who were rated as "experienced and eager to fight," failed to score against the P-38s. An unidentified 7th FS intelligence officer added an interesting comment to the Unit Narrative Combat Report filed by the squadron, noting that "the combat was a successful one, altho one or two more enemy planes might have been added to the score had some of our pilots been better gunners."

The victories scored on November 11th, which boosted Dick's score to 36, were the last claims he made in November. In slightly over two weeks of hectic combat at Tacloban Dick had added four Oscars and two Zeros to his score. Given the Fifth Air Force's need for experienced fighter pilots at Leyte - and Dick's love of flying combat - readers may wonder why he made no further claims in November. The answer to that question is instructive, for it helps scotch criticism that Dick enjoyed free rein to run up large numbers of kills. When queried by the authors on this matter, General Kenney responded as follows:

"The months of November and December were tough ones for me, trying to keep Dick from flying too many combat missions. General MacArthur, General Arnold and everyone in the Fifth Air Force from my sergeant to General Whitehead kept saying 'why don't you send him home before he gets knocked off?' Dick wanted to go for 50 victories. I said 'no, at 40 you go home.'

"The reason he didn't fly more than nine days in November and December was that I kept him on the ground unless I needed him on an especially important mission. In spite of everything, in the five weeks from November 10th to December 17th, he shot down seven Jap planes. Not bad for a guy who just about had to get permission from his commanding general to even rev up his engines." In a subsequent letter Kenney reiterated that Dick's duties "were mostly to teach gunnery to the newly arrived pilots and be cheerful instead of chafing because I didn't want him to press his luck."

Comparing Dick's score with those of his closest rivals during the last three months of 1944 reveals no significant differences. Dick claimed 12 victories in three months. By contrast Tom McGuire downed 17; Charles MacDonald, 11; and Jerry Johnson, 10.

In spite of the frontline conditions at Tacloban, Dick, like many Fifth Air Force aces, felt the skies over Leyte were a fighter pilot's paradise. Although the Japanese committed many air units to the struggle, the majority of their pilots were brave but inexperienced. Dick summed it all up by saying that it was "easy hunting here because we only have to take off and they aren't very far away. In fact they come looking for us more often than I like."

Since he was grounded during much of November Dick had a good opportunity to observe first-hand the continuing attacks by Japanese aircraft. The Japanese came by day and night, Dick recounting an experience when he "had dinner with the mayor of the town near us a couple of nights ago. These Filippinos are pretty sincere people and the mayor gave quite a speech following the dinner. Everyone else had to say something too. Had a raid right in the middle of the dinner and the anti-aircraft guns shot down a Nip plane. Made a big explosion when he was hit. Just like the Fourth of July only much more so." The enemy aircraft was a Val dive-bomber which had attempted to hit Tacloban at dusk on the 17th. The 49th FG history recorded that this aircraft "crashed in flames, a most edifying sight."

Events at Tacloban were often hectic, Japanese raiders hitting unexpectedly at all hours. Mixed in with the conventional bombing and strafing raids were Kamikaze attacks, suicide-minded pilots intent on crashing into Allied shipping. Nowhere is the quicksilver nature of life at Tacloban so vividly captured as in a letter Dick wrote on November 24th:

"Well we have just been bombed again in broad daylight. It is about 8:30 a.m. and the raid is just over. About 25 Nip planes came over and bombed. The ack ack shot down one bomber right over hour heads. He caught on fire and was a right pretty sight to watch. I had a premonition last night that I ought to fly this morning but the roads were so muddy that I didn't go down to the strip. It sure would have been easy if I had because these Nip bombers are very easy to shoot down and no danger to yourself. Doggone if another one didn't go across just now! He must have been taking pictures though, because he didn't drop any bombs.

"Had dinner with the mayor last night. Woops another one just went across but there are two P-38s chasing him so he won't get home..."

Dick's assessment of the Japanese pilot's fate was on the mark. The pursuing P-38s caught up with the reconnaissance plane - a Dinah - and Flight Officer Henry Hammett downed it for his first victory. In between these Japanese interruptions Dick continued his letter-writing, touching upon the ace race with the following remarks:

"Maybe if I shoot down 40 Nips I can get sent home again to stay. Hope so anyway. And listen, just in case you are worrying or think I'm crazy for flying combat why I can tell you that I'm not sticking my neck out at all because I'm just as anxious to get home as you are to have me home. I expect to arrive just as hale and hearty as I have the other times."

General Kenney's main concern in restricting Dick's combat time following his victories on November 11th was that Dick was pushing his luck too far and might go the route of Lynch and Kearby. On November 28th Kenney's worst fears were almost realized. On the 28th Captain John Davis, the 49th FG assistant operations officer, scrambled in Dick's aircraft during a dusk alert. The aircraft had barely gotten airborne when an engine burst into flames and the P-38 crashed, killing Davis instantly. Dick's ship was well-known at Tacloban since it bore 36 Japanese victory flags on its nose.[3] For a few anxious moments it was believed that Dick had been piloting the aircraft but the error was quickly cleared up.

The crash of Dick's P-38 only confirmed Kenney's belief that he should pull Dick out of combat once he had gained his 40th kill. In the meantime, Dick could continue to attach himself to different squadrons to observe and evaluate their gunnery. Dick chose the 431st FS, 475th FG as his next assignment. It was a surprising move, for the 431st was commanded by Tom McGuire!

Chapter 13

Medal of Honor
(December 1944)

Of all the Fifth Air Force fighter aces who tried to topple Dick from his catbird seat, Tom McGuire stands out as Dick's most persistent rival. Dick already had 16 kills to his credit before McGuire made his first claims in August 1943. While others fell by the wayside McGuire, who made no secret of the fact that he wanted to be number one, steadily closed the gap, boosting his score through a series of multiple victories over the course of a year. By early December 1944, when Dick moved in with McGuire's 431st Squadron, the scoring stood at 36 for Dick and 28 for McGuire.

Over the years Tom McGuire, like Dick, has come in for some bad press, criticism which the authors feel is undeserved in both cases. Like Dick, McGuire was not destined to survive the war. The late Carroll Anderson, a noted aviation historian who flew with the 433rd FS, provided the following description of Tom McGuire. Anderson's summary, like McGuire himself, is opinionated but accurately captures the spirit of the man.

Anderson recalled that "McGuire certainly was no shrinking violet. Neither was he a brilliant intellectual. He was an earthy, brash type of guy who led by example. The 431st could not have compiled the brilliant record it did with bad leadership. Beginning with Franklin Nichols, through Verl Jett, to McGuire and Pappy Cline the 431st had up front, very aggressive leadership. Those crazy bastards loved to fight and kill Japs. No one more than Mac.

"He could be abrasive and caustic but he fought and he led, which Bong never did. Bong did not command. He was up at Fifth Fighter Headquarters and when a good mission was forthcoming, he dropped down to the 9th or the 39th, his first assigned squadron, and flew with the boys. Hell, Dick scored something like 14 victories when flying with the 475th, primarily with the 431st. (NOTE: Dick only scored four kills while flying with different squadrons of the 475th FG. AUTHORS) Except for a brief period before his death, Mac was compelled to lead his squadron and go where 5th Fighter Command sent him. When you consider the Billy Bishop free-lance possibilities of Bong's efforts against the necessity of running a squadron by the book McGuire's record becomes all the more fantastic.[1]

"Bong told Joe Price that he had lost two wingmen. Looked back once coming off Wewak and his wingman was gone. (NOTE: Both wingmen lost were flying missions to Rabaul. AUTHORS) Mac had his squadron shot up but apparently never lost an actual wingman. Joe Price said that Bong told him the only way he could get a Nip was to drive right up its ass. McGuire could shoot from 90-degrees and hit them. McGuire scored doubles and triples left and right. I doubt if Mac was in more than 20 fights during his entire tour, which is saying something for his shooting ability.

"I don't deprecate Bong. He was a wonderful guy who smoked, drank and chased with the best of them in Sydney but Bong had that boyish, shy look about him and he often was that way. Mac, on the other hand, grew a big black mustache to make himself appear older than he was. His face was narrow with an undershot jaw that gave him a sharp, pugnacious look. He was aggressive as hell. He wanted to be number one, to win the CMH and get a colonelcy before going home. So what else is new?"

That spirit of aggressiveness Anderson commented on caused McGuire to fly up to Tacloban in advance of his squadron, apparently arriving on October 30, 1944. In any case, he was in action over Tacloban on November 1st when he destroyed a Nakajima Ki-44 (Tojo) fighter for his 25th kill. McGuire's squadron - the 431st - flew up to Leyte on November 9th and eventually settled at the Dulag airstrip south of Tacloban. By mid-November Dulag housed all three squadrons of the 475th Fighter Group.

As the new month began the situation on Leyte shifted in favor of the Americans. The Sixth Army had steadily pushed across Leyte and were now threatening the port of Ormoc. The Japanese had continued to pour in reinforcements but their convoys were savaged by American air- and sea-power. Over 1,000 additional aircraft had been funneled into the Philippines by the Japanese but they too ran afoul of Kenney's experienced fighter units.

On December 7, 1944 troops from the American 77th Infantry Division were landed south of Ormoc town, their goal being to cut Leyte off from further reinforcement. The Japanese also chose that day to land reinforcements north of Ormoc on San Isidro Bay. The air over Ormoc swarmed with Japanese and American aircraft, each trying to sink the other's shipping while protecting their own forces.

At 2:30 p.m. the four P-38s making up Daddy Green Flight lifted off from Dulag to patrol over Ormoc. Tom McGuire was flight leader, Dick leading the second element as Daddy Green Three. Arriving over Ormoc Bay at 2:50 the P-38s began circling, waiting for action. At first the skies over the American shipping anchored in Ormoc Bay were clear of enemy aircraft, but within ten minutes Daddy Green Flight would have all the action it could handle. Dick was the first to call in bandits and later reported that he "sighted a Sally low on the water, at 12 o'clock, and gave chase. Closing to 1,000 feet I set the left engine on fire and she crashed on Bohol Island at 3:10 p.m.

"We returned to patrol the convoy and sighted one Kate among A/A bursts. Major Rittmayer shot him down out of control from astern amidst the A/A fire at 3:40.

"We again resumed patrol at 3,000 feet over the northwest corner of the convoy and sighted five Tojos, at two o'clock level, coming towards us. We attacked from 30° deflection to dead astern but I did not like the idea of diving into the A/A so I turned left and met the tail man head-on and observed several hits on his engine. I observed Major McGuire shoot one Tojo down, just astern of the convoy and Lieutenant Fulkerson shot one down that exploded just before it contacted with the water. The Tojo that I hit from head-on spiralled down with a dead engine and crashed just to the rear of the convoy. I then observed Major Rittmayer attacking a Tojo from astern and the Tojo started smoking and made a 360° turn and ended up right in front of me. I took a shot at him but he was already finished and he crashed in the water at 4:30.

"We were ordered to go up and cover a destroyer which had been previously hit. We arrived just as it and its escorts were firing at a single Nip airplane. We gave chase but another flight of P-38s beat us to him and Lieutenant Hart of the 431st Fighter Squadron shot him down. We patrolled for a few more minutes and returned to Dulag, landing at 5:20."

The Japanese paid a terrible price for the 4,000 troops they managed to land on December 7th at Ormoc. All their transports were sunk or destroyed. In the air over 70 kills were claimed by Fifth Air Force and Marine Corps pilots. Daddy Green Flight's contribution to that score was seven confirmed kills - one Sally, one Kate and five Tojos, two of which fell to Tom McGuire.

Dick now had 38 victories to McGuire's 30, a state of affairs that did not please McGuire. For some months McGuire had been kidded about always being eight kills behind Dick. Despite some sharp shooting on December 7th, McGuire still had not been able to cut into Dick's lead. Dick's next letter home was full of news on the ace race, leading off with the comments: "Well I did it again as I suppose you know by now. Got two more Nips yesterday. Shot at two planes and got both of them. One was a head-on pass and a pretty fair shot if I do say so myself. McGuire got two also, making him 30 and Johnson got three making him 22. Still have an eight shy lead on McGuire.

"I'm living with McGuire right now and so I'm not with my old outfit anymore. Haven't had any mail for about six weeks except that one letter you sent to the 49th Group so I don't know much about what is going on back home. The boys are receiving clippings back here so I see I'm spread all over the papers again... Would like to know what's going on back home and how badly the reporters are treating you all. I'll bet you're both getting plenty of trouble from them. I've heard vague rumors to the effect that I'm going to be decorated again so you know what that will be.

"I'm feeling fine except that I caught a bad cold yesterday. Nose is stopped up so most likely I won't fly for several days. Bad news. I got into a poker game and lost $1500 before I knew what had happened. Looks like my sins have caught up with me. McGuire lost $2500 so the majors practically financed the game. War is hell but poker is worse."

Less than a week later the vague rumors Dick mentioned in his letter came true as he was presented with the Medal of Honor by General MacArthur in a ceremony at the Tacloban airfield. Shortly after Dick had made his 36th kill, Kenney had decided his actions warranted the Medal of Honor. Kenney drew up a citation that cited Dick "for conspicuous gallantry and intrepidity in action... from October 10, 1944 to November 15, 1944. Though assigned to duty as gunnery instructor and neither required nor expected to perform combat duty, Major Bong voluntarily and at his own urgent request engaged in repeated combat missions, including unusually hazardous sorties over Balikpapan, Borneo and in the Leyte area of the Philippines. His aggressiveness and daring resulted in his shooting down eight enemy airplanes during that period." MacArthur approved the citation as written, obtained Washington's approval for the award and agreed to present the medal in a public ceremony, something he rarely did. The awards ceremony was to take place at noon on December 12th.

Dick, who was staying with the 431st Squadron at Dulag, had some difficulty getting to the ceremony, as Hal Gray pointed out. Gray recalled that "Dick wasn't too happy with the prospect of riding over 20 miles of muddy roads so they were going to send him up in an L-5. We fixed up a P-38, though, and flew him over piggy-back. Protocol was the order of the day. General MacArthur, trench coat and polished shoes: Dick, baggy unpressed sun tans; and a very light drizzle."

At the airstrip four P-38s had been drawn up in a semi-circle as a background for the ceremony. A guard of honor made up of 12 pilots from Dick's old unit, the 9th FS, formed up behind Dick. In front of him stood MacArthur with Kenney, Whitehead and other Fifth Air Force brass a respectful distance behind the general. Several hundred airmen and soldiers crowded around the area, elbowing their way forward to get a front-seat view. Air Force photographers and motion picture cameras recorded the scene as Dick stepped forward.

MacArthur, ever the showman, had a surprise up his sleeve as he discarded his prepared text and ad-libbed a short speech of congratulations which Kenney, among others, thought was one of his finest. Placing his hands on Dick's shoulders MacArthur intoned: "Major Richard Ira Bong, who has ruled the air from New Guinea to the Philippines, I now induct you into the society of the bravest of the brave, the wearers of the Congressional Medal of Honor of the United States." MacArthur then pinned the medal on Dick's uniform, the two shook hands, exchanged salutes and the ceremony ended.

As impressive as the ceremony had been, harsh reality intruded into the scene soon after. Having satisfied the demands of photographers, Dick hurried off in search of food. The medal ceremony had so engrossed Dick that he had forgotten to eat breakfast before journeying up to Tacloban! Lieutenant Colonel George Walker's hut yielded a can of tuna and in between mouthfuls the two friends started to talk. Major Jerry Johnson, who had flown with Dick back in New Guinea, stopped in to offer his congratulations. Dick let slip that he would probably be stateside sometime in early January, hopefully in time to be at Marge's graduation on the 15th. He had talked over the matter with Kenney and was fairly certain Kenney would have him packing in time to make the graduation ceremony. Dick and Jerry Johnson began brainstorming plans for a postwar get-together in Poplar, each trying to top the other in describing the mouth-watering culinary delights that would grace their reunion. Tragically, it was an appointment never to be kept.

The Bong-McGuire scoring race resumed on December 13th when Tom McGuire downed a Mitsubishi J2M Jack, narrowing Dick's lead to seven kills. McGuire barely had time to rejoice before Dick came back on the 15th to down an Oscar, making the score 39 to 31.

On December 15th Dick took off from Dulag at 6:30 a.m., leading the second element of Daddy Special Flight. He later reported: "We arrived over Negros Island at 7:00 and circled over the airdromes on the northern and eastern coasts for an hour. We then flew over to Panubulon Island and my wingman, Lieutenant Fulkerson, called in a Nip aircraft below us. We made a 360° turn but could not see him so we flew a 60° heading because that was the way the Oscar was headed.

"I soon spotted him at three o'clock low and dived from 7,000 feet to attack him. I fired a short burst from 90° to 60° deflection and observed a hit in the right wing. I overshot him, made a 360° turn to the left, closed to 1,000 feet and opened fire from 50° deflection. I observed a couple of hits, causing him to turn to the right and lose altitude. I fired a short burst from directly astern and the Oscar crashed into the water and exploded.

"We rejoined Major McGuire over Negros and Lieutenant Fulkerson made a strafing run on Tanza Drome. He lost his canopy and I escorted him home, where we landed at 8:55."

In addition to Dick's Oscar kill, Lieutenant Fulkerson's strafing pass flamed two Jacks and an Oscar and damaged two others. At least 20 enemy aircraft were sighted on Tanza Drome but no further strafing runs were made after Fulkerson had his canopy shot off. McGuire made no claims on this mission.

Two days later Dick caught up on his letter-writing, recounting the momentous events of the past week and his friendly rivalry with Tom McGuire, among other topics. He opened by stating that "you of course know that General MacArthur presented the Congressional Medal to me a few days ago and you probably know that I got another Nip plane on the 15th making it 39 now. Seems like one or two Nips doesn't make any difference anymore.

"Major McGuire is doing his darndest to pass me or gain on me anyway, but since I am living with him at the present, why, he has a hard time of it because I fly when he does and we break even. Sure is good hunting up here and it is the best place we have ever been because we are much safer than we ever have been before. Major Johnson got four a few days ago making him 23 so he is quite happy. I have gotten 11 since I last left home and McGuire and Johnson have both gotten 10 in the same period.

"The gunnery training I got in the States sure improved my shooting about 300 or 400 percent. It confirms my opinion that if I had known it before I came over the first time I could have 75 or 100 now. Sounds like a lot, doesn't it? When I think of all the chances I have had and missed it doesn't sound impractical at all.

"Gee, here it is only eight days to Christmas and a Happy New Year to everyone and drink a toast that we never spend another apart like this. I hope you bought presents for everyone for me and also for Marge. Have you seen her lately? I haven't heard from her since she wrote on October 23 so I'll have a lot of mail when it catches up with me. She was beginning to get a kick out of some of her practice teaching last I knew.

"Have you had much trouble from the newshawks? I suppose you have and it worries me slightly about what you do to them. I don't have too much trouble with them here because they can't get to me but I suppose it will be another bad session with them when I get home again.

"Here all I do is try to teach the boys gunnery and fly a mission with them now and then and I run into some Nips and have to protect myself and what happens? I shoot down a couple here and there and they give me the Congressional Medal and write big stories about me. War is hell. Did you think when I joined the Air Corps that I would cause so much trouble and be such a figure in the American Public's eye? I sure didn't."

On December 17, 1944 Dick was once again in the spotlight, downing an Oscar over the Mindoro beachhead for his 40th confirmed kill. The large-scale air battles fought over Ormoc Bay on December 7th and December 11th had heralded the turning of the tide on Leyte. After the 11th the Japanese would risk no further reinforcement convoys nor commit large formations of aircraft. Even as the ground action continued on Leyte the Americans began planning their next move up the Philippines chain - the island of Mindoro. Troops waded ashore on December 15th. Two days later Dick logged his last combat mission, as recounted in the following report:

"I took off from Dulag Strip at 2:50 p.m. as leader of Daddy Special Flight on a fighter sweep to Mindoro beachhead. We climbed to 9,000 feet on course and arrived over Mindoro at 4:05. I contacted the controller and started to patrol.

"At 4:15 the controller said that the friendly beachhead ws being strafed. At the same time I sighted two bogeys at 12 o'clock high. As friendly flights were down to take care of the strafers I dropped tanks and started climbing for altitude.

"The Oscars made a 180° turn and headed straight north. We gave chase and I closed on the leader, who had dived to the right separating from the other e/a, and shot him down at 4:25 from an altitude of 9,000 feet. The Oscar disintegrated and then caught fire and dived straight down and crashed about 20 miles north of San Jose.

"I then watched Major Rittmayer, my wingman, shoot down the other Oscar. We reformed formation and patrolled over San Jose until 5:15 and returned to home base, landing at 6:30. Lieutenant Fulkerson saw the Oscar crash and will confirm it."[2]

Fulkerson reported that he had seen Dick "close in on the Oscar from dead astern and fire a short burst which brought pieces from the Oscar. The Oscar turned right and with another burst from Major Bong, did a half-roll, trailing fire, and crashed in the jungle."

Upon hearing the news of Dick's latest kill General Kenney sent word that he was to fly his P-38 to Tacloban and leave it there. Until further notice Dick was through flying combat. In actual fact Kenney had already decided that 40 kills was enough and that it was time for Dick "to go home while he was still in one piece, marry Marjorie, and start thinking about raising a lot of towheaded Swedes like himself."

After being told of Kenney's decision Dick made one last flight back to Mindoro, escorting the transport carrying Kenney on an inspection trip of the new airdromes around San Jose. Ostensibly Dick flew up to pass along a few last gunnery tips to some "Forty-Niner" pilots. In reality there were some last farewells to be made.

Since October 10th Dick had added 12 confirmed kills to his credit while flying various J and L model Lightnings. Seven Oscars were destroyed along with two Zeros, one Irving, one Sally and one Tojo. He also damaged four Oscars.

Shortly before midnight on December 29, 1944 Major Richard Ira Bong boarded an Air Transport Command C-54 bound for the states. Behind him lay two years of combat, over 200 combat missions flown over some of the toughest terrain in the world against skilled and ruthless opponents. In contrast, the future was rich with promise - thoughts of home, of Marge and of a new career testing the Air Force's jet fighters. An exhilarating chapter in Dick's life was ending. Yet the future promised so much more.

Chapter 14

Test Pilot
(January - August 1945)

For all intents Dick's immediate future had been decided before he boarded the C-54 that would fly him to the States. Shortly before Dick's flight departed from Tacloban on December 29, 1944 General Kenney handed him a letter to be delivered to General Arnold. In it Kenney praised Dick's war record, explained the reasons behind Dick's reassignment to the States and added that Dick was "particularly anxious to get in on the development of the jet-propelled fighter and that . . . he should be given that opportunity."

Kenney felt Dick would be invaluable in such work due to his extensive combat experience and logical, unemotional approach to problem-solving. Accordingly, he requested that Dick be "sent to the Material Division and given every opportunity to learn something about the jet engine and the construction and maintenance of both engine and the airplane." After acknowledging that Dick would be of great value to Arnold for publicity reasons Kenney, with typical thoughtfulness, appealed to Arnold not to let "any of his public appearances interfere with Dick's appearance at the church in Poplar, Wisconsin."

Just before midnight on the 29th Dick shook hands with Kenney and boarded the waiting ATC transport. For the past two-and-a-half years the military careers of Dick Bong and George Kenney had intertwined to the mutual benefit of both. Now the warriors parted, neither one realizing the finality of their hasty words of farewell.

Dick's flight landed in San Francisco on New Year's Eve, and after a brief layover he was soon on his way to Washington. Before he left San Francisco Dick found time to call Marge and wire a holiday bouquet of roses. Marge remembered that "our telephone conversation on December 31, 1944 was one of jubilant confusion. Happy to hear each other's voices again, we both tried to talk at once. We did settle one thing: the date of our wedding. One week after my graduation seemed like plenty of time to take care of the necessary last-minute details. The date was set for February 3, 1945. But I had reckoned without the opinion of our mothers who squealed 'Horrors! We need more time!'" After talking to Dick on the 31st Marge was dying to tell her friends that he was back, but was told to keep mum. The official announcement of Dick's arrival had to be made in Washington!

Upon arrival Dick went through the obligatory public relations chores. Having had considerable experience with the media, he handled the press conferences in typical fashion. When asked how he managed to shoot down 12 Japanese aircraft while assigned instructor duties Dick good-naturedly replied: "Oh, demonstration is a pretty good way of teaching. Anyhow I had to get my flight pay." In reply to questions about Japanese airpower Dick noted some improvement in both planes and pilots, adding that "it takes longer to catch up with them and more lead to shoot them down." He felt Japanese naval pilots were "pretty fair" and eager to scrap while their Army counterparts were "dodos." The highlight of one conference came when one ill-informed reporter asked if Dick had instructed Tom McGuire in the art of aerial combat! Dick stared in disbelief for several seconds before heatedly replying that "McGuire is a hell of a good combat pilot without instructions from anyone."

Dick had hoped his stay in Washington would be brief. Unfortunately, appearances on the Army Hour radio program and at a dinner given in his honor by Wisconsin Congressman Alvin E. O'Konski delayed his departure. In the meantime the official announcement of Dick's and Marge's wedding plans was made public. After some soul-searching the date was pushed back a week to February 10th at Superior's Concordia Lutheran Church.

In the midst of his Washington stay Dick was saddened by news from the Southwest Pacific Theater. Tom McGuire had been killed in action. McGuire had run his score to 38 kills in the last days of December 1944 before being grounded by Kenney, who wanted to ensure that Dick, then on his way home, received the hero's reception he deserved. On January 7, 1945, free once again to fly combat, McGuire led three other P-38s on a sweep over Negros Island. A lone Oscar intercepted and in the ensuing combat McGuire stalled out at low altitude trying to protect another P-38 and crashed.[1] McGuire's combat record earned him a posthumous Medal of Honor. No other pilot would ever come as close as McGuire in contesting the title of America's ace of aces.[2] The ace race was finally irrevocably over!

Sig Vattendahl, Marge's dad, was one of the well-wishers on hand when Dick's train pulled into the Superior railroad station on the 14th of January. General Arnold had assigned Dick to "detached service" at Superior until the first week of February, after which he would have 21 days leave. In accordance with Dick's wishes no welcoming ceremonies had been scheduled by city officials though the enthusiastic crowd at the station left no doubt of their happiness at Dick's return. Mr. Vattendahl drove Dick to the family home where Marge was anxiously waiting. Later that day a second even more joyous reunion took place at the Bong household in Poplar.

The remainder of January was taken up with finalizing the arrangements for the upcoming wedding, Marge's graduation on the 26th, family chores, hunting trips and renewing old friendships. Although on detached service, Dick was still on call for public relations duties. On the 30th he and Marge traveled to Milwaukee at the invitation of the Milwaukee Elks Chapter. Earlier that month the Wisconsin Civil Air Patrol had voted Dick its annual award, citing his record as "the outstanding performance by a Wisconsin man in aviation in 1944." The presentation of the CAP award, in Mayor Bohn's office, was one of the highlights of the day. Interestingly enough, when Dick signed the guestbook in the mayor's office he wrote "Richard I. Bong, 9th F.S., 49th F.G., 5th A.F., Poplar, Wis."

Following a noon luncheon at the Press Club Dick visited with wounded veterans at the Soldiers Home, attended a reception at the Elks Club from 2:00 to 5:00, spoke briefly over radio station WTMJ and capped off the day with a dinner in his honor at the Elks Club. Surveying the capacity crowd at the Elks dinner, Dick quipped: "My hand is just about broken but outside of that and being awfully tired, we've had a grand time here today."

On February 10, 1945 Dick and Marge were married by Reverend Paul Boe in a night-time ceremony at Superior's Concordia Lutheran Church. Marge recalled that "both Richard and I were agreed a simple wedding would be a more beautiful one. But with all our intentions for a simple wedding - one just like anybody else's - it could not be. Essentially it was that but the exterior took on a different veneer." As it had happened so many times before, the doings of America's number one ace was big news, his wedding being no exception. The press corps was out in force on February 10th. Reporters from Associated Press, International News Service and Acme jostled with newsreel cameramen from Fox Movietone, Hearst, Paramount, Pathe and Universal outside the church. Inside Concordia Lutheran, Dick and Marge would allow just one pool photographer and he had strict instructions to shoot only two pictures during the ceremony.

Over 1,200 people were crowded inside the church, with hundreds more outside, as Marge walked down the aisle on the arm of her dad. Dick stood waiting with his best man Walter Markey along with the rest of the wedding party - Nelda and Geraldine Bong, Beverlee Barrett, Ed Edgette and Lowell Vattendahl. Dick took Marge's arm and together they walked towards Reverend Boe. In the background the soloist began Edvard Greig's *I love Thee*. The vows went quickly, Marge inadvertently adding "lawful" to the phrase "to be my wedded husband." She later claimed that insertion was equivalent to a shotgun in case Dick tried to back out!

As Major and Mrs. Richard Bong walked out of the church at the end of the ceremony the night sky exploded into light. Dozens of flash-bulbs and magnesium flares illuminated the scene as Dick and Marge made their way to the waiting car. Held back by members of the Wisconsin National Guard and the Superior police and fire departments, the hundreds of spectators could only shout out their wishes for health and happiness as the car sped away taking Dick and Marge to the studio for their official wedding portrait. Much later that night, running two hours behind schedule, Dick and Marge left on their honeymoon, bound for the Hotel Nicolet in Minneapolis. Five hours later, alone at last in their room, Marge recalled Dick passed the "true test of love," that test being "when a man can look at his wife in pin curls and shiny face sans lipstick and still say that he loves her."

Well into the honeymoon Dick found time to write home on the 25th, reporting: "Well we have arrived down here (Anaheim, CA.) and we haven't been plagued (by reporters) nearly as bad as it could be. Took Marge to Earl Carroll's and to Ken Murray's 'Blackouts.' I think she likes it out here. Also took her for a piggy back ride in a P-38 and she liked that too.

"We were out to Warner Brothers studios and I guess we will get to MGM, Paramount and Fox studios yet while we're out here. We met Bette Davis, Glen Ford, Joan Crawford, Joan Leslie, Bob Hutton, Johnnie Miles, Dana Clark and will meet a lot more. Oh yeah, and Bing Crosby. We were down to his radio show last Thursday evening and saw him. It seems that he wanted to send us congratulations in the wire and they wouldn't let him so he sent the wire anyway. Saw Costello but didn't meet him. You know we stayed up in Tulare for a couple days with Tex Rankin and were up in Sequoia National Park.

"Marge looks wonderful and we are very happy together. She has quite an appetite too. I think she will really be in good shape by the time we leave California. I'm going to stay at Santa Monica just as long as I can before going back to Wright Field..."

While staying with "Tex" Rankin Dick had treated the students at the Rankin Academy to a 45-minute airshow with Marge flying the rear seat in the AT-6. She recalled that "garbed in pilot's flying clothes and laden with parachutes we climbed into the plane. I had a moment of panic, one that I had experienced before I had become an official P-38 piggy-back rider. When Dick told me how to open the hatch and jump out in case of emergency, something just rolled over inside of me.

"After 45 minutes of slow-rolling, spinning and Immelmanning the panic gave way to a most becoming shade of green. Richard would question me by inter-comm if I still had everything intact and I hastened to assure him that everything was just fine! When he started to hedge-hop and jump the stick I told him that perhaps I had had enough. Asked what I thought of the ride I said with simulated enthusiasm that it was probably the biggest sensation of my life and hurried off to the dressing room."

The side trip to Sequoia National Park came about because of a chance remark Marge made to Mrs. Rankin about missing the snowy Wisconsin weather. Mrs. Rankin promptly "ordered a mountain visit for us. With borrowed snow togs and equipment we drove to Sequoia National Park where Richie did some low flying around hair pin curves. I decided the man I married just didn't have any nerves!

"My husband was a rascal that day. He threw snowballs at anyone who came in his sights, washed my face in snow and got us tangled up in our snow shoes. And as he slid down a hill on a tin cover he seemed much like a little boy who had run away from his governess."

The weeks seemed to flash by and then it was time for Dick to report to the Air Force Redistribution Center in Santa Monica for his orders for Wright Field. Upon completion of that assignment Dick was looking forward to returning to Burbank and the Lockheed Aircraft plant where the revolutionary P-80 Shooting Star was taking shape.

The Lockheed P-80 would take the Air Force into the jet age, a transition that was fraught with danger. Since the initial flight of the Shooting Star on September 13, 1944 the P-80 program had been plagued with problems. Lockheed was under a tremendous amount of pressure to test, refine and put the aircraft into production. Luftwaffe jet and rocket fighters were already in action in Europe by the fall of 1944 when the first pre-production YP-80A was flown. America's only other jet fighter - Bell's P-59 Airacomet - was proving to be a disappointment, which left the P-80 as the main hope.

Pressure to get the aircraft into production was compounded by design, engine and production problems. Only a month after the P-80's first flight, test pilot Milo Burcham experienced engine failure shortly after takeoff and crashed to his death on October 20, 1944. Over a dozen accidents, several of them fatal, followed Burcham's crash. Even Tony LeVier, Project Pilot for the P-80 Program, ran into trouble, bailing out of his jet after it shed its tail during a routine test flight on March 20, 1945.

In order to meet the demanding production schedule Lockheed began flying the P-80s out of their Burbank facility, a decision that LeVier, among others, did not agree with. LeVier felt that the P-80 wasn't "ready to fly out of Burbank yet, there were too many things about it that are not safe, it was too unreliable." LeVier was speaking here of the engine rather than the basic design of the P-80 itself, specifically the instability of the engine rpm on takeoff. Surrounded as it was by residential housing, the Burbank facility was not an ideal location for wringing the bugs out of a new jet fighter. Should an emergency occur on takeoff at Burbank the test pilot was left with few options since, as LeVier put it, "there were not too many places to land out there in those days."

Yet despite its problems, the Shooting Star was the hottest ship in the Air Force and Dick was eager to try it out. On April 6, 1945 Dick reported to Wright Field at Dayton, Ohio and was assigned to the flight section of the Air Technical Service Command. Wright Field would be a comparatively brief stop-over for Dick, being mostly preparation for the main event back at Lockheed's Burbank plant. In the two months Dick was at Wright Field he absorbed all the information available on jet flight - basic theory, advances made by the Americans, British and Germans and so on. By mid-June Dick and Marge were on their way back to Burbank and the Shooting Star.

Dick's commanding officer at the Lockheed Plant was Lieutenant Colonel C. J. Langmack who noted that Dick's "top goal in life was to be a test pilot and that is the reason he asked to be assigned to the Air Force Department at Lockheed-Burbank. At that time I was in charge of all flying, experimental and acceptance of Army Air Corps aircraft, therefore Dick worked for me.

"When I first learned he was going to be assigned to my office I phoned high up in the military and asked that he not be assigned here. We were having plenty of problems with the P-80 and I didn't think he should fly them for the time being. I couldn't see putting him in a high-risk assignment after all the glory he had won for himself and our nation. Anyway, I was told to give Richard whatever he wanted.

"He flew P-38s most of the time as we were getting very few P-80s. At that time I had more military pilots than P-80s. He (did study) the operational manuals on the P-80 aircraft and knew them very well."

Dick reported to Burbank in early July 1945 at a time when the entire P-80 production program was reaching a critical stage. Ignoring a severe shortage of parts problem, the Air Force had approved plans to deploy a full fighter group of P-80s to the Pacific Theater by December. Lockheed's ability to meet the demands of such an overly ambitious plan was increasingly in doubt due to the need to rework tooling, critical shortages in skilled workers and the on-going changes in the aircraft itself. Shortly before Dick reported for duty at Burbank an Air Force pilot was killed when his production model P-80 crashed on takeoff on July 1st. Before the P-80 was grounded on August 7th two more pilots would be killed, making a total of six fatalities since Milo Burcham's crash in October 1944.

Despite the troubles at Lockheed, Dick was enthused about being involved in testing the P-80, writing home on July 12th: "Well I finally checked out in the P-80 and it is quite an airplane all right. I work out at Lockheed every day except Sundays and holidays. Not hard work but it sure takes a lot of time. Pretty good job though. I don't know how long I'll stay in the Army but probably until Christmas anyhow. Got to see what kind of a job I can get now that I'm out here."

Between July 7th and August 6th Dick logged slightly over four hours of flight time in the P-80, making some 11 test flights in all. As Colonel Langmack previously mentioned, few pilots assigned to the Lockheed Plant were able to build up time in the aircraft due to the lack of available P-80s. By August 1945, however, Dick had well over 1,300 hours of total flight time under his belt, having checked out in over 20 aircraft ranging from P-36s to twin-engine PBY Catalinas.

On August 2, 1945 the fifth fatal Shooting Star crash occurred when a YP-80A exploded in mid-air. At a dinner party three days later Dick shrugged of talk about the latest incident, saying only that he "never worried about those things." Party-goers also recalled that Dick received the third light three times in succession when he, Marge and friends lit cigarettes during the party. The third time this occurred Mr. and Mrs. Henry Fennenbock remembered that Dick held out the match to Marge with a smile and asked her to blow it out, explaining "that'll take off the curse."

Dick and Marge left the restaurant fairly early on August 5th, both aware that tomorrow was the start of another week of test flights. At the Lockheed Plant workers had already prepared a number of Shooting Stars for Monday's schedule, one of them being P-80 serial number 44-85048.

Half a world away, on the Pacific island of Tinian, 20th Air Force personnel were also busy preparing one of their aircraft for a special mission it was scheduled to fly the next day. The aircraft was a B-29 bomber named *Enola Gay* and, like Dick, it too had a date with destiny on August 6, 1945.

An informal shot taken after the October 10, 1944 mission to Balikpapan, showing Dick with George Walker, (1 victory) Wally Jordan (6) and Jerry Johnson (22). The 49th FG was the top-scoring AAF fighter group of World War II and here are four good reasons why it won that honor! (Walker)

A poor quality still showing Dick, General MacArthur and General Kenney (facing MacArthur) immediately after the 49th FG landed at Leyte, November 1944.

Dick and Tom McGuire talk shop during a pause in the fighting over Leyte, November 1944. In terms of personality they were diametric opposites, McGuire being as opinionated and forceful as Dick was quiet and reserved. Both were brilliant fighter pilots in their own right.

The last P-38 Dick regularly flew in combat was an L-1-LO model, serial number 44-23964. The 36 victory flags date the photo as being taken after November 11, 1944. This aircraft was lost at the end of November while being flown by a 49th FG pilot.

On December 12, 1944 Dick was awarded the Medal of Honor by General Douglas MacArthur in a public ceremony at Tacloban, Leyte. Standing immediately behind MacArthur are Kenney and Whitehead.

General Douglas MacArthur congratulates Dick after presenting him with the Medal of Honor on December 12, 1944. MacArthur discarded his prepared text and adlibbed a short speech citing Dick as one "who has ruled the air from New Guinea to the Philippines."

Safely back in the states after two years of combat, Dick poses for a formal photograph. In addition to the Medal of Honor Dick's decorations include the Distinguished Service Cross, Silver Star with Oak Leaf Cluster, Distinguished Flying Cross with six Oak Leaf clusters and numerous Air Medals.

Wedding day, February 10, 1945. Marge and Dick walk down the aisle of Superior's Concordia Lutheran Church as 1,200 people wait outside to greet the newleyweds.

A candid snapshot taken during Dick and Marge's trip to Sequoia National Park, spring 1945.

Although Dick disliked the hoopla that accompanied his growing list of victories, sometimes being the top ace wasn't so bad after all! Wearing a million dollar smile, Dick poses with Beryl Wallace, one of the headliners at Earl Carroll's Hollywood nightclub.

During the war bond and publicity tours Dick undertook while on leave in the States, he flew specially-marked P-38s such as this J-20 model, adorned with the famous photograph of Marge Vattendahl. (Lockheed)

Dick poses with a suitably marked Lightning for a stateside publicity shot. This particular aircraft, a J-20 model, was one of at least two Lightnings used by Dick for Air Force public relations chores.

An official Lockheed photo of an early model P-80 Shooting Star, similar to the one in which Dick lost his life on August 6, 1945.

Lockheed P-38 Lightning as displayed at the Bong Memorial in Poplar, Wisconsin.

Chapter 15

"It Was a Terrible Sight"
(August 6, 1945 and After)

At 2:30 p.m. on August 6, 1945, Dick pointed the nose of P-80 44-85048 down runway 33 at the Lockheed Air Terminal and applied power to the Allison J33 engine. Two minutes later 048 was so much smoldering wreckage scattered about a vacant field between Satsuma Street and Oxnard Boulevard. Dick's body, partially wrapped in the shrouds of his parachute, was found 100 feet from the aircraft's turbine assembly. In an ironic twist of fate Dick had survived two years of combat only to perish on a routine acceptance flight!

Eyewitnesses to Dick's last flight were in general agreement as to what transpired in those few short minutes. Hal Gray, an ex-475th fighter jock who had flown with Dick on Leyte, was visiting Lockheed that day at Dick's urging. Gray recalled that "we were to get together that evening and have dinner together. I had plenty of time so I wandered out on to the flight strip. While I was looking around Dick came out to run his test flight, so I decided to watch.

"On his takeoff there were a number of puffs of black smoke coming out of the tail pipe. It looked like something was haywire to me. He got into the air maybe 300 or 400 feet but the thing still was not operating right. All of a sudden he started to get out of it, then got back in and turned it. He started to get out again and the plane rolled on him. That was the last I saw of him."

Frank Bodenhamer, a Lockheed mechanic, reported that at first Dick's takeoff seemed normal. Bodenhamer, like Hal Gray, realized "there was something wrong when I saw a puff of black smoke just as he leveled off in flight. The right wing tipped. The next thing I knew the escape hatch came off and the plane started to glide and then nosed straight down. A column of smoke went into the air for about 400 feet. It was a terrible sight."[1]

Most witnesses at Lockheed commented on vapor streaming from the P-80's fuselage just as the aircraft lifted off. No vapor or smoke was visible as Dick passed over the runway intersection at an altitude of about 50 feet. As 048 passed over the boundary fence the aircraft appeared to sink briefly before resuming a normal climb. The J33 engine cut off as the aircraft was over Valhalla Memorial Park, but again no smoke or vapor was reported. As the engine cut back in, there was a big puff of smoke followed by a fairly steady stream of vapor or smoke. Dick began a turn to the right and consequently was lost to witnesses at Lockheed.

Mrs. George Zane, a housewife near the scene of the crash, witnessed Dick's last moments. She remembered thiking that "Major Bong obviously was in trouble as he headed toward my house. He was fighting with the plane, dipping first one wing, then the other. He flew over telephone wires and under high tension lines heading toward a vacant lot in a desperate effort to avoid crashing into surrounding houses.[2]

"Thirty feet up there was an explosion that shook the whole neighborhood. Then smoke poured from the plane. I saw Major Bong jump out, holding both hands above his head. He jumped on the side of the plane that faced me. I could plainly see him trying to free himself from the plane. Then the smoke swept over him."[3]

Lieutenant Colonel Langmack had a somewhat different view. Langmack was in a C-47 staff ship "parked near the intersection off the east-west/north-south runways. I was still looking over or checking a few things on my airplane when Richard Bong went by on takeoff run. I watched; he cleared the boundary O.K. and then just a second or two later, the engine quit just as he had started a very shallow right turn at 50 or 60 feet altitude and nowhere near efficient climbing speed. Within a split second after the engine quit, the P-80 stalled and went in at a very steep angle, striking the ground with terrific impact and fuel explosion.

Lockheed's Wayne Pryor supplied further details on the crash in a letter to the authors. Pryor noted that "the airplane hit in a nose-down position and scattered pieces all over the area, including fuel, and there was a brief flash fire. The theory is that Major Bong had yanked the ripcord as a sort of desperation move just moments before impact. The chute pack was open and the chute had streamed but not blossomed. Apparently he hit just as the chute deployed because the canopy had burned while still folded.

"The shrouds had not spread. They were still wrapped together as an almost solid mass. A chute where the canopy has opened has a regular spider web of shroud lines, widely separated. It is even possible that the ripcord could have hooked on something as Major Bong was hurled from the cockpit and deployed the chute but it is more likely that he pulled it. He had jettisoned the canopy and was apparently starting to get out but was far too low and too late.

"Things happened much faster in a jet than in a piston engine plane. The glide angle is that of a greased brick and the rate of sink is fierce."

Initially some were unsure of the identity of the pilot of the doomed aircraft. Two P-80s had been aloft at the time of the crash, the other being piloted by Captain Ray Crawford. Ironically, Dick had asked Crawford to test the ship assigned to him because he had an afternoon golf date with Bing Crosby. When Dick realized he had left his golf shoes at home he canceled out only to discover Crawford had already taken off. Dick then decided to return the favor by testing the aircraft assigned to Crawford. It was only after Crawford had taxied in, after being ordered to land, that some learned the news.

Marge heard of the crash over the radio and called Lockheed in the vain hope that the reports were in error. She could only listen numbly as the Air Force Officer at Lockheed confirmed that Dick had been killed. Colonel Langmack later gave her further details of Dick's flight.

Radio carried the news quickly. Dick's parents were visiting friends in Superior when they heard the reports. They drove to the Vattendahl household and talked quietly for a few minutes before leaving for Poplar. News of Dick's death struck home for people in Poplar and elsewhere. After surviving so many months of combat his death seemed tragic and needless. Calls flooded the news rooms of radio stations and newspapers to confirm the reports. The feelings of many people were perhaps best summarized by an unidentified *Milwaukee Sentinel* reader who called in and poignantly stated: "I thought he was safe now."

Even as the shocking news was going out Lockheed reacted organizing a crash investigating committee which included representatives from the Air Force, General Electric and Allison. The remainder of the afternoon was spent examining the crash site after which the wreckage was transported to Building 352 at the Lockheed Terminal.

Dick's death was to prove the last straw in the trouble-plagued P-80 program. On August 7th, even as the committee was meeting, the order came down that no further flying was to be done with the P-80 until a thorough investigation was made of all fatal P-80 flights and corrective steps instituted. The Shooting Star was grounded!

The crash committee went about its investigation in a systematic fashion. The wreckage was thoroughly examined with various pieces of equipment being disassembled and sent for further testing. Over 25 witnesses were called to testify. Tests simulating different takeoffs, conducted before several of these witnesses, were run to determine if similar circumstances had happened on August 6th. Additionally, tests would be undertaken at Muroc Test Base to investigate other possible contributing factors to the crash.

Shortly after 8:30 a.m., on August 8th, 1945, the C-54 transport bearing Dick's coffin arrived at the Duluth airport. Over 1,000 people were on hand as the transport taxied in and shut down its engines. As Marge stepped from the aircraft she recognized familiar, loving faces clustered at the front of the crowd. Her parents were there and Dick's dad with some of the huge Bong tribe - Jerry, Nelda and Bud. Mrs. Glen Bryce, Dick's grandmother, was there too. Lost in their own thoughts, they could only watch heartsick as the casket was removed from the aircraft for its journey to the Downs mortuary in Superior.

Dick's body lay in state at the Concordia Lutheran Church from 11 a.m. until the service at 2 p.m., an honor guard in constant attendance. The church was filled to capacity long before Marge and the Vattendahl and Bong families arrived for the ceremony. Some people were in their work clothes, having stopped in the middle of their farm work to pay last respects to one of their own. Reverend Paul Boe, who had married Dick and Marge barely six months ago, and Reverend Arvid Hoorn, pastor of Bethany Lutheran Church in Poplar, officiated at the service.

As requested by the family, the church service was brief. Reverend Boe conducted the altar ceremonies and read verses from the Bible. Before giving the sermon Reverend Hoorn gave a simple but moving eulogy of Dick, recalling that he had confirmed Dick some nine years ago. Hoorn remembered Dick "was never one to do much talking or to intrude himself upon others. He was not much for sentimentality but to him everything was real. So also in his religion. He seldom made an open show of it but as we learned to know him, we rather sensed the hidden power and faith."

Drawing his inspiration from Romans 8, verses 38-39, Hoorn told the mourners that "even though his years were not many, yet he lived and lived well. Lived strenuously. Whether at play or at work he put his whole heart into it. The calm peaceful life of the tiller of the soil, the active arduous life of the huntsman. In these last three years he met life in its most tragic aspect. Surely he knew life."

Thousands of onlookers lined the funeral route as the 30-car procession left Concordia Lutheran to take Dick home to Poplar. At Poplar the procession was met by a military band, a color guard, an honor guard and contingents from the VFW and American Legion. With the Army band playing the funeral march, the procession turned off Highway 2 and slowly wended its way through the green Wisconsin countryside southeast of town to the Poplar Cemetery.

Despite the military presence, the graveside rites were simple and straightforward, as befitted the man. As the mourners assembled at graveside a cloud passed acrossed the face of the sun, giving temporary relief from the hot August rays. Drawing upon the 91st Psalm, Reverend Hoorn reassured Dick's family and friends that "he that dwelleth in the secret place of the Most High shall abide under the shadow of the Almighty. I will say of the Lord, He is my refuge and my fortress; in him will I trust."

As Reverend Hoorn finished his remarks 18 P-47 Thunderbolts roared over the cemetery, briefly dipping their wings in an airman's salute to a fellow pilot. Following the Lord's Prayer and a volley from the honor guard, the mournful notes of "Taps" sounded over the hillside. At the conclusion of the service a brief silence fell over the gathering, broken only by the rippling sounds made by the nearby Poplar River. Marge, clutching the flag that had been draped over Dick's coffin, was led away. Overhead the P-47s circled one last time and then banked away to the west, the thunder of their engines steadily dwindling as the mourners made their way from the graveside.

Despite the atomic bombings of Hiroshima and Negasaki and rumors of imminent Japanese surrender, newspapers continued to give Dick's death front-page coverage. Increasingly such stories began taking on a vehement tone as details of the problem-plagued P-80 program leaked out. On August 9th, for instance, the *Los Angeles Examiner* ran a front-page editorial entitled "Irreplaceable Loss." In the editorial the paper ripped Air Force commanders for the "arbitrary methods by which they assign irreplaceable personnel" and flatly declared Dick "should never have been assigned to the hazardous duty in which he met death." Various public officials, including Wisconsin Senator Alexander Wiley, demanded an investigation into Dick's assignment to test pilot duties and the circumstances that led to his death. (In fairness to AAF officials it should be noted that Dick's assignment to the P-80 program was at his own request and that of General Kenney. In its reply to Wiley the War Department stated it would have been "arbitrary and presumptive" to have forbidden Dick to fly the P-80 since it was an assignment "eagerly sought" by him.)

Against the backdrop of hue and cry, the crash investigating committee at Lockheed continued its methodical search for the cause of Dick's crash. Initial speculation had centered on a combination of mechanical failure compounded by human error. In many respects Dick's crash resembled that of Milo Burcham, who was killed on October 20, 1944. Burcham's crash had been attributed to two factors - a sheared drive shaft which resulted in loss of fuel pressure and a faulty overspeed governor, a device which limits engine rpm. Some felt governor failure might have been the culprit in Dick's crash. Yet Lockheed engineers had designed a backup system to serve as a source of fuel pressure in an emergency and Dick's P-80 had that I-16 fuel pump installed as of August 6th. The I-16 system should have worked as advertised on the 6th but it hadn't. What went wrong?

On August 11th the investigating committee summarized its preliminary findings in a document entitled *Review of Bong Crash Investigation Proceedings up to August 11th,* copies of which were furnished to the authors by Wayne Pryor. They set forth a number of facts, among them the following:

1. There was no evidence of fire in the plenum chamber.
2. There was probably no cockpit fire.
3. There was no fire in the aft fuselage, as burning was from the outside in.
4. The I-16 electrically driven pump was hooked up and could be operated.
5. The basic engine was satisfactory.
6. The plane was controllable.
7. The engine cut out or reduced power sharply, but resumed power and perhaps at low thrust.
8. Take-off speed apparently was maintained for approximately 6,000 feet, the length of the runway. (The climb was steeper and the technique employed by Major Bong in making a right turn was sharper than his usual practice.)
9. Some fuel was observed coming out of a vent, both during take-off and after the ship became airborne.
10. The pilot jumped after releasing the canopy.
11. The landing gear was retracted.
12. The flaps were extended.
13. The plane was flying slowly at the top of its climb and may have stalled.
14. Fuel had been checked and indicated a total of 420 gallons, inluding the leading edge tanks.
15. Previous flights had been satisfactory. (AUTHORS' NOTE: The statements given in this rather lengthy section detailed the aircraft's history and discussed various engine parts. They can be summarized as follows: (a) Total time on Dick's P-80 had been 1:35, only one previous flight, by Lockheed, having been made. Complaints regarding the aircraft had been slight. (b) A new Bendix barometric had been installed prior to Dick's flight. The unit's governor had not been dump-checked immediately prior to Dick's flight. Like the barometric unit, the governor had also been a replacement unit. (c) Prior to Dick's flight engine idling had been set at 3900 rpm. Additionally, a tail pipe extension modification had been made.)
16. The aircraft involved in the crash was a P-80, Lockheed No. 1071, A.A.F. No. 44-85048, having installed in it Allison J33 engine No. A-070757.
17. A.A.F. inspector stated the I-16 electrically driven fuel pump cockpit switch was not in the "on" position when he stepped from the wing of the airplane in the starting area prior to Bong's takeoff; however, it might have been turned on by the pilot prior to his actual take-off.
18. No wingtip drop tanks were used.

Several points regarding the committee's report need to be examined. A number of witnesses had reported noticing a discharge coming from Dick's P-80 during its flight, this being variously reported as "white fumes," "white smoke" and "puffs of black smoke." Lockheed, assuming this vapor may have been fuel venting from a tank which had gotten inside the fuselage of Dick's aircraft, tested the theory at Muroc Lake. The right inboard wing tank of another P-80 was filled with a special water and dye solution. The tank's filler cap was removed and the cap cover left unfastened. During the take-off tests that followed, under normal flight conditions, the solution did not enter the fuselage nor did it "impinge on the engine at all." Thus the committee's statement that "some fuel was observed coming out of a vent" does not adequately reflect the views of the eyewitnesses nor the results of Lockheed's own tests at Muroc Lake.[4]

Likewise, tests were undertaken which simulated take-off conditions should the governor dump on take-off, both with the I-16 pump turned on and with the unit switched off. Again the major aim in these tests, flown by Tony LeVier, was to duplicate the conditions of Dick's last flight. Unfortunately, despite five test runs, most of the eyewitnesses reported little similarity to what they witnessed on August 6th.

The committee was quite frank in its report, going on to admit that "on tests that have been made to date, none have been very enlightening as to any unsatisfactory condition that might have contributed to the crash" and that "no definite conclusion as to the exact reason for the crash has been determined." The committee felt that "the basic engine was satisfactory. Various minor defects were noted but none of these were considered contributing factors to the accident." In its discussion of the I-16 unit, the committee concluded "that the (I-16) pump had been hooked up and was in operating condition prior to the crash (whether it was used or not by the pilot remains questionable.)"

Tests run on the I-16 unit from Dick's aircraft seem to undermine the comment regarding the aircraft's engine. The motor and pump assembly was recovered and adjudged "not damaged by fire." Investigators reported that "about four cc of loose dirt was removed from gear box end of motor by shaking," a curious finding since the gear box is an enclosed unit. The same investigators reported that the assembled pump and motor "were operated manually and appeared to be free and operable." The units were tested, "operated electrically with fuel in pump but at no pressure. Flow was about 3100/hr and 50 psi approximate. Motor current was about 30 amps for about ten seconds at which time the current started to increase to approximately 80 amps and *smoke issued from motor* (italics added). It was then shut down. The process was repeated and with the same result in about 15 seconds, causing *motor to smoke* at which time it was shut down (italics added).

Examination of the motor by the manufacturer, Electrical Engr. & Mfg. Co., revealed "a misalignment of commutater and bell along with slight separation of about .040 inch," which probably caused rubbing on the field laminations. When the unit was run at normal voltage, "it started to smoke and sound of motor indicated that it was under heavy load." Following motor disassembly, it was found that the commutator end laminations had been rubbing on the field laminations. Is it possible that the smoke or vapor reported by several witnesses of the take-off was, in fact, smoke being emitted from the electric motor driving the I-16 fuel pump? If such a malfunction had occurred and Dick had spotted it, he may have switched off the motor or cut power. That, of course, is pure speculation.

In its deliberations the committee concentrated on the mechanical aspects of the crash. The possibility of pilot error was implied in several statements in the August 11th report (i.e., the I-16 pump "had been hooked up ... whether it was used or not by the pilot remains questionable."). However, no hard evidence was introduced to support that theory.

After much discussion and testing, the crash investigating committee was unable to pinpoint the exact reasons for Dick's crash on August 6, 1945. There are no final conclusions drawn in the August 11th report, nor in any other documents furnished to the authors by Lockheed. Nor do the authors claim to have the final verdict on what caused Dick's crash. The commonly-cited cause of the crash is given as power-plant failure and there the matter rests.

Although an immediate explanation of Dick's crash was not forthcoming, the P-80 grounding order was partially lifted on September 1, 1945. Following accelerated service tests begun on September 24th, the grounding order on all P-80s was lifted with the proviso that all P-80s be equipped with certain engineering modifications found in test aircraft. This program had barely gotten underway when all P-80s equipped with Allison J33-9 engines were grounded until further notice. The Shooting Star program was in trouble once again. The further tribulations of the P-80 program lie outside the scope of this book. Suffice it to say that the Lockheed P-80 Shooting Star survived its problem-plagued beginnings to become an effective fighter that served its country for many years.

* *

Then as now, Dick's death seemed a senseless tragedy. Yet he died performing a job he had eagerly sought, an assignment which enabled him to fly the one American aircraft that pushed the aeronautical technology of the day to its limit. In short, it seemed an ideal position for a man who loved flying and Lockheed aircraft. After repeatedly facing death in Pacific skies it was grimly ironic that he should perish on a routine test flight. The tragic manner of his death, however, does not detract from the legacy of service to country that Dick left in his stead. During the years he fought for his country Dick had received every major American decoration for bravery, been lionized by the press and public and been cited by Douglas MacArthur. Dick took it all in stride, insisting his success had been more a matter of luck than ability. In some respects, that ability to keep his wits about him despite all the acclaim is perhaps the best measure of the man. He disliked being referred to as a hero or as a "Jap killer." Dick did not regard himself as either. Yet it would seem that, in those last moments over Burbank, fighting to pilot his crippled aircraft away from innocent civilians, Dick Bong demonstrated once and for all that he was indeed "one of the bravest of the brave."

Epilogue

"There is a Time for Patriots"
Jay Reed

They don't talk about Dick Bong up in Poplar, Wis., much, anymore. Nor over in Superior. A lot of the people who knew him are dead and the wind whines around their graves now just as it does around his.

They play rock-and-roll music in the Poplar Cafe and they gather in the hardware store to damn the Department of Natural Resources or to purchase nails or to compare crops. They buy their supplies of groceries in the Poplar Market and they do their financial business at the Poplar State Bank.

And once in a while, they drive around the block off Highway 2 and pass beside the red-brick school building and the silver, twin-tailed airplane that stands nearby as a monument to a local boy who made it big long ago.

Major Richard Ira Bong, the greatest fighter pilot in American military history and a 21-jeweled honest-to-God Wisconsin hero, is a fading memory in the state that spawned him.

There is no intent here to take to task the tendency of people to forget. That is human and, perhaps, even merciful. It just happens that Poplar, Wis., and, more specifically, the Richard I. Bong Memorial in Poplar, is one of my favorite places.

Dick Bong was of another time, another generation, and they would measure him square now. He came from nowhere. He lived on a farm. He knew more about tractors than cars. He played the clarinet and he sang in the church choir. He went to war without once chanting, "Hell, no, we won't go."

He came home from that war. He courted a girl and married her. He hated to make a public speech. The only time he ever went to a rally was when they gave him another medal. He washed windows instead of breaking them. Bread, to him, was something you toasted and ate for breakfast. The only establishment he knew about was the groundcrew that serviced his airplane.

The only thing Dick Bong knew about getting high was to crawl in an airplane and fly it as far into the clouds as it would go. Getting busted had nothing to do with the law. It meant dropping a grade in rank. He wouldn't know about "patching out" because there's no way to do it with a tractor but, Lordy, how he could fly a high performance airplane.

That's what he did best. Better, in fact, than any American before him or since.

Back during the "Big War," World War II, the war that was supposed to end all wars, he shot down 40 Japanese airplanes in high-sky combat and he would have had more if they hadn't desked him from time to time. He was and is America's ace of aces. He became a national hero, acclaimed as few men have ever been acclaimed.

That's the reason for the Bong Memorial, you see. And it is the reason why I envy the children who go to school in the building abutting the memorial.

These kids, nameless and faceless to me, are getting the foundation for their education in the shadow cast by a ghost who lived in days when America adored its sons who lived by the gun in the name of patriotism.

They can, if they wish, when their regular day of learning is ended, stroll into the little room at the end of the building and see all that remains of the stubby, pink-cheeked young man who once stood a hundred feet tall in the eyes of America. That's a large plus factor in any educational process, whether those children know it or not. They are the sons and daughters of men and women who maybe didn't even know Dick Bong, so perhaps the room with its green chairs and blue-brown tile floor and registration book and glassed showcase doesn't really mean very much.

But, if you are in the middle years or older, it just may be that a trip to the Bong Memorial will do something for you. Maybe it might do something for anyone who has lost faith in this land.

Go there, then, and if you care enough . . .

The first thing you'll see once you walk through the double doors is the bronze plaque that honors the men of Poplar who went to war. You'll see that three of the names have stars emblazoned before them, showing that they were killed. There's Lawrence Hofstedt, for instance, and there is Dale Falk.

Then there is Richard I. Bong.

No man can tell how it was that Hofstedt and Falk died. But there is much to see and know and learn of the man that once was Dick Bong. There is his uniform for an opener. There is the crushed hat that fliers of that era wore with distinguished pride. And there are the decorations. He was awarded 26 in all.

There is the Medal of Honor, and there is the Silver Star and the Distinguished Service Cross and the Distinguished Flying Cross and the Air Medal, and there are the citations which accompanied each of them.

There are pictures and news clippings and items of equipment. And there are fragments of metal which came from the plane in which Bong died.

There are all of these things and much, much more plus a thousand memories for those who remember how it was in those days.

If you are from Milwaukee, you might remember how it was that day in January of 1945 when the city came to a halt to honor the Wisconsin war hero. Or maybe you'll remember how it was when the newspaper carried almost daily accounts of the farm boy as he was shooting his way to a 40-kill record.

Maybe you'll remember the cheers when he came home to hunt for deer and claim a bride.

Or maybe you'll remember August 6, 1945, when Dick Bong died. Maybe you'll remember the disbelief and shock in your heart when you heard how this Wisconsin son who had so recently been in your midst died when a jet plane he was testing exploded over Burbank, Calif.

If all that is not enough, you'll see outside the P-38 fighter plane, the type Bong flew to immortality. If you are observant, you'll note the yellow tips on the black, twin props. You'll see the 40 stamp-sized replicas of the Imperial Japanese Rising Sun flag. And you'll see the number of his ship: 2103993.

Look off in the distance, beyond the airplane, and you'll see the fields where Dick Bong worked, the streets where he played, the skies where he learned to fly, the woods where he hunted.

And maybe - just maybe - you'll feel an old throb in your heart, a tug at the elbow of your soul that reminds there is a time for patriots, for farmboy heroes who laugh at death and do something for the entire world.

NOTE: This article is reprinted by permission of the *Milwaukee Journal* in which it originally appeared.

Notes

CHAPTER TWO

1. To avoid confusion young Carl was nicknamed "Bud."

CHAPTER THREE

1. Quoted in Willard Wiener's *Two Hundred Thousand Flyers*, Infantry Journal Pub., 1945.
2. The Army Air Corps was redesignated the Army Air Force in June 1941.
3. Copyright © 1944 by King Features Syndicate. Reprinted by permission.

CHAPTER FOUR

1. Reprinted by permission of Zenger Publishing.

CHAPTER FIVE

1. To help facilitate identification of Japanese aircraft a list of code names was devised by Fifth Air Force's Technical Air Intelligence Unit in the fall of 1942. Japanese fighters were assigned masculine names such as Zeke, Tony, Nick and Oscar. Bombers had feminine names like Betty, Sally, Kate and Val. Other types of aircraft were handled in similar fashion.
2. The "Type 1" designation was another method used by the Allies to identify Japanese aircraft. Nakajima Ki-43 Oscars were also known as "Type 1" fighters. Nakajima Ki-44 Tojos were "Type 2" fighters while Kawasaki Ki-61 Tonys were "Type 3" and so on. During the early months of the war, Mitsubishi Zekes and Nakajima Oscars were frequently mistaken for each other, both being referred to as "Zeros."
3. Dr. Frank Olynyk of Aurora, Ohio has resolved part of the uncertainty surrounding the P-38s Dick flew in the 39th FS. For more details, refer to Appendix C.

CHAPTER SIX

1. Air Force Historical Study #85 credits the 49th Fighter Group with 673 confirmed victories as follows:

Headquarters	28
7th FS	178
8th FS	206
9th FS	261

Other unofficial sources credit the 49th FG and 9th FS as having 697 and 271 victories respectively.
2. The "Hamp" designation referred to a Model 32 Mitsubishi Zero fighter. The original Model 21 Zero fighters ("Zekes") had rounded wingtips, the Model 32 had squared-off wingtips.

Notes

CHAPTER EIGHT

1. Dick was promoted to Captain on August 24, 1943.

CHAPTER NINE

1. Reprinted by permission of William Morris Agency.
2. Reprinted by permission.

CHAPTER TEN

1. Dick had 25 victory flags painted on *Marge* because he had downed an Oscar on March 5th, a claim later downgraded to probable status. Dick's 25th *official* kill did not come until April 3, 1944.
2. Boyington had actually broken the record in January but was then shot down along with his wingman. Since no other American witnessed Boyington's last combat his score officially stood at 26.
3. Although Dick stated he had three probables, in fact he was credited with five at this time: two Oscars and three Bettys between January 7th and September 6th. During his subsequent tours he added three more Oscars to the list of probables.

CHAPTER ELEVEN

1. The 80th FS also had cause to celebrate after the mission, since its total score now stood at 203 confirmed kills. The "Headhunters" thus became the first AAF squadron in any theater to surpass 200 victories. Their opponents on April 12th were apparently from the 77th *Sentai*. Interestingly enough, Dick's victories were credited to Fifth Fighter Command rather than the 80th FS.
2. Kenney's action was quite unusual in that normally the commander of an air force did not go to such lengths to help an individual pilot under his command. Apparently this was the only time Kenney took such action on behalf of one of his pilots. Although the gesture was magnanimous, it left Kenney open to charges of playing favorites.
3. Copyright © 1944 by the New York Times. Reprinted by permission.
4. Reprinted with permission of United Press International, Inc.
5. In early May Hollandia fell to the Americans. Kenney kept his promise to Dick and sent a diver down in the area where Dick said his 28th kill lay. The diver found the Oscar and Kenney had orders cut belatedly confirming Dick's 28th victory.
6. Reprinted with permission of the Milwaukee Journal.
7. The early P-80s were tested at Muroc Field, later renamed Edwards Air Force Base.

CHAPTER TWELVE

1. The kills scored on the 10th pushed the 9th FS score over the 200 mark.
2. Walter Simmons, Chicago Tribune, Nov. 14, 1944, quoted with permission.
3. On the 29th Dick told his family that it "looks like I'm kind of out (of it) as far as flying goes because somebody wrecked my airplane yesterday. It was a good airplane and I got eight Nips with it. Had 36 flags painted on it but no picture of Marge because I haven't been able to get one blown up yet."

CHAPTER THIRTEEN

1. The advantages and disadvantages of freelancing versus command of a squadron were also discussed in Chapter 10.
2. Dick's tactics during this mission and the mission on December 7th were criticized by some members of McGuire's squadron. The mission summary report for the December 17th mission included a comment by the assistant intelligence officer that "though the flight was successful in destruction of both of the e/a, good flying technique was neglected when the leading flight separated, thus forcing the second element to

separate to protect them." The 431st FS history for December 1944 is even harsher. The history noted that on December 7th Dick attacked a Sally bomber before calling it in. On the 17th both Dick and Major Rittmayer were criticized for breaking flight integrity. The history concluded with the comment that "those (visiting) pilots... seemed more interested in running up their individual scores than in protecting themselves and their flight members and following our standard operating procedures." It is uncertain how justified these criticisms were.

CHAPTER FOURTEEN

1. Major Jack Rittmayer, who had flown Dick's wing in December 1944, was also killed in this combat.
2. The top Navy ace, Commander David McCampbell, had logged his 30th kill on October 24th, 1944, briefly tying the record. Dick claimed his 31st on October 27th and thereafter held the U.S. title exclusively. McCampbell finished with 34.

CHAPTER FIFTEEN

1. Reprinted by permission of the Milwaukee Sentinel.
2. The vacant lot Mrs. Zane referred to was actually a right of way for Pacific Electric high voltage transmission lines.
3. Reprinted by permission of the Milwaukee Sentinel.
4. Subsequent tests held at Lynn on August 18, 1945 were partially successful in reproducing the smoke reported in Dick's crash. At certain rpm settings closing the fuel stopcock for several seconds followed by re-opening the stopcock produced white smoke. Likewise closing and re-opening the stopcock followed by ignition to recover the unit, at certain rpm settings, produced white smoke.

Appendix A

Decorations and Promotions of Major Richard I. Bong

Decorations

Medal of Honor (awarded December 8, 1944)
Distinguished Service Cross (awarded October 20, 1943)
Silver Star (awarded January 24, 1943)
    Oak Leaf Cluster (awarded November 19, 1943)
Distinguished Flying Cross (awarded June 14, 1943)
    First Oak Leaf Cluster (awarded June 28, 1943)
    Second Oak Leaf Cluster (awarded February 22, 1944)
    Third Oak Leaf Cluster (awarded March 1, 1944)
    Fourth Oak Leaf Cluster (awarded March 15, 1944)
    Fifth & Sixth Clusters (awarded December 28, 1944)
Air Medal (awarded April 23, 1943)
    First Oak Leaf Cluster (awarded August 26, 1943)
    Second-Ninth Oak Leaf Clusters (awarded November 19, 1943)
    Tenth Oak Leaf Cluster (awarded March 2, 1944)
    Eleventh Oak Leaf Cluster (awarded March 11, 1944)
    Twelfth Oak Leaf Cluster (awarded April 28, 1944)
    Thirteenth & Fourteenth Clusters (awarded December 28, 1944)
American Campaign Medal
American Defense Service Medal
Asiatic-Pacific Campaign Medal (with one Silver Service Star for participation in the Leyte, Luzon, New Guinea, Northern Solomons, and Papua Campaigns)
Philippine Independence Ribbon
Philippine Liberation Ribbon (with one Bronze Service Star)
    Philippine Republic Presidential Unit Citation Emblem
World War II Victory Medal
Australian Distinguished Flying Cross
Distinguished Unit Citation (with one Oak Leaf Cluster). Awarded to 49th FG.

Promotions

Flying Cadet	May 29, 1941
Second Lieutenant	January 9, 1942
First Lieutenant	April 6, 1943
Captain	August 24, 1943
Major	April 12, 1944

Appendix B

Combat Record of Major Richard I. Bong

(Based on Combat Reports Filed)

FIRST TOUR: December 1942 - November 1943

Date	Location	Enemy Aircraft	Own Aircraft
12/27/42	Buna/Cape Endaiadere, New Guinea	1 Aichi D3A "Val" Dest. 1 Mitsubishi A6M "Zeke" Dest.	P-38F #15 *Thumper*: One hit/Left engine (s/n 42-12664)
12/31/42	Lae, N.G.	1 Mitsubishi A6M "Zeke" Dam.	P-38F (s/n 42-12624)
1/7/43	Huon Gulf, N.G. (Two missions)	2 Nakajima Ki-43 "Oscars" Dest. 1 Nakajima Ki-43 "Oscar" Prob.	P-38F: Two .30 caliber hits/Right Boom (s/n 42-12664)
1/8/43	Lae, N.G.	1 Nakajima Ki-43 "Oscar" Dest.	P-38F *Thumper* (s/n 42-12664)
3/3/43	Huon Gulf, N.G.	1 Nakajima Ki-43 "Oscar" Dest. 1 Nakajima Ki-43 "Oscar" Dam.	P-38G-5
3/11/43	Dobodura/Bismarck Sea, N.G.	2 Nakajima Ki-43 "Oscars" Dest. 1 Nakajima Ki-43 "Oscar" Prob. 1 Mitsubishi G4M "Betty" Dam.	P-38G-5: Damage to left engine/wing.
3/29/43	Bismarck Sea, N.G.	1 Mitsubishi Ki-46 "Dinah" Dest.	P-38G-5
4/14/43	Cape Frere/Milne Bay, N.G.	1 Mitsubishi G4M "Betty" Dest. 1 Mitsubishi G4M "Betty" Prob.	P-38G-5: Single 20mm hit in elevator.
6/12/43	Bena Bena, N.G.	1 Nakajima Ki-43 "Oscar" Dest. 1 Nakajima Ki-43 "Oscar" Dam.	P-38G-5: Damage to both wings, hydraulic system and right tire.
7/26/43	Markham Valley, N.G.	2 Mitsubishi A6M "Zekes" Dest. 2 Kawasaki Ki-61 "Tonys" Dest.	P-38G-5

Combat Record of Major Richard I. Bong

Date	Location	Enemy Aircraft	Own Aircraft
7/28/43	Rein Bay, N.G.	1 Nakajima Ki-43 "Oscar" Dest.	P-38G-5 #73: Damage to aircraft.
9/6/43	Lae/Morobe, N.G.	2 Mitsubishi G4M "Bettys" Prob.	P-38H-1: Damage to right engine. (Crash-landed at Marilinan.)
10/2/43	Gasmata, New Britain	1 Mitsubishi Ki-46 "Dinah" Dest.	P-38H
10/29/43	Rabaul, N.B.	2 Mitsubishi A6M "Zekes" Dest. 1 Mitsubishi A6M "Zeke" Dam.	P-38H
11/5/43	Rabaul, N.B.	2 Mitsubishi A6M "Zekes" Dest.	P-38H-5 #79

SECOND TOUR: February 1944 - April 1944

Date	Location	Enemy Aircraft	Own Aircraft
2/15/44	Cape Hoskins, N.B	1 Kawasaki Ki-61 "Tony" Dest.	P-38J-15-LO *Marge* (s/n 42-103993)
2/28/44	Wewak, N.G.	1 Mitsubishi G4M "Betty" Dest. (GROUND KILL)	P-38J-15-LO *Marge* (s/n 42-103993)
3/3/44	Tadji, N.G.	2 Mitsubishi Ki-21 "Sallys" Dest. 1 Kawasaki Ki-61 "Tony" Dam.	P-38J-15-LO *Marge* (s/n 42-103993)
3/5/44	Dagua/Wewak, N.G.	1 Nakajima Ki-43 "Oscar" Prob. 1 Nakajima Ki-43 "Oscar" Dam.	P-38J-15-LO *Marge* (s/n 42-103993)
4/3/44	Hollandia, N.G.	1 Nakajima Ki-43 "Oscar" Dest.	P-38J
4/12/44	Hollandia/Tannemerah, N.G.	3 Nakajima Ki-43 "Oscars" Dest. 2 Nakajima Ki-43 "Oscars" Prob.	P-38J-15-LO *Down Beat* (s/n 42-104012)

THIRD TOUR: October 1944 - December 1944

Date	Location	Enemy Aircraft	Own Aircraft
10/10/44	Balikpapan, Borneo	1 Nakajima J1N1 "Irving" Dest. 1 Nakajima Ki-43 "Oscar" Dest.	P-38L-1-LO (s/n 44-23964)
10/27/44	Tacloban, Philippine Islands	1 Nakajima Ki-43 "Oscar" Dest. 1 Nakajima Ki-43 "Oscar" Dam.	P-38J
10/28/44	Leyte/Masbate Island, P.I.	2 Nakajima Ki-43 "Oscars" Dest. 2 Nakajima Ki-43 "Oscars" Dam.	P-38-1-LO: Damage to left engine. (s/n 44-23964)
11/10/44	Ormoc Bay, P.I.	1 Nakajima Ki-43 "Oscar" Dest. 1 Nakajima Ki-43 "Oscar" Dam.	P-38L-1-LO (s/n 44-23964)

Date	Location	Enemy Aircraft	Own Aircraft
11/11/44	Ormoc Bay, P.I.	2 Mitsubishi A6M "Zekes" Dest.	P-38L-1-LO (s/n 44-23964)
12/7/44	Bohol Isl./Ormoc Bay, P.I.	1 Mitsubishi Ki-21 "Sally" Dest. 1 Nakajima Ki-44 "Tojo" Dest.	P-38L-1
12/15/44	Panubulon Isl., P.I.	1 Nakajima Ki-43 "Oscar" Dest.	P-38L-1
12/17/44	San Jose, P.I.	1 Nakajima Ki-43 "Oscar" Dest.	P-38L-1

For the record, Dick shot at some 88 airborne enemy aircraft, as mentioned in his letters and encounter reports. He hit 58 (counting probables and damaged) and destroyed 40. In other words, he hit 66% of his targets and destroyed 60% of those he hit.

A breakdown of Dick's claims by tours shows how he improved in his two years at war, from December 1942 to December 1944.

	Destroyed	Probables	Damaged	Missed	TOTAL	
First tour	21	5	5	26	57	(54% hits)
Second tour	7	2	2	1	12	(91% hits)
Third tour	12	0	4	3	19	(84% hits)
TOTAL	40	7	11	30	88	(66% hits)

P-38F	5 victories
P-38G	11 victories
P-38H	5 victories
P-38J	7 victories
P-38L	12 victories

Appendix C

Aircraft Flown by Major Richard I. Bong

One of the intriguing questions regarding Dick's career is how many P-38s he used to run up his total of 40 victories. Several articles have appeared over the years, but they are woefully inaccurate. The generally-accepted number is three P-38s, but in fact Dick flew several other Lightnings in combat. Unfortunately, like most fighter pilots, Dick rarely identified the aircraft he used on a specific mission, so the true figure may never be known. From various sources, however, we can present the following summary.

Dick scored his first victories on December 27, 1942 while flying a 39th FS P-38F (serial number 42-12664) named *Thumper*. This aircraft was assigned to Lieutenant John "Shady" Lane. It was painted in standard Army Air Force camouflage of medium green with neutral gray undersurface. Its squadron number was 15, painted in white on both sides of the nose.

Many of the 39th FS P-38s had shark's teeth painted on the engine nacelles, *Thumper* carrying that decoration only on its right engine on December 27th, since the crew chief had been too busy to complete the painting. Dick also flew *Thumper*, apparently, on January 8th, 1943.

On December 31st and January 7th he used a different P-38F, serial number 42-12624. But no other information is available on this second Lightning.

Beginning on March 3, 1943 Dick scored victories while flying one or more P-38G-5 models. March 11th was the only exception, when Dick used a G-15 variant to claim his seventh and eighth victories during the wild scramble over Dobodura. Dick may have flown the same P-38G-5 on later missions. Although his logbook lists damage to the aircraft he flew on different missions there was a time gap between each successful mission which would have enabled the damage to be repaired.

Dick's first claims while flying an H model P-38 were made on September 6, 1943, the aircraft being listed as a P-38H-1. This may have been the aircraft featured in the photos showing Dick standing next to a P-38 with 16 kill markings. Unfortunately in the photos available the serial number of this aircraft is covered by a kill flag. The model designation is also obscured but appears to be P-38H-1.

In October and November 1943 Dick scored five kills, running his total to 21 victories. On October 2nd and 29th he claimed three kills while flying an aircraft listed only as a P-38H. On November 5th he flew a P-38H-5 on a mission to Rabaul, claiming two Zeros destroyed. During early November Dick flew three missions, all at the controls of an H-5 model. In all probability this was aircraft number 79, illustrated elsewhere in this book. Its serial number is unknown.

During his abbreviated second tour Dick claimed all his victories while flying P-38Js. From the evidence available, Dick probably used *Marge*, a P-38J-15-LO s/n 42-103993, to claim his 22nd, 23rd and 24th kills. Dick never scored a victory with this P-38 after he had the special *Marge* markings put on it. Photographs showing the *Marge* aircraft with twenty-five kill markings have led some to conclude that Dick flew the aircraft at least up through April 3, 1944 when he scored his 25th kill. As previously related, however, *Marge* was lost on March 24th while being flown by Lieutenant Tom Malone. The 25th kill flag on *Marge* probably indicated Dick's claim for one Oscar destroyed on March 5, 1944, a claim that was changed to probable status due to lack of eyewitnesses.

It has also been alleged that Dick flew a P-38J-15-LO, s/n 42-104380, on April 12, 1944 when he broke Eddie Rickenbacker's record of 26 kills. The only eyewitnesses to this historic flight whom the authors could locate indicated otherwise, stating that Dick flew William Caldwell's *Down Beat* on April 12th. This aircraft was a P-38J-15-LO, s/n 42-104012, which carried the code-letter "T" on its nose. It was assigned to the 80th FS, 8th FG.

In one newspaper account from this period Dick mentioned having flown seven P-38s since arriving in New Guinea. It is uncertain if Dick was referring to just those P-38s in which he scored kills, but it seems likely this is the case.

After he broke Rickenbacker's record Dick was photographed with a natural metal P-38J-15-LO, s/n 42-104380, adorned with 27 victory flags. In some photos a dark rectangular area is visible on the nose, leading some to suggest that this aircraft had Marge Vattendahl's photo on it at one time. No evidence has yet surfaced to confirm this suggestion.

It is uncertain if Dick flew 42-104380 upon his return to the Southwest Pacific in September 1944. General Kenney wrote that while Dick was stateside Kenney had his aircraft stored at a Port Moresby depot pending Dick's return. Assuming that is true, a J model Lightning figured in only one victory after Dick's return, that being on October 27, 1944 over Tacloban. All other claims made during October and November were attributed to P-38L aircraft.

On November 28th Dick's regularly assigned aircraft, P-38L-1-LO s/n 44-23964, crashed while being flown by another 49th FG pilot. Dick mentioned to his family that the aircraft carried 36 flags but no picture of Marge and that he "got 8 Nips with it." This last statement is puzzling since records indicate seven kills scored with P-38Ls prior to November 28th. Dick may have forgotten his Oscar kill on October 27th had been made with a J model.

Dick's December kills were all made with P-38L-1 aircraft, presumably using an aircraft borrowed from Tom McGuire's squadron. No photographs have yet come to light showing any "Dick Bong P-38" with more than 36 kill markings on it.

It would appear that Dick used far more than three P-38s to run up his score as some sources would have it. Lacking detailed information, it appears he may have used as many as nine different Lightnings over the course of two years. The number may be higher, but that is speculation.

At least two specially-decorated Lightnings were used by Dick during his stateside war bond tours. Both were P-38J-20-LO models. The first Lightning, s/n 44-23461, carried Dick's final score of 40 kills but no picture of Marge. The second aircraft, s/n 44-23491, conversely carried a picture of Marge (the same one carried on the original aircraft) plus Marge's name in stylized letters. This P-38 carried no victory flags. There have been reports of other Lightnings similarly decorated, but no photographic evidence has yet been found to confirm these reports.

Appendix D

The Richard Bong Memorial

On May 22, 1955 dedication ceremonies for the Richard Ira Bong Memorial were held in Poplar, Wisconsin. The ceremonies culminated almost ten years of effort by a variety of groups and individuals, headed by Poplar businessmen and the VFW, to commemorate Dick's exploits in World War II.

Over $47,000 was raised, the money being used to create a "living memorial" to Dick. The funds helped finance an addition to the Poplar Elementary School which included an auditorium-gymnasium, additional classrooms and a 12 ft. by 20 ft. trophy room containing mementos of Dick's military career. A Lockheed P-38 Lightning, which had been donated to the village in 1949, was refurbished by the Air Force and mounted on a pylon adjacent to the school.

In the intervening years thousands of people have visited the Memorial, pausing to view photographs of wartime scenes and marvel at the collection of medals and citations. The massive P-38 Lightning adorned with 40 Japanese victory markings dominates the scene, its angular shape still menacing forty years after the event.

The Richard Ira Bong Memorial is entirely self-supporting, receiving no monies from any governmental agency. Donations to help with the upkeep are welcome and may be sent to: Bong Memorial, Poplar, Wisconsin 54864.

THE CHAMPLIN FIGHTER MUSEUM

The Champlin Fighter Museum ranks as one of the world's unique historical institutions. Unlike most museums, it is privately operated, owing its origin to Douglas L. Champlin, a long-time collector of vintage aircraft. Champlin began acquiring WW II fighters in 1969 and opened his museum in Mesa, Arizona (25 miles east of Phoenix) in January 1981. With addition of original and reproduction WW I aircraft, the collection includes some 30 historic airplanes representing five nations. Most are maintained in airworthy condition.

Designated official home of the American Fighter Aces Association in 1982, the museum hopes to add jet aircraft of Korean and Vietnam War vintage. CFM Press has begun a series of volumes which will cover the history of the men and machines which have made fighter aviation a subject of enduring fascination.

Other CFM books in print:

Big Friend, Little Friend	Lt. Col. Richard E. Turner, USAF (Ret)
The Champlin Fighter Museum Coloring Book	Bob Stevens, artist
America's First Eagles Lt. Lucien H. Thayer (co-published with Bender Publishing, San Jose, California)	
Fox Two	Randy Cunningham with Jeff Ethell
Angels, Bulldogs & Dragons	Bill Marshall

Forthcoming titles include:

The Austro-Hungrian Aces of WW I	Dr. Martin O'Connor
Winged Samurai: Saburo Sakai Japanese Navy Aces	Henry Sakaida
Fighting Mustang: Chronicle of the P-51	William N. Hess

Champlin Fighter Museum
Falcon Field
4636 Fighter Aces Drive
Mesa, Arizona 85205
(602) 830-4540

About The Author

Mike O'Connor has been interested in military aviation history all his life. Born in 1951, he received his B.S. in history and M.S. in library science from the University of Wisconsin. He is currently head of the Technical Processing Division of the Marathon County Public Library in Wausau, Wisconsin.

O'Connor is active in the American Aviation Historical Society and has published several articles in its journal. His work also has appeared in *Air Classics*, *Air Combat* and *Weapons and Warfare Quarterly*. He is currently finishing a history of U.S. Navy MiG kills in the Vietnam War, and he plans volumes on the North Vietnamese and North Korean Air Forces.

About The Artist

During the last two decades aviation artist James H. Farmer's illustrations have become a familiar staple of the printed medium. His technically authentic magazine and book illustrations are internationally recognized. As comfortable at a typewriter as he is at a drawing board, Mr. Farmer has authored more than 40 articles in the fields of aviation and motion pictures, and has served as associate editor of the Journal of the American Aviation Historical Society. He has authored two books, *Celluloid Wings* and *Broken Wings*, and recently broke into television writing.

Index

Adams, Burnell W.	90	Bong, Nelda	2, 4, 69, 110, 129
Adkins, Frank E.	19	Bong, Roy	67
Africa, John T.	7-8	Bong, Sue	2
Amberly Field	18, 19, 20	Boyington, Gregory	67, 75
Anderson, Carroll R.	104	Brown, Harry W.	54
Andrews, Stanley O.	22, 25, 29	Bryce, (Mrs.) Glen	129
Arnold, Henry H.	16, 92, 94, 109	Burcham, Milo	111, 112, 130
Baker, Captain	97	Butler, James	14
Ball, Edgar D.	47	Caldwell, William A.	89, 144
Barden, Elwood	43, 58	Carroll, Earl	111
Barnes, Clayton J.	17, 47, 49, 54	Clark, Dana	111
Barrett, Beverlee	110	Clark, Kenneth	1
Bauhof, Art	18	Cline, Robert	104
Bente, Frederick H.	49	Coleman, William	94
Bills, Ralph	22	Collins, Russell	15
Bjork, Erland	3	Coolidge, Calvin	4
Blair, Samuel V.	73	Corley, Ishmael	101
Bleeker, William	61, 65	Costello, Lou	111
Bluher, O. G.	15	Cragg, Edward	57
Bodenhamer, Frank	128	Crawford, Joan	111
Boe, Paul	110, 129	Crawford, Ray	129
Bohn, John	110	Crosby, Bing	111, 129
Bong, Barbara	2	Cummings, John	100
Bong, Betty	2	Curton, Warren D.	96-97
Bong, Carl	2, 67	Davis, Bette	111
Bong, Carl (Bud)	2, 46, 67, 69, 93, 129	Davis, John	103
Bong, Dora Bryce	2	Dobodura Airdrome	22, 46, 48, 52, 54
Bong, Geraldine	2, 110, 129	Donnell, LeRoy	47, 50
Bong, Gust	2	Down Beat (P-38 Lightning)	89, 144
Bong, James	2	Dulag	105
Bong, Joyce	2	Dunham, William B.	73
Bong, Marjorie Vattendahl	68-69, 76, 80, 105, 109, 110-111, 112-113, 121, 122, 129, 144	Earnhart, Charles	14
		Eason, Hoyt A.	22, 47, 48

Edgette, Gene	3	Haney, William F.	47, 58
Fagan, James	61	Haniotis, George C.	63, 65
Falk, Dale	135	Hanning, William F.	49
Fanning, Grover E.	52	Harbour, David F.	46
Faurot, Robert	47, 48	Harris, Ernest A.	50
Fennenbock, Henry	112	Hart, Lieutenant	105
Firey Ginger IV (P-47 Thunderbolt)	73	Harvey, Clyde L.	45
		Harvey, James	46, 54
Flack, Nelson	50-51, 53, 102	Hays, Ralph L.	57
Flying Knights (See 9th FS)		Headhunters (See 80th FS)	
Ford, Glenn	111	Hess, William N.	66
Forty-Niners (See 49th FG)		Hofstedt, Lawrence	135
Foss, Joseph	67, 75	Holt, Jack	12
Foster, Preston	12	Hoorn, Arvid	3, 129
Fowler, Thomas R.	34, 49, 57	Howes, Edward B.	1, 53, 97
Franklin, Obert	49	Hutton, Bob	111
Fulkerson, Floyd	106-107, 108	Hyland, Norman D.	20
Gallup, Charles S.	22	Ince, James C.	54
Gentile, Donald S.	75	Jager, Charles	46
Gersch, William J.	47	Japanese air units:	
Golden Gate Bridge	15	11th Sentai	21, 22, 24, 25
Goldwater, Barry	11	24th Sentai	50
Gray, Hal	106, 128	33rd Sentai	50
Groups:		68th Sentai	54
4th FG		78th Sentai	54
8th FG	52	253rd Kokutai	63
14th FG	13, 14	309th Hikotai	97
35th FG	20, 22, 62, 97	582nd Kokutai	21, 22, 24, 25
43rd FG			
49th FG	1, 20, 48, 53, 60, 62, 98, 101, 105, 110	602nd Hikotai	97
		902nd Hikotai	97
58th FG	89	Jett, Verl E.	104
78th FG	16, 17	Johnson, Gerald R.	1, 31, 46, 50, 57, 59, 98-99, 102, 103, 106, 107, 114
348th FG	54, 59, 62	Johnson, Robert S.	93, 94
354th FG	45	Johnson, Stanley W.	63, 65
475th FG	54, 60, 62, 96, 103	Johnson, (Mrs.) Stanley W.	69
Hamilton Field	13, 15	Jones, Warren	67
Hammett, Henry	103		

Jordan, Wallace R.   46, 50, 54, 59, 65, 97, 101-102, 114

Kearby, Neel E.   54, 59, 62, 70, 73

Kelsey, Benjamin   14

Kenney, George C. 15, 16, 19, 22, 23, 25, 54, 64, 70-72, 74, 90, 92, 95-98, 102, 106, 108, 109

King, Charles W.   71

Kluckhohn, Frank   91

Ladner, Herman   74

La Follette, Robert M., Jr.   93

Landers, John D.   36, 45, 46

Lane, John H.   22, 29, 30, 143

Langmack, C. J.   112, 129

Leslie, Joan   111

Le Vier, Tony   111-112, 132

Lindbergh, Charles   87, 96

Loisel, John S.   54

Luke Field   9-12

Lynch, Thomas J.   21, 22, 23, 29, 30, 52, 70-74, 78

MacArthur, Douglas 90, 92, 98, 106, 115, 119

McCarthy, Frank   91

McGomsey, Robert M.   50, 100

MacDonald, Charles   103

McElroy, Charles   65

McGuire, Thomas B.   46, 54, 60, 62, 64, 97-98, 103, 104-107, 109, 110, 116

McMahon, Robert F.   19

Magnas, Richard   21

Malone, Thomas   74-75, 143

Mankin, Jack C.   17, 18, 34, 49

Marge (P-38 Lightning)   74, 143

Markey, Walter M.   15, 17, 18, 20, 50, 53, 65, 110

Mathre, Milden E.   100

Miles, Johnnie   111

Miller, Paul   4

Moore, Del   65

Morrissey, Robert L.   98-99, 100

Murray, Ken   111

Nichols, Franklin A.   54, 104

O'Neill, John G.   15, 17, 31, 49, 62

Peaslee, Jesse   45

Pegg, George   56

Peterson, Marvin   68, 69

Petrovich, Peter   1

Pierce, Sammy A.   45

Planck, Carl G.   22, 49, 53

Poleschuk, Stephen   45

Prentice, George W.   20, 54

Price, Joe   52

Price, Theron D.   17, 31, 61

Pryor, Wayne   129

Rankin, John Gilbert   6, 7, 111

Reynolds, Andrew J.   45, 46

Rickenbacker, Eddie   69, 75, 85, 90, 92

Rittmayer, Jack   108, 138

Robbins, Jay T.   18, 57, 60, 62, 64, 83, 89, 90

Roberts, Daniel T.   52, 54

Roth, Russ   90

Russell, Richard B., Jr.   93

Sauber, John S.   45

Schwimmer Airdrome   20, 23

Sells, William D.   53

Sibley, Frederick J.   17, 18, 57

Smith, Cornelius M.   89, 90

Sparks, Kenneth C.   22, 24

Squadrons:

> 7th FS   23, 56, 57, 98, 100, 102
>
> 8th FS 23, 48, 53, 60, 102
>
> 9th FS   1, 20, 23, 25, 45, 46, 47, 52-54, 56, 57, 60, 61, 63, 65, 70, 96, 98, 101, 110
>
> 36th FS   57, 64
>
> 39th FS   20, 22, 23, 45, 46, 47, 52, 54, 57, 70-71

40th FS	52, 96	Wire, Ralph L.	31, 61
41st FS	52, 96	Woods, Sidney S.	34, 36, 49, 54, 55, 58
49th FS	13, 15	Wright Field	111, 112
80th FS	52, 54, 57, 60, 62, 64, 71, 89	Wurtsmith, Paul B.	23, 40, 45, 70, 96
84th FS	16	Yaeger, Paul	54
110th TRS	100	Yamamoto, Isoruku	52, 53
353rd FS	45	Zane, (Mrs.) George	128
421st NFS	74, 100		
431st FS	103, 105, 138		
432nd FS	75		
433rd FS	104		

Stimson, Henry	92
Suehr, Richard C.	25, 29, 30
Taft, Robert A.	93
Tagaya, Osamu	22
Tanimizu, Takeo	63
The Beast (P-38 Lightning)	60
Thumper (P-38 Lightning)	22, 143
Thunder Birds (motion picture)	12
Tice, Clayton	36
Tierney, Gene	12
Tojo, Captain	25
Van Atta, Lee	15
Vattendahl, Lowell	110
Vattendahl, Sig	110
Wade, Kenneth	13
Walker, George	96-97, 98-100, 106, 114
Wandry, Ralph H.	31, 46, 48, 54, 58, 60, 62, 65
Watkins, James A.	57, 58, 59, 64, 65
Welch, George S.	50, 51, 60, 64, 93
Wellman, William	12
White, Robert H.	60
White, Wallace H.	93
Whitehead, Ennis C.	11, 20, 40, 48, 98, 106
Wiley, Alexander	130